WRITING THE FUTURE

WRITING THE FUTURE

Perspectives on Nationally Competitive Scholarships

Edited by Suzanne McCray, Doug Cutchins, and Cindy Schaarschmidt

The National Association of Fellowships Advisors

THE UNIVERSITY OF ARKANSAS PRESS
FAYETTEVILLE
2025

Copyright © 2025 by the University of Arkansas Press. All rights reserved. No part of this book should be used or reproduced in any manner without prior permission in writing from the University of Arkansas Press or as expressly permitted by law.

ISBN: 978-1-68226-282-5
eISBN: 978-1-61075-844-4

29 28 27 26 25   5 4 3 2 1

Cataloging-in-Publication Data on file at the Library of Congress.

CONTENTS

Acknowledgments vii

Introduction 3

Part I: Scholarship Advising

1. "Thank U, Next . . ."—There's Got to Be a Better Way: Appreciative Advising as an Effective Fellowships Advising Tool 15
Craig Filar, Jesse Wieland, and Bonnie Garcia-Gloeckner

2. Trust the Process: Examining Fellowship Applicant Success from the Student Development Lens 37
Kristin Bennighoff, Laura Collins, and Kelsey Fenner

3. Writing the Future in Fulbright Applications 55
Paul Fogleman

4. From Imagination to Reality: Leveraging the Fellowship Application Process as an Imaginative Tool 67
Nicole Galante

5. Advising for Knowledge Transfer: Building Better Writers for Life 85
Claire Kervin

6. What Do We Get Out of This? Helping Students (Re)Examine Purpose and Positionality in Study Abroad Fellowships 99
Megan Bruening

7. English Belongs to "Those Who Use It": Cultivating Authentic Voices with Inclusive Writing Pedagogies and Linguistic Pluralism 113
Elena Reiss, Mitch Hobza, and Julia Goldberg

8. That's Going to Leave a Mark: Writing About Trauma
   in Fellowship Applications 129
   Tara Yglesias, Kristin Janka, Mathilda Nassar,
   Elise Rudt-Moorthy, and Melissa Vert

Part II: On the Profession

9. You May Ask Yourself, "Well, How Did I Get Here?"
   Advisors as Application Reviewers for Foundations 147
   Sarah Chow, Kurt Davies, Lindsay Lawton,
   and Tara Yglesias

10. The Logic and Lessons of the Prestige and
    Practicality Forums 173
    Rachel Ball-Phillips, Jessie McCrary, Eric Myers,
    Terumi Rafferty-Osaki, Jayashree Shivamoggi,
    and Christian Tanja

11. Approaching Endorsement Letters: How to Do Justice
    to Your Student, Represent Your Institution Well,
    and Keep Your Wits About You 193
    Lisa Gates, Katya King, Christine Overstreet,
    and Cindy Stocks

12. NAFA at Twenty-Five: The Origin Story....................................... 213
    Jane Morris

National Association of Fellowships Advisors Members 227

Contributors 243

Index 255

ACKNOWLEDGMENTS

This volume includes many essays that resulted from presentations delivered at recent National Association of Fellowships Advisors (NAFA) conferences, most notably the July 2023 conference in New Orleans. Events of this size and complexity require incredibly hard work from many talented people. The New Orleans conference would not have been possible without Cindy Schaarschmidt (Pierce College District), who was the president of NAFA at the time of the conference. As vice president for the two years leading up to that conference, Megan Friddle (Emory University) served as chair of the conference planning committee and was instrumental in the planning and execution of that meeting. Friddle then transitioned to the role of NAFA president, at which time Robyn Curtis (Clemson University) assumed the vice presidency and took the lead for planning our 2025 conference.

The bulk of the credit, however, belongs to the conference planning committee, which for the 2023 conference included Megan Friddle (Emory University, chair), Heidi Bauer-Clapp (University of Massachusetts Amherst), Rebecca Blustein (University of California, Los Angeles), Robyn Curtis (Clemson University), Teresa Delcorso-Ellmann (Rutgers University), Allison Edgren (Loyola University New Orleans), Garrett Fontenot (Louisiana State University), Katya King (Williams College), Bridget Hansen (Emory University), Anastasia Lin (University of North Georgia), Brian Souders (University of Maryland, Baltimore County), and Daniel Villanueva (Congress-Bundestag Youth Exchange).

As always, John Richardson (University of Louisville, emeritus) continued to be an invaluable asset for NAFA, working first as treasurer (2001–2013) and then as NAFA's first employee (2014–present). Additional administrative support was provided by Georgia Brunner (Emory University) as conference planning coordinator, Ariel Lawrence (Emory University) for on-site support, and Tracy Mitchell (ConferenceDirect) as event manager.

The foundations, agencies, and organizations that sponsor national scholarships and fellowships are, as always, key members of NAFA, sharing their expertise with advisors at conferences, during campus visits, and in the proceedings. A special thank you goes to Daniel Villanueva (CBYX), Christian Tanja (Knight-Hennessey), John Mateja (Goldwater), Tara Yglesias (Truman), Wyatt Bruton (Schwarzman), and Michelle Douenias (Luce Scholars) for serving on the foundations conference planning subcommittee.

Special thanks also go to the foundation members who participated in the structured foundation interviews or "chat" sessions. Representatives (at the time of the conference) who gave generously of their time included Kaveri Advani (Critical Language Scholarship and Benjamin A. Gilman Scholarship), Mags Dillon (Princeton in Asia), Christopher Grider (Carnegie Endowment for International Peace/James C. Gaither Junior Fellows Program), Eurica Huggins Axum (USAID Donald M. Payne Fellowship), Payge Jennings (Office of Alumni Affairs at the Bureau of Educational and Cultural Affairs), Karoly Jokay (Fulbright Commission Hungary), Heidi Ramaeker (Foreign Affairs Information Technology Fellowship/William D. Clarke Sr. Diplomatic Security Fellowship), Michael Saffle (IIE/Boren Awards), Patricia Scroggs (Howard University/Rangel Program), Lora Seery (Fulbright US Student Program), Heather Theisen-Gandara (Benjamin A. Gilman Scholarship), Sterling Tilley (Thomas R. Pickering Foreign Affairs Graduate Fellowship Program), and Caitlin Ting (Critical Language Scholarship Program), Amelia Wallace (DAAD), and Tara Yglesias (Harry S. Truman Scholarship Foundation).

The NAFA publications committee also deserves recognition for its support of this project: Jennifer Staton (University of Alabama at Huntsville, chair), Kathleen Barry (Johns Hopkins University), Bridget Hansen (Emory University), Alsace-Lorraine Gallop (North Carolina Agricultural and Technical State University), Kristin Janka (Michigan State University), Suzanne McCray (University of Arkansas), Leigh Pratt (University of New Hampshire), and

Meredith Raucher Sisson (Virginia Commonwealth University), Connie Storey (Northern Illinois University), and Jasmine Stork (Smith College).

The authors also wish to thank Charles Robinson (chancellor) and Terry Martin (provost and executive vice chancellor for academic affairs) of the University of Arkansas for their ongoing support. Special thanks also to the Division of Enrollment Services at the University of Arkansas and the staff of the Office of Nationally Competitive Awards in particular. Emily Wright (senior associate director) and Matt Halbert (associate director) provided excellent proofreading support. William Clift designed the striking cover. The continuing support of Ketevan Mamiseishvili (dean), Michael Hevel (associate dean), and Kristin Higgins (chair of the Department of Counseling, Leadership and Research Methods) in the College of Education and Health Professions has been greatly appreciated. And of course, this publication would not be possible without the excellent work of the University of Arkansas Press: Mike Bieker (director), David Scott Cunningham (editor in chief), and Charlie Shields (director of sales and marketing).

The authors also wish to thank New York University Abu Dhabi's Dana Downey (associate dean of Student Affairs and director of the Career Development Center); Baishakhi Taylor (associate vice chancellor of Student Affairs); Fabio Piano (interim vice chancellor); Arlie Petters (provost); Erich Dietrich (vice provost of Undergraduate Education); and the entire staff of the Career Development Center. A final thanks also goes to Matthew Campbell, (president, Pierce College Fort Steilacoom) and Julie White, (chancellor and chief executive officer of Pierce College District.)

WRITING THE FUTURE

INTRODUCTION

The New Orleans 2023 National Association of Fellowships Advisors (NAFA) conference, "Redefining Purpose: Tradition and Change in Nationally Competitive Awards," provided the opportunity for members to learn, share, and grow together in person after holding the 2021 conference virtually. The conference theme pointed to important changes since NAFA's last in-person gathering, including an increased emphasis on student engagement and belonging, the expansion of graduate advising, and new strategies for personal statements and letter writing. NAFA core values of supporting student development, emphasizing the value of the process, and pursuing excellence remained central ideas. Such topics, both traditional and new, are included in this volume.

The world of nationally competitive scholarships and fellowships continues to change and evolve, and the work of foundations and advisors is adapting with it. AI created a whirlwind of questions about how it can and cannot be used, and both advisors and foundations are working to understand how it will affect the application and selection process. Another challenge is the current volatility of award funding, with some scholarships ending entirely and others on pause, while at the same time an ever-increasing number of exceptional students seek such funding to expand their academic preparation and to help enhance their service and career trajectories. For small and large awards offices alike, this means exploring ways to scale up services while maintaining a high level of student interaction. This volume, *Writing the Future: Perspectives on Nationally Competitive Scholarships*, centers on the future of students as they envision it, on access during a rapidly shifting sense of what that means, and on the best practices advisors can employ to help talented students realize the future they are writing about in their applications.

The first eight chapters of this book focus on various aspects of the advising process—encouraging applications, as well as helping students envision their future and then write about that future in language that is authentic and true to their experience and their own rhetorical style. Craig Filar, Jesse Wieland, and Bonnie Garcia-Gloeckner in Chapter 1, "'Thank U, Next . . .'—There's Got to Be a Better Way: Appreciative Advising as an Effective Fellowships Advising Tool," insist that prescriptive advising or simply conveying information to a student falls short of what students need and expect when they seek support from fellowships advisors. The "better way" articulated in this chapter is appreciative advising, which combines prescriptive advising with a more collaborative form that is both deliberately intrusive and intentionally developmental. The authors describe the various phases of appreciative advising (disarm, discover, dream, design, deliver, don't settle), elements of which echo in other essays on advising later in this volume. Even though the terminology may change, the basic premise of interactive, respectful advising—which encourages students to envision and write an ambitious future—remains the same.

Chapter 2 focuses on the developmental aspect of advising, providing students with outcomes (critical thinking, communication, leadership, and self-realization skills) that go beyond receiving a specific award. Authors Kristin Bennighoff, Laura Collins, and Kelsey Fenner, in "Trust the Process: Examining Fellowship Applicant Success from the Student Development Lens," ground their approach in existing theoretical frameworks, including Identity Development Theory, Self-Authorship Theory, and Experiential Learning Theory. These and other student development theories help provide a framework to better serve students who are asking questions about who they are now, who they want to be, and what experiences will help them shape the futures they envision. The authors provide examples of best practices including courses, workshops, assessments, and even celebrations that provide structure to a process intended to help students be successful. At times, being successful will include winning a scholarship or being admitted to a highly competitive program, but every time it should include honing skills that will assist the student no matter what their future brings.

Paul Fogelman, in Chapter 3, "Writing the Future in Fulbright Applications," focuses specifically on the Fulbright Scholarship process. He examines the complexity of writing about the future as students are asked to do in a variety of applications. Students are expected to explain what they wish to do in terms of the scholarship—where they will go, what they will study, what degrees they will seek, the faculty who will mentor them, and (even more tenuously) how the scholarship will benefit them in the career trajectory they have also outlined. Students are encouraged to detail such plans in a tone of confidence that rarely acknowledges the role serendipity will take in shaping their futures. Students feel this disconnect and often voice discomfort in "writing their future" so specifically for a scholarship when in fact they are uncertain about what direction their career path will take even if they are lucky enough to win the award in question. Fogelman, an experienced Fulbright Program Adviser, created a survey to see if the post-scholarship plans his Fulbright applicants (win or not) wrote about in their applications matched what they were currently doing. He found that 22 percent of students responding to the survey indicated that they were doing something completely different from what they had described as a future plan in their applications; the rest had either fully or at least partially realized those plans. The students in Fogelman's survey were, for the most part, in the social sciences, and Fogelman reflects on the impact this may have had on the outcome of the survey. Advisors often deal with exceptional students who are uncertain about their career paths, and this study provides insights that will be helpful to advisors in those circumstances.

Chapter 4, "From Imagination to Reality: Leveraging the Fellowships Application Process as an Imaginative Tool," also examines the process of "writing the future." In this chapter, Nicole Galante discusses the process of imagining the future, differentiating imagining from fantasizing. The imagining phase is similar to the discover and dream phases of appreciative advising, discussed in Chapter 1. Though the language to describe the process is different, the approach to the student is similar. In this chapter, Galante demonstrates how the practice works in her office by allowing the students to speak for themselves. Three students describe their experiences with the office, with their advisor, and with the process of imagining their futures. The students had varying degrees of success with receiving awards, but all three pointed to a process that helped them examine their strengths and passions as well as imagine a future that flies past "the nets" (as James Joyce phrased it in *A Portrait of the Artist as a Young Man*) that would limit it and develop a plan based on those "imaginings," a plan that might have looked very different were it not for this process. The essay ends with a key insight on part of one of the students: "I was the prize . . . I was not just applying for a fellowship. I was giving these fellowships the opportunity to support the change that I was already making and will make in this world." The lesson is clear: Students who are free to fully imagine their future will be writing ours in some part as well as theirs in their applications and in the work those applications empower.

Author Claire Kervin examines the transfer of knowledge that can occur through the application process. As the title of Chapter 5, "Advising for Knowledge Transfer: Building Better Writers for Life," indicates, Kervin focuses on the transfer of writing skills from the application process to other types of writing. She gives Goldwater as an example. Goldwater candidates learn to articulate their research for an application and can in turn use the same writing principles to articulate that research for a presentation to a general audience or for grant purposes. While most fellowships advisors ask students to reflect on their past experiences as they translate those experiences to future plans, perhaps fewer ask their students to examine their past writing experiences. Kervin has incorporated such examinations into her daily work with students. In doing so, she is able to understand a student's attitude toward writing, the writing skills they feel they have, and negative writing habits they may need to unlearn. She makes honing writing skills an overt part of the application process and treats it as another practice that offers students a significant benefit whether or not they receive a particular award. Any process that promotes deeper learning on a college campus is one to be celebrated, and Kervin recommends making sure students are reminded that this deeper learning is an important goal of the process.

In Chapter 6, "What Do We Get Out of This? Helping Students (Re) Examine Purpose and Positionality in Study Abroad Fellowships," Megan Breuning recommends asking applicants to study abroad programs to thoroughly consider the purpose of their proposed travel. Her goal is for students to benefit fully from their time abroad, and, to do that, she argues, they need to have a sense of what their identity and positionality abroad might be. The "we" in "What Do We Get Out of This?" is not just the student and the student's family but also includes the programs offering funding, the host country, and the United States on the student's return. She provides examples of two exercises that encourage students to think beyond their own experiences and the potential benefits (academic, professional, and personal) that may accrue to them and to broaden their sense of purpose to include the possible benefits to these other constituents as well—benefits that may extend well beyond their time abroad. Students should understand that their time abroad needs to be more than an extractive experience that involves taking from, but not giving back to, the international communities they encounter. Bruening also puts forward a third exercise that asks the student to consider possible scenarios that could occur while they are abroad. This exercise encourages students to imagine tough situations in which their sense of their own identity is questioned or different from the one perceived by a group abroad. The exercise reminds students that one of the identities they must maintain even in difficult circumstances is that of cultural ambassador.

Fellowships advisors are increasingly working with international students and students who have diverse linguistic backgrounds. In Chapter 7, "English Belongs to 'Those Who Use It': Cultivating Authentic Voice with Inclusive Writing Pedagogies and Linguistic Pluralism," authors Elena Reiss, Mitch Hobza, and Julie Goldberg examine how advisors can encourage a wider range of "Englishes" among applicants from multilingual backgrounds. Applying for highly competitive awards and programs is a challenging process, which is made even more challenging if English—the application language for students in the United States and for many beyond it—is not a student's native language or only native language. These students can be limited then by a language that might not as closely describe their experience, their sense of themselves, or the complexity of their ideas. In addition, an application's own writing requirements and structures (think intellectual merit and broader impacts with National Science Foundation Graduate Research Fellowships) can further limit a student's ability to express themselves. Students may struggle to write in a voice that is authentically theirs, robbing them of the opportunity to share who they really are and the foundations from understanding the full slate of talent before them. The goal, as the authors outline it, is "mutual intelligibility," which allows students some ability to move between languages in a fluid way that better communicates their experiences to the reader. Even native speakers of English may want to move between the colloquial language of their upbringing and the more standard English that applications (and English teachers) seem to require. The authors encourage advisors to consider translingual pedagogies, and they provide examples of students writing in a more compelling way as a result, giving the reader greater insights into the students' lived experiences and opening the door to a broader group of successful applicants.

Chapter 8, "That's Going to Leave a Mark: Writing About Trauma in Fellowship Applications," is the final chapter about student advising. Authors Tara Yglesias, Kristin Janka, Mathilda Nassar, Elise Rudt-Moorthy, and Melissa Vert also focus on the writing process, but in this chapter, it is the subject matter, not language or style, that is emphasized. "That's Going to Leave a Mark" is an effective though brutal title for an essay that questions the validity of some personal statements focused on trauma, the wisdom of others, and the applicability of bringing up trauma at all. The title has an echo of trauma, but there is also an underlying question: Will readers feel abused by the essay, or will the mark be a positive one? In the latter case, trauma and trajectory align, the purpose of the revelation is clear, and the inclusion of the story is compelling. Anyone who has worked in college admissions is long familiar with essays built around trauma and of students rising from the ashes or looking for something that will make it seem so. Such essays can point to serious (but sometimes not so serious) challenges overcome, or they can reflect challenges faced by others in ways that have benefited the student. Sometimes such stories can overwhelm grades and scores, and students are admitted, but there are other times when officials are at a loss about what to make of what they have been told—unable to see relevance or overlook a lack of preparation that may mean the student will not succeed if admitted. This chapter cautions advisors to "hear" but not misuse trauma. Deliberately attempting to exploit experiences that are not relevant to a student's application does not serve the student or the reviewers well.

In Chapter 9, "You May Ask Yourself, 'Well, How Did I Get Here?,'" Sarah Chow, Kurt Davies, Lindsay Lawton, and Tara Yglesias discuss the role advisors can assume as reviewers for foundations. Tara Yglesias, executive deputy secretary of the Truman Foundation, and Sara Chow, application and selection program specialist for Boren, write from the foundation's point of view of including advisors as reviewers. Lindsay Lawton and Kurt Davies write as fellowships advisors serving as reviewers for foundations. Each speaks directly to their own experience. But together they provide insights into how the collaboration works. Lindsay Lawton provides practical advice for reviewers who choose to serve in such a capacity, including how to select suitable awards, how to get started, how to measure the value of participation, and how to approach the reading. Sarah Chow outlines the selection process for Boren awards and how they select qualified reviewers. Like Lawton, Davies stresses the benefits of getting a hands-on look at how the sauce is made. Davies reinforces the idea that the nomination letter is a key part of the application and the first item they read. He follows with other Truman questions and his approach to them—outlining what he considers a strong response. Yglesias rounds out the piece with a discussion of the Truman review process, reminding readers that advisors have been part of the Truman review well before NAFA existed. Yglesias provides a snapshot of the Truman review process—whom they select as readers, how readers and then applications are sorted, and how finalists are selected. All four enthusiastically stress that the collaborative process of reviewing benefits both advisors and foundations. Advisors gain key insights on what makes students competitive for a particular scholarship, including a better understanding of what a winning application might look like. Foundations learn what advisors are sharing with students, problems that may exist with the application, and a new perspective on the questions they are asking. It is a win-win experience.

The 2023 NAFA conference began with a "Prestige and Practicality Forum," which tackled prestige biases, considered how the language we use to describe fellowships can seem exclusionary or limiting, and how to forge ways to make the application process inviting and empowering to all. In Chapter 10, "The Logic and Lessons of the Prestige and Practicality Forums," authors Rachel Ball-Phillips, Jessie McCrary, Eric Myers, Terumi Rafferty-Osaki, Jayashree Shivamoggi, and Christian Tanja outline the origins of the various access initiatives within NAFA in general and the creation of the Prestige and Practicality Forum in particular, placing it within a legal and historical context. The 2023 Forum included breakout sessions focused on support, bias awareness, and the language of prestige and practicality; participants were asked to complete a survey and to share a word that best described how they felt about their breakout exchanges. From the survey the authors determined specific themes related to access efforts and NAFA. The findings were mixed as evidenced by the two most frequently mentioned words—"frustration" and "hopeful"—but it was generally noted that NAFA membership is looking for guidance and support from NAFA on these issues of access and belonging, and this topic will be part of the conversation at NAFA conferences, summer workshops, and in the proceedings for the years ahead.

Authors Lisa Gates, Katya King, Christine Overstreet, and Cindy Stock provide a mini how-to manual on writing letters of endorsement or nomination in Chapter 11, "Approaching Endorsement Letters: How to Do Justice to Your Student, Represent Your Institution Well, and Keep Your Wits About You." Institutional letters are an important part of a select number of applications, including the Rhodes, Marshall, Churchill, Fulbright, Boren, Truman, and Goldwater. Earlier in this volume, Kurt Davies (a Truman reviewer) reads the Truman nomination letter first as a road map to the student's application. That practice is likely a common one. Though an excellent letter of endorsement cannot turn a less than stellar applicant into one who receives an award, it can certainly provide important support for a strong candidate. The detailed advice in this essay provides helpful insights, especially to those new to the profession, about how to get started, how to collect information and what to collect, how to work with upper and central administration, what details are best to include, and how to organize the letter. For more seasoned advisors, the authors provide a checklist to help advisors make sure each letter represents the student well, aligns with the foundation's criteria for competitive candidates, represents the institution and the writer appropriately, and is as persuasive as possible. This chapter abounds with practical advice that will make the make the process more straightforward, more organized, and therefore saner (the "Keep Your Wits About You" part) for advisors and administrators.

In the final chapter, in "NAFA at Twenty-Five—the Origin Story," Jane Morris writes elegantly about NAFA's beginnings—the purpose for its creation, the early stars such as Bob Graalman, Mary Tolar, Nancy Twiss, and Louis Blair who pushed it forward, and the attention it drew from *The Chronicle of Higher Education* and others. What Morris adds to Beth Powers's 2013 history of NAFA are the voices of some of the founding NAFA members, including Ann Brown, Bob Graalman, Suzanne McCray, Mary Tolar, Betsy Vardaman, and Paula Warrick, as well as Powers herself. Five past presidents who are part of that mix cover a significant portion of that early history. Their stories not only reveal how important NAFA was to them professionally and personally but also how important it was initially in creating access for a broader range of students in a broader set of institutions and how far it has come since with added emphasis on inclusion, on graduate student applications, and on more nuanced kinds of advising. Morris effectively captures the evolution of NAFA in these pages as well the motivation behind its creation, which was informed by a "practical decision-making" that we hoped then and hope now will lead "to human flourishing."

Suzanne McCray
University of Arkansas

PART I

Scholarship Advising

1

"Thank U, Next…"— There's Got to Be a Better Way

Appreciative Advising as an Effective Fellowships Advising Tool

CRAIG FILAR, JESSE WIELAND, AND BONNIE GARCIA-GLOECKNER

Fellowships advisors often find themselves at the intersection of many facets of the advisee experiences. Students look to advisors for the answers to numerous questions, some of them practical (When is the application due? Do I have to do another round of editing?) and some more esoteric and philosophical (Am I a strong candidate for this fellowship? What does it mean to be successful? How can I articulate my purpose in a compelling manner?). Over the months and years that advisors support students, applicants receive useful tools to complete both challenging and dense fellowship applications and, in some part, to engage in well-lived lives. But how do advisors advise so broadly, and what is the framework that they use to conduct this business?

While universities provide basic advising training and the National Association of Fellowships Advisors (NAFA) provides unparalleled support, the bespoke nature of the fellowships advising process needs to be organized in such a way that advisors can ensure a standard and consistent quality and an approach to advising that accommodates both growth in student interest and the varied personalities and perspectives of advisors. Appreciative advising is a developmental advising model that is founded on the idea of the collaborative practice of asking positive open-ended questions to help students optimize the potential for opportunities of self-discovery and to achieve their dreams. We have found that the appreciative advising model aligns elegantly with the more general work of fellowships advising and have implemented this approach on our campus at Florida State University.

Fellowships Advising at Florida State University

Located in Tallahassee, Florida, Florida State University is a Research 1 institution that has been designated a preeminent university in the state of Florida. Situated in the state capital, nearly adjacent to the capitol building, Florida State University enrolls approximately 43,000 students, with an undergraduate enrollment of around 32,000 students and a graduate enrollment of around 10,000 students. Approximately 78 percent of the students are from in-state, with out-of-state students coming from all other 49 states and the District of Columbia. We have a campus in Panama City, Florida, as well as international study centers in London, England; Valencia, Spain; Florence, Italy; and Panama City, Panama.

The Office of National Fellowships (ONF) was founded in 2005 to consolidate fellowships advising on the campus. The office was established within the Division of Undergraduate Studies, which traditionally serves as the academic unit for all first- and second-year students before they are formally admitted into their college and major at the start of their junior year. In addition to administrative services, the Division of Undergraduate Studies includes the undergraduate research office, the first-generation student programs, transfer student services, the honors program, the premier merit scholarship program, and the student athletic academic support services, among others. The inclusion of the fellowships office in undergraduate studies allows us to serve students from every corner of campus, regardless of major. ONF primarily serves undergraduate and recent alumni populations. We have a sister office, the Office of Graduate Fellowships and Awards, which is housed in the same building and serves the Florida State graduate student population with fellowships advising needs.

Over the past fifteen years, the office has grown from a full-time staff of two to a full-time staff of four, including three full-time fellowships advisors in addition to the director. Even with the additional administrative support of more advisors, the challenge—with an increase in student volume—is maintaining a quality advising experience for students. The staff has grown in response to the substantial increase in the number of students advised and applications submitted. To maintain high-level impact and quality, ONF has routinely surveyed our fellowships applicants to ascertain the quality of their experience and to improve our outreach and advising. A consistent outcome of the survey is the great value the students found in building relationships with the fellowships advising team as they conducted the work of self-exploration and self-expression. The collaborative spirit that informs our advising practice became the foundation for our team to craft an advising paradigm. This concept enhances the expectation that both the student and the advisor find value. For the process to be a learning experience for the student requires that we have a thoughtful presence and an open comfortable space for dialogue in our advising meetings.

Over the years, our office has developed a meaningful approach to our advising appointments that relies on strong collaboration between student and advisor. We began to develop a framework that describes our advising process, ensuring a standard used across the team. We decided to submit a presentation proposal to a NAFA conference to discuss our advising strategies and ideas. When conducting the literature review for the presentation, we were pleased to discover our approach aligned perfectly with a thoughtful approach to advising called *appreciative advising*.

Advising Methods and Fellowships Advising

Appreciative advising is a student-centered advising model based on the idea that students have more command and understanding of themselves than they may recognize or connect with on a regular basis.[1] As advisors we seek to connect them with that understanding and build their confidence in it. To comprehend appreciative advising, it is helpful to take a moment to review a couple other stylistic approaches to advising.

Prescriptive Advising

Prescriptive advising conveys information. It is a unilateral and somewhat power-based model that works from the notion that the advisor has the pertinent information and must convey it to the student.[2] We all do this type of advising to a certain extent, as we explain policies, procedures, and application structures. We clarify questions about deadlines, about materials, about recommenders, and about other data points to ensure students understand the parameters in which they are working in terms of the application materials and the application timeline.

Intrusive Advising

Intrusive advising relies on proactive interactions and interventions to connect with students before situations arise that are difficult to remedy. The outcome of intrusive advising is to develop a caring relationship that increases persistence and provides support. This advising model is also initiated by the advisor.[3] Fellowships advisors do not routinely engage with this model of advising, yet we develop closer relationships with students than some others on campus, and this model is at heart meant to ensure students know that they are seen and heard in large institutions like colleges and universities. As fellowships advisors, we are well positioned to do this and occasionally find ourselves needing to proactively reach out to students to check on them and get a sense of their well-being.

Developmental Advising

Developmental advising is more collaborative than prescriptive advising. It is a process in which the advisor and the student work together to help the student make the best-informed decisions. The advisor acts as a guide and a sounding board. They are not the source of definitive information, but rather the voice of experience and opportunity.[4] When we work together with students assessing the various fellowship opportunity options and weigh the cost/benefit of each against the students' own experiences, we help them develop their self-assessment skills in a collaborative environment. Here they grow in their ability to make the most informed, best decision for themselves. Appreciative advising is a specific type of developmental advising that benefits the growth of both student and advisor.

Implementing Advising Methods

It is not uncommon for a fellowships advising appointment to pivot between these styles within one meeting. Over the arc of our meetings, the goal is not only to ensure the development of skills and conveyance of information, but to create a holistic environment based on open communication and inspirational, yet grounded support.

What Is Appreciative Advising?

The advising model used in ONF at Florida State University is described in detail in *The Appreciative Advising Revolution* by Jennifer L. Bloom, Bryant L. Hutson, and Ye He.[5] It is a way to highlight a student's strengths and empowers students to define who they are, what they want to accomplish, and the tools and skills they must develop to enhance their strengths and achieve goals. The model draws from several different academic fields, including psychology, counseling, and education theory and practice, and was originally developed to assist students who faced difficulty in school, either with the coursework or in discovering the appropriate major.

Although appreciative advising has a strong theoretical structure supporting it, the main focus of our chapter is its practical application for fellowships advising and how we assess its efficacy.[6] Appreciative advising has six clearly defined phases, which we review below, describing how we engage in each of the phases in our office with our students. We also discuss how we have incorporated these six phases into our assessment tool and provide an overview of our recent office assessment.

The Six Phases of Appreciative Advising

The six phases of appreciative advising are (1) disarm, (2) discover, (3) dream, (4) design, (5) deliver, and (6) don't settle.[7] Also known as the Six D's, these phases provide a comprehensive structure for fellowships advising that starts from before the student arrives in the office.

1. Disarm Phase

The disarm phase emphasizes the first impressions we are making with students and how those impressions may set the tone for our advisor-advisee relationships. It is important to remember that these initial meetings can be an intimidating experience, especially for students who are unfamiliar with the catalog of awards advisors support or those who have not been trained to apply for these awards or craft the necessary written components. This is particularly salient at FSU, where 25 percent of the undergraduate population identify as the first member of their family to attend college. Therefore, we want to ensure that when they enter our offices, we greet them warmly and have intentionally created spaces that feel safe and comfortable.

During these first meetings, we do not want our students to feel like our conversations are entirely one-sided. Establishing a level of trust and an atmosphere in which applicants feel comfortable sharing their stories, both those that are joyful and some that may be difficult to verbalize, will help us become better mentors. This patient and tactful approach helps our students understand that we are invested in getting to know them as people and not solely as potential award recipients. Our hope is that this approach will alleviate some of the inherent pressure, or "high stakes," often associated with these application cycles and thus allow our students to focus on their growth as writers, scholars, and young professionals.

Figure 1.1. The waiting area outside of our offices.

Figure 1.1 shows the waiting room of our advising space, and Figure 1.2 shows the interior of one of our offices. In the first photo, readers can see comfortable couches, as well as tables and chairs where students wait until we come out and greet them for our meetings. We have fliers and handouts on those tables about different opportunities and resources around campus, which we encourage students to take with them. What can be difficult to see in that first photo is that our third and second floors are connected by an atrium in the center of the building. Students can hear clearly from the second to the third floor, even occasionally including whispers. While that is not an issue for extroverts, for some introverted students this can seem intimidating, which is why we intentionally greet our students face to face before we walk them back to our offices, where, if they are comfortable, we may close our sliding doors to drown out the building noise.

When students first walk into our offices, we want them to see an intentionally curated space where they view both a balance of our personal interests and pieces that show our investment in their success. These items may serve as conversation starters, allowing

Figure 1.2. The view from a staff member's office doorway.

students to connect with us over shared interests or prompt them to inquire about our own academic background, international travels, or long-standing experience with these fellowships. It is helpful periodically to sit in the chairs our students occupy to take in our office space and understand what our students see when they meet us for the first time.

2. Discover Phase

The discover phase has us ask effective and open-ended questions to learn from our students. We know students come to us with complex, nuanced experiences, and it is important for us to navigate these conversations with grace because students may never have shared these stories with anyone before, let alone a new advisor. With an effective disarm phase, we can be unintrusive and provide them the space to open up and share their stories.

There are plenty of methods besides questioning we can incorporate that will help our students reflect on their lived experiences.

For example, one of our advisors has a small bookshelf that he has filled with poetry, short stories, and graphic novels. For students who may be more reserved and may not be as comfortable verbally sharing their experiences, these books are available to "check out." This bookshelf is stocked with authors who are representative of our student populations and speak to relatable experiences; this content is intended to show students the power of their stories and help them feel more comfortable.

We want to be sure we are attentive and actively listening to our students during our meetings. We want to limit the time we are on our computers or multitasking, unless we can engage our students in what we are doing (i.e., researching fellowships guidelines, campus resources, and so on).

When we reach the point with our students where they have begun to identify narratives or experiences that they want to write about, we want to be active in helping them develop their ideas. Maybe these stories are rooted in their daily routine (i.e., research, campus involvement, community service) and, due to the familiarity of these routines, the students have not yet recognized the ways they are maturing or the skills they are acquiring. Similarly, students who are excellent time-managers or heavily involved in their communities may not understand how unique they are relative to their peers. As fellowships advisors, we can bring a fresh perspective to these conversations and help our students develop a "strength-based" reconstruction of their narrative that better clarifies the key traits or points reviewers often look for. If we do our job well in the discover phase, our applicants not only feel comfortable sharing their past and current engagements, but also feel safe in sharing their academic and professional aspirations.

3. Dream Phase

In the dream phase advisors seek to understand the hopes and aspirations a student carries with them, some of which they may have never given voice to before. Doing so effectively depends on our ability to acknowledge and support an applicant's dreams without judgment.

While it is appropriate to challenge and push our applicants to dream without boundaries, we can do so while keeping them grounded. We may need to help our advisees see the connections between the discover and the dream phase; it is not uncommon for undergraduates to diligently work toward a goal (i.e., law school, medical school, and so on) without pausing to consider their *why*. If advisees can connect these two phases, it will be easier for them to craft essays that feel intentional and honest.

For example, in personal statements we do not want our students to be vaguely sharing, "I'm *just* so passionate about this" or "I've *always* wanted to do this." Instead, we want them to reflect on how those lived experiences from the discovery phase have influenced and shaped the dreams and aspirations that they have. During the dream phase, we push them to think beyond what they may have been told or believed they could accomplish. We want our advisees to articulate for themselves what they want out of their academics, their college experience, and, ultimately, their careers. If they write with this level of purpose and specificity, they will begin to emphasize to the reader *why* the opportunities they pursue are necessary to achieve their goals.

4. Design Phase

The design phase embodies the fellowships application process. Here, too, advisors guide students without prescribing answers. During this phase, we teach our students how to make effective editorial and organizational decisions, focused on their wants and needs, relative to the awards for which they apply. For example, if a student is unsure whom to ask for a recommendation letter, we can have them list and describe the people who instantly come to mind; then, we may discuss the purpose of the fellowships and begin to draw connections between the mission of the award and what qualifications their recommenders can highlight. In terms of essay organization, our students often have great narratives and ideas, but they do not always know how to organize their thoughts on paper. We do not ask for perfection, but we do encourage our students to read their applications from a stranger's perspective, which often leads to more logical, cohesive organizational choices. Our goal is to help our students feel confident as they make these decisions in their writing, and we believe this confidence may also transfer to their day-to-day decision-making. It may be a hard transition for some of our advisees, but we want them to feel capable of making the best decisions for themselves in their academic journey and not just follow what their parents, guardians, friends, or advisors want for them.

The focus of the design phase should be on what advisees need. Providing positive, constructive feedback is important. We want to focus on the aspects of their applications where there is significant potential in their ideas and how their ideas connect within their essays. If we overly fixate on the negative and where they missed the mark, and not the strengths, students may be less inclined to return. We want to find the silver linings in their applications and in those early drafts, particularly for our students who have never worked with us before.

We also want to avoid the curse of knowledge. That is, as advisors, we are extremely knowledgeable when it comes to these fellowships foundations, the selection processes, and what "traditionally" makes for a competitive application. We should not gatekeep this information, but we cannot fault our students for what they do not know. If we can encourage our students to find the answers or contact foundations and alumni, we can empower them to be advocates for themselves and not be afraid to seek advice to fill gaps in their knowledge.

The design phase is also where we can make effective referrals. For example, at Florida State, we have an excellent Reading and Writing Center that we recommend to students when they want strictly grammatical edits. We, of course, share and make those suggestions for edits when appropriate, but we want to keep our focus on the big-picture ideas and structure of their applications. Or, if our student is from an academic field that our fellowships advisor is unfamiliar with, we may connect them to faculty or staff who can provide better insight, such as our campus' faculty committees, or we can make specific referrals to alumni. Similarly, if our applicants want to become more involved on campus or in their field of study, for service, leadership, or other projects, we want to know where to refer them. This requires advisors to be knowledgeable about the institution and what various offices have to offer. We do not need to have all the answers, but the more diverse our professional network becomes, the easier it will be for us to help our students find what they need as they navigate these application processes.

5. Deliver Phase

While the deliver phase incorporates the necessary technical aspects of submission, both those the applicants are responsible for and those that need to be finalized by advisors, it is also a time when we can reinforce the culture within our offices. Are we an office that prioritizes student growth and development or one that values award recipients and "name brand" recognition? This is not to say we cannot value all these things as advisors, but it is a fine line to walk with our students. At FSU, we want to cultivate and emphasize the former because when our students know we are invested in their growth, development, and success, we have higher return rates from our applicants. If our office culture overvalues award recipients, students could perceive this as being a transactional relationship that puts the office's or university's needs above those of the students.

Follow-up meetings with every student in the weeks after an application process concludes, but before they are notified of their selection, nonselection, or alternate status, also exemplify a supportive office culture. During these meetings, we want to discuss what went well, what did not go well, and how we, both advisor and advisee, can continue to improve. Admittedly, these conversations can bring up tough questions, such as "Are you satisfied with the application you submitted?" or "Do you have a contingency plan if this fellowship does not pan out?" For our students who exceeded expectations during the application process, we want to celebrate their achievement and not overshadow the significance of crossing the finish line. For our students who may have stumbled through the process, or ultimately did not submit or did not become a university nominee, we want to use these conversations as a moment for reflection, growth, and further goal-setting. How advisors end an application process is going to determine whether that student wants to continue working with them. This deliver phase can solidify for students that advisors are advocates for their personal success, which goes much farther than whether or not they receive a fellowship.

6. Don't Settle Phase

In the don't settle phase, we cannot only engender hope that students are capable of achieving their goals but also help then see that there are many intersecting paths that lead them there. Success does not hinge on one single fellowship or award. As we work with our applicants for weeks, months, or years, we hope we learn when it is appropriate to challenge them and when it is appropriate to support them. We want to make sure that, regardless of the news they receive from any fellowship, they are going to "raise the bar" for themselves. Doing so occurs when we help our advisees identify other relevant opportunities, often with concurrent deadlines, that will support their academic growth or development as young professionals. This may include other fellowships; at FSU, it also includes our university's own scholarships and special programs, as well as other leadership programs and internships in Florida and beyond.

We want to prepare our students for the possibility of selection, but whether they are our most competitive or our least competitive applicant, we are always navigating these conversations with them. If we can build their confidence and resilience and help them develop the necessary grit they need for these competitive applications, the likelihood that they will remain a consistent presence within our office throughout their undergraduate education significantly increases. What we have come to see at FSU, in nearly thirty-five years of combined fellowships advising experience, is that our students take these soft skills with them into graduate school and into their professional careers.

What We Are Hearing

Keeping the Six Ds in mind, our office sought to measure whether we were, in the eyes of our students, meeting the mark with each of the appreciative advising phases. While the office had previously sent out an end-of-semester satisfaction survey to all students who have worked with our office and applied earlier in that term, it was not capturing data on the distinct appreciative advising phases until 2022. As our office, since its establishment in 2005, was already using the appreciative advising model without its formal name, the questions asked previously are largely the same as our current set. The updated survey, however, has better aligned our questions with the appreciative advising phases. This update has been particularly helpful in determining which phases we are executing well and which ones still need work. It is also helpful as we consider how we can incorporate appreciative advising approaches and language more thoroughly into our promotional materials and digital media.

The survey has twenty-nine questions that measure student perceptions of our office and services and collects information on the student's year in school, major, and campus engagement. The appreciative advising–directed questions are listed in Table 1.1, with the

Table 1.1

Student satisfaction survey questions, used 2022 to present, aligned with appreciative advising phases

Appreciative advising phase	Statements made to determine if appreciative advising phase objectives are being met
Disarm	I feel that the ONF staff were available and welcoming throughout my process.
Discover	As a result of working with ONF, I believe I have increased clarity about my personal values, academic goals, and career goals.
Dream	As a result of working with ONF, I believe I have considered goals which are "bigger" than those I had when I arrived at the university.
Design	As a result of working with ONF, I believe I am connected to other FSU offices/resources that relate to my goals and interests.
Deliver	I feel that the ONF staff supported my efforts and were concerned about my personal success.
Don't Settle	Based on your application experience, would you consider working with the ONF staff on another application if you are able?

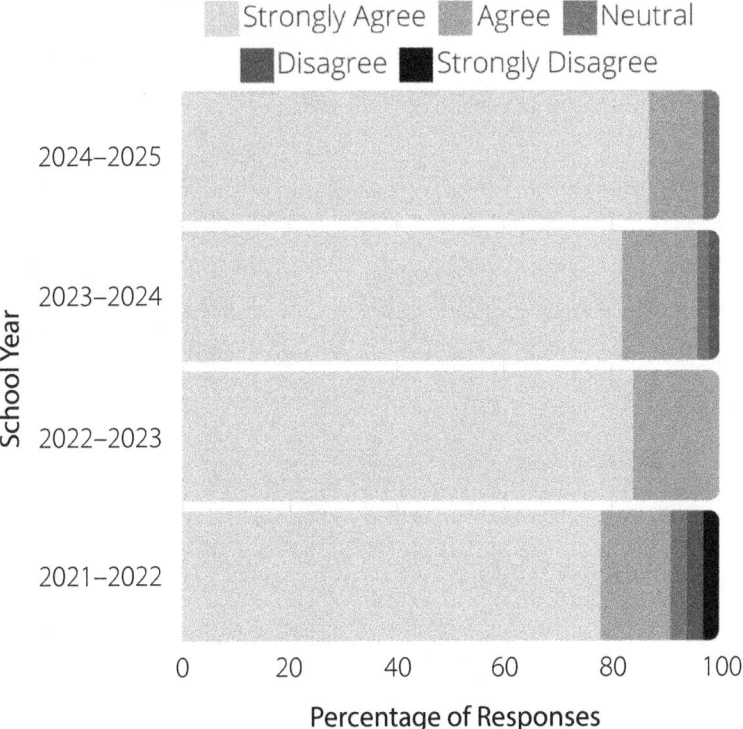

Figure 1.3. Disarm phase

first five asking for responses on a 5-point Likert scale (Strongly Disagree, Disagree, Neutral, Agree, and Strongly Agree) and the last question (Don't Settle) as a binary "yes" or "no" choice.

The results of the satisfaction survey over four years are shown in Figures 1.3–1.8. Note that the 2024–2025 data reflect only half of the academic year, as spring applicants will not receive the survey until April 2025 (after this chapter was submitted for publication).

Overall, during the 2023–2024 school year, our survey respondents indicated that they believed that we were helping them grow and develop in ways that can be highlighted and monitored through the appreciative advising cycle. These results are consistent with

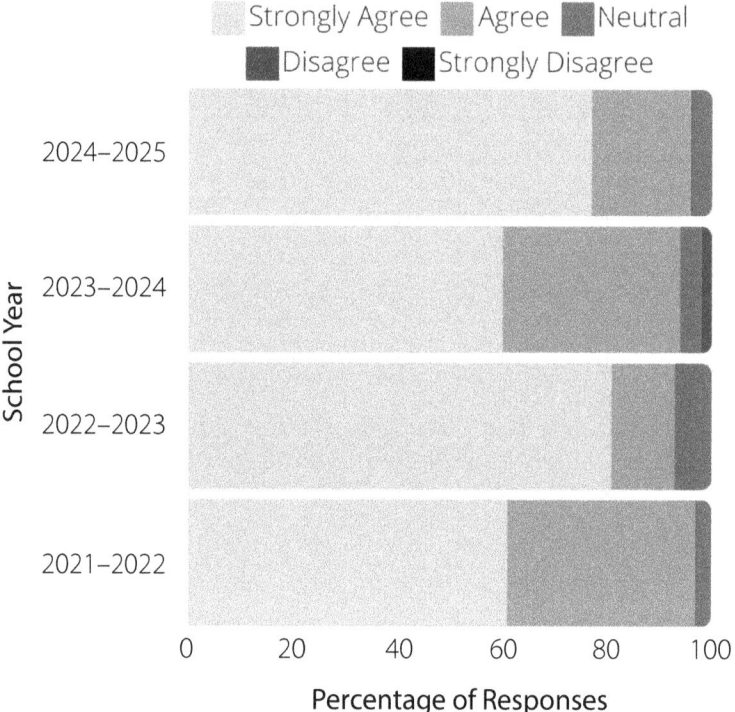

Figure 1.4. Discover phase

what we have seen for the past several years. Even if an applicant did not feel as though we achieved one of our goals, it is encouraging to note that every respondent would consider working with us again. If nothing else, they believe that we, like them, can grow and develop our talents.

The biographical information collected also means our office can parse out specific information on applicants per year in school. From a university administration view, this breakdown aids in our yearly reporting of institutional effectiveness, by measuring and showcasing the impact of our office. From this information, we can see where the strengths and weaknesses of our office lie and then

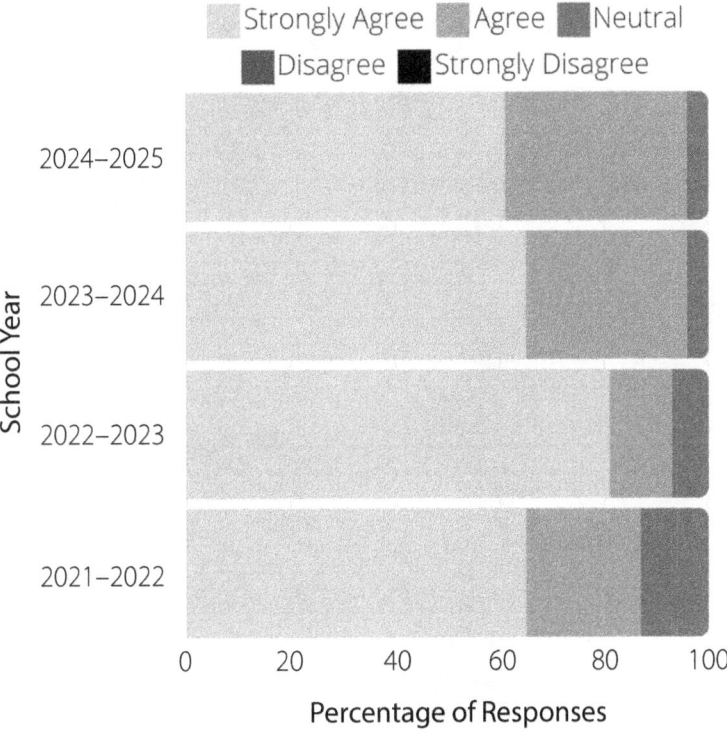

Figure 1.5. Dream phase

incorporate better programming and outreach for our students. For instance, we have found that our first-year (freshman) applicants do not feel as supported as they could in being connected to other offices on campus (our design phase question), which is hardly surprising given that they are so new to the school. (See Figure 1.9.) By sophomore and junior year, we see a larger group of our respondents answering that they "agree" or "strongly agree" that we are connecting them with other FSU offices and resources. This a positive result for second- and third-year students but does mean that we should consider how we can better share university resources and offices to our first-year applicants. Programming targeted for

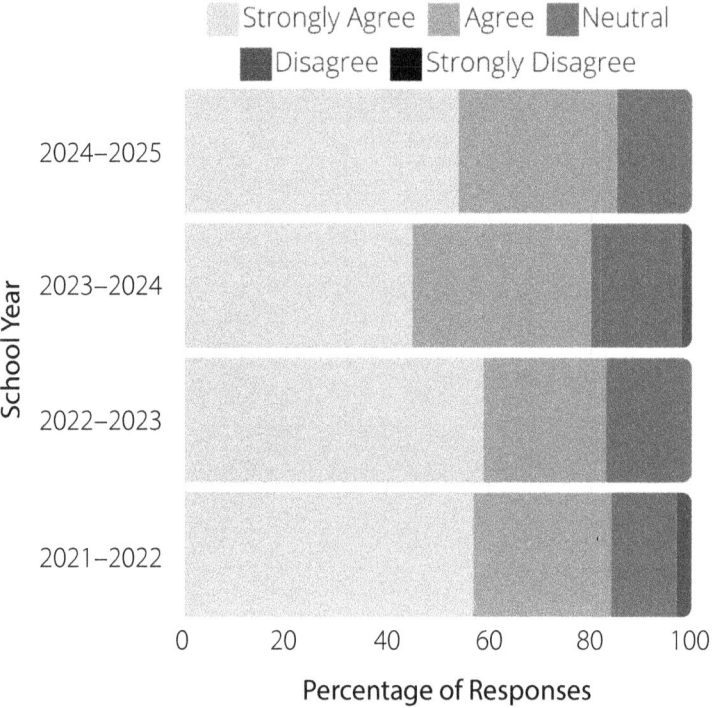

Figure 1.6. Design phase

them may, in the future, emphasize how to get involved on campus and bring in contacts that could be of use during their time at Florida State.

There are, of course, limitations to the data collected by our satisfaction survey. First and foremost is the sample size of respondents every year. The survey is sent to individuals who completed an application during the summer, fall, and spring of each yearly school cycle, and then those who complete the survey make up the data presented here. The applicants we work with are by no means required to complete this survey. Further, we survey only students who complete the fellowships application process, which means that we do not account

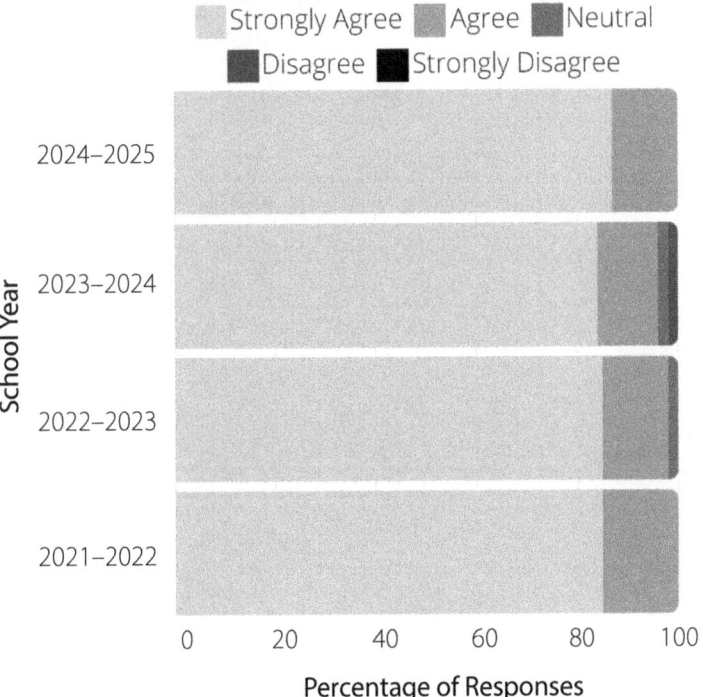

Figure 1.7. Deliver phase

for those applicants who decide not to complete an application. We would benefit from finding a means to gather information from students who come to introductory meetings or who begin but do not complete a fellowship application, but at this time we are not capturing that data. In addition, while our survey is set up to measure student perception, which for our office and administration is acceptable for our needs, we recognize that measuring how students "feel" may not hold the same weight at other institutions. By this measure, it seems that students regard our model as effective for their growth. That works for FSU administration and what is required of us for our annual reporting.

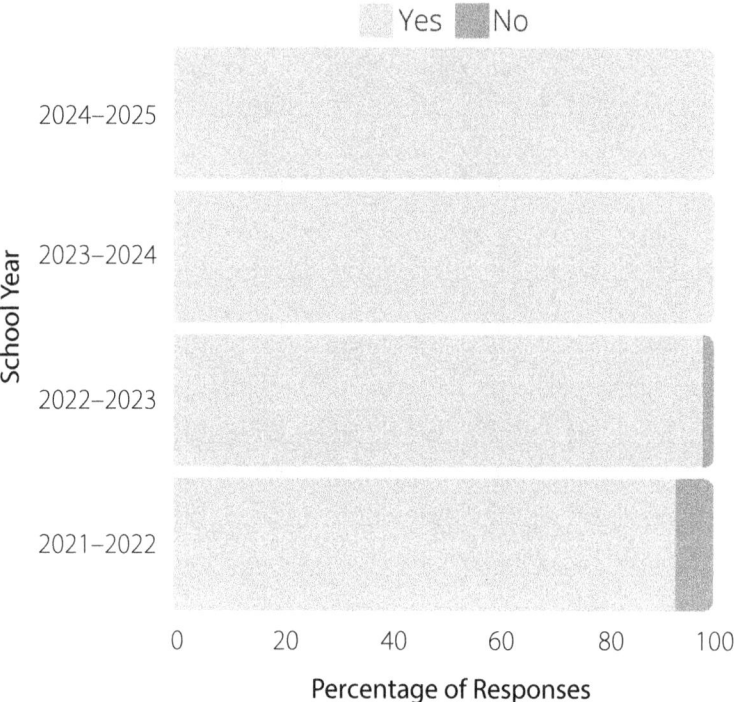

Figure 1.8. Don't settle phase

Conclusion

As our office enters its third decade, the discovery of the appreciative advising model has offered us a tool and a template that will allow us to expand our service and our reach to student populations. While we recognize that not every fellowships office may find the model to be a perfect or possible fit for their office culture or staffing, and while we understand that this model is not needed to build a strong rapport with a student, we are satisfied with how the appreciative advising model aligns with FSU's ONF and our campus culture. The Six Ds provide depth and impact for our students and allow us to give clarity

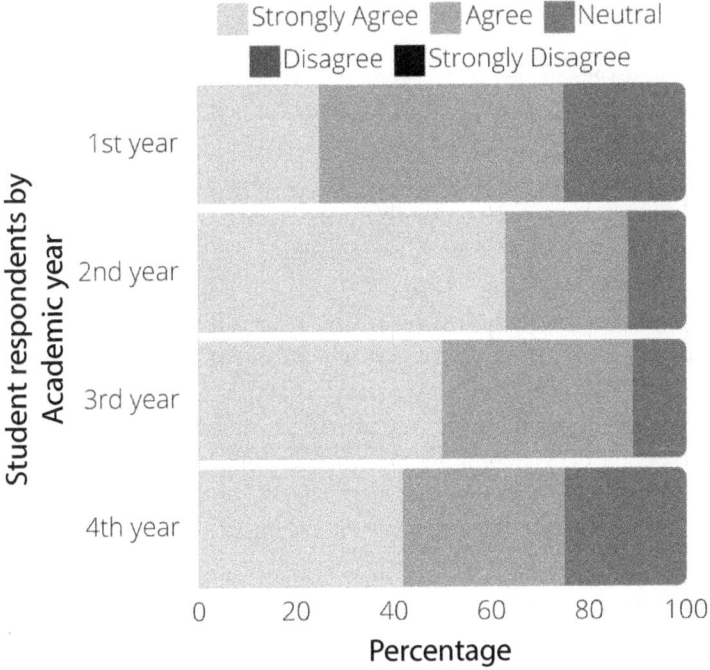

Figure 1.9. Designing phase survey responses by first-, second-, third-, and fourth-year status, 2023–2024. Note that the percentage of first-year (freshman) respondents who believed we hit a neutral mark was larger than for second-year (sophomore) and third-year (junior) respondents. Our fourth-year students (largely comprised of seniors) also felt relatively neutral regarding our connecting them to other campus offices. This may be due to their working with us so close to their graduation date.

and consistency to our approach while allowing each advisor to adapt the stages to their own personality and strengths. The logical and creative path that takes us from the initial stage of *disarm* to create a space, to *discover* what is available, and then to *dream* it as a possibility then allows us to equip students to *design* their narratives and to *deliver* an application. And true to form for our field and our students, regardless of the outcome, we learn that we *don't settle*; rather, we circle back with a stronger rapport to discover the next great step.

Notes

1. Matthew Church, "Integrative Theory of Academic Advising: A Proposition," *The Mentor: An Academic Advising Journal* 7, no. 1 (2005); Marc Lowenstein, "An Alternative to the Development Theory of Advising, *The Mentor: An Academic Advising Journal* 7, no.4 (1999). Both in Jennifer Bloom, Bryant Hutson, and Ye He, *The Appreciative Advising Revolution* (Champaign, IL: Stipes Publishing LLC, 2005), 12.
2. Burns B. Crookston, "A Developmental View of Academic Advising as Teaching," *NACADA Journal* 14, no. 2 (1994): 5–9 (reprinted from *Journal of College Student Personnel* 13 [1972]). In *The Appreciative Advising Revolution*, ed. Jennifer Bloom, Bryant Hutson, and Ye He (Champaign, IL: Stipes Publishing LLC, 2005), 12–13.
3. Robert Glennen, "Intrusive College Counseling," *The School Counselor* 24, no. 1 (1976): 48–50; Jennifer Varney, "Proactive (Intrusive) Advising," *Academic Advising Today* 35, no. 3 (2012): 1–3.
4. Church, "Integrative Theory of Academic Advising: Crookston, "A Developmental View of Academic Advising as Teaching," in *The Appreciative Advising Revolution*, ed. Jennifer Bloom, Bryant Hutson, and Ye He (Champaign IL: Stipes Publishing, 2005), 12–13.
5. Bloom et al., *The Appreciative Advising Revolution*, 14–20.
6. Bloom et al., *The Appreciative Advising Revolution*, 25–34.

2

Trust the Process

Examining Fellowship Applicant Success from the Student Development Lens

KRISTIN BENNIGHOFF, LAURA COLLINS, AND KELSEY FENNER

Fellowships advisors who have joined the profession since the inception of the National Association of Fellowships Advisors (NAFA) have entered a community that shares and is driven by the same set of values. NAFA members are guided by the commitment that to minimize harm and maximize benefit, advisors—along with all stakeholders—must value the process above all else.

In this chapter, we pay special attention to valuing the process above a winning result with specific core NAFA values in mind: *learning*, the belief that opportunities for growth and development are prioritized above outcome(s); *inclusion*, the belief that the process is an occasion to foster a sense of belonging; and *collaboration*, an intention that encourages us to create access and opportunity widely.[1]

According to NAFA's Values and Code of Ethics, "Fellowships systems and processes should prioritize opportunities for applicants, advisors, and additional partners to learn, grow, and develop, regardless of outcome."[2] What do advisors hope applicants will learn from applying to competitive fellowships? The American Association of Colleges & Universities (AAC&U) and the National Association of Colleges & Employers (NACE) identify skills and competencies such as oral communication, critical thinking, ethical judgment, working effectively in teams, demonstrating self-awareness, pursuing and applying feedback, and developing future plans and goals, which prepare students to succeed in their future endeavors.[3]

Inclusion means working to reduce unnecessary barriers to participation in fellowships processes, as well as fostering a sense of belonging within our profession and for our advisees.[4] For large universities and institutions with significant first-generation student populations, the relationships built through fellowships advising can foster that feeling of belonging and show students what is possible for their futures.

Insofar as collaboration means striving to "foster a community of practice which encourages people to work together, minimize harmful competition, and cultivate opportunities to share fellowships expertise,"[5] this chapter is a prime example of this value at work. Three fellowships advisors in the same region, with potential for candidates competing for awards, have collaborated on processes, ideas, practice interviews, and this chapter. NAFA members aim to show other fellowships advisors what is possible with collaboration and fellowship applicants what it means to be truly supportive colleagues.

Over time, fellowships advisors may be called on to explain trends in their fellowship recipients, justify time and resources, and even defend the existence of fellowships advising altogether. By centering responses on the value of the process over the result with evidence, advisors can demonstrate the importance of our work and the work of our applicants. This chapter describes the strategies at three different universities (Rutgers University–Camden, the University of Delaware, and Villanova University) and offers suggestions for how NAFA might standardize a set of learning outcomes that emphasize the value of the process.

Relevant Theories

As NAFA moves into its next quarter century supporting advisors, foundations, and applicants, it may be beneficial to consider creating standardized learning outcomes associated with the process of fellowships advising and applying. These outcomes should be based on identified needs—the things foundations, graduate schools, and employers state as the most sought-after skills, as well as past evidence or what applicants say they have developed or strengthened throughout the application process.

Fellowships advisors rely heavily on their instincts to identify the awards that best fit individual applicants and to coach and advise regarding the opportunities that will help them develop in the ways to which they aspire. If applicants seek opportunities to engage in leadership, there are awards for that; if they are interested in cultural exchange, there are awards for that. Through thoughtful exchange, advisors learn the strengths of their applicants, what motivates them, and how they see—or wish to see—themselves in the world.

Fellowships work, then, is grounded in the knowledge advisors possess about those they advise. Anecdotally, advisors know there are common outcomes (experiences, skills) that applicants routinely seek and that advisors can often deliver through structured processes. But how do we know? What we know about our applicants' interests and what our advising processes can offer are based as much on our practice as they are in an already existing body of work. As fellowships advising continues to professionalize, including standardizing and promoting the learning outcomes associated with it, existing theory provides an understanding of the needs of our applicants and how to be inclusive in establishing and evaluating outcomes.

Grounding fellowships in theory allows advisors to achieve their goals with evidence for programs that engage students in critical developmental stages, processes that support students' identity development, and the ability to create and advocate for inclusivity and access for our students. Using theory as a guide, advisors can develop and solidify strategies that encourage applicants to engage in the whole advising process and achieve the maximum developmental benefits. While there are many theories that address these goals—many of which fall within the student development framework—several are particularly applicable to fellowships advising.

Identity Development Theory describes the essential processes that adolescents and young adults engage in as they strive to form what psychologist Erik Erickson called a coherent sense of self.[6] Relevant to fellowships advisors' work is the identity development with which our students and applicants engage within the educational and vocational domain, as part of their personal identity development, as well as their social identity development, or how they perceive themselves as it relates to their social experiences.[7] Advisors begin nearly all conversations with questions about goals, current and long-term, and how applicants anticipate that the awards and opportunities we support will contribute to those goals. Embedded within these conversations are questions about who they are, who they want to be, and how they see (or wish to see) themselves in the world. Applicants can consider these questions within the safety net of our offices and the university setting overall. Where these essential developmental processes might otherwise occur in early work and other life experiences, our applicants are using fellowships advising and awards opportunities to facilitate their identity development. Through the application process, students are challenged to reflect on the roles they have held and those they aspire to; they are asked to imagine "what if" scenarios and outcomes that force them to consider alternatives they may otherwise not. In a 2021 study of exploration in peer groups, researchers found patterns that support exploration, including clarifying and elaborating an idea and a safe environment.[8] While this study was not conducted in the context of advisor-advisee interactions, it seems plausible that these patterns might also be observed within fellowships advising.

Building on the work students do to form a coherent, stable sense of self and identity, *Self-Authorship Theory* speaks to the iterative and reflective processes that we observe in applicants. While Robert Keagan first proposed the idea of self-authorship, it is most widely associated with Marcia Baxter Magolda,[9] who describes it as the process that young people engage in as they form their own perspectives, including values exploration, investigating possible paths, and taking steps toward and along these paths. Furthermore, self-authorship is distinguished by the questions that emerge through these processes, including "How do I know?"[10] While the relationship between self-authorship and our work as fellowships advisors is likely evident in those questions alone, Mary Hale Tolar makes the connection clearly in "A Path Revealed: Reflections of a Former Scholarship Advisor," where she describes how her fellowships advisor—the revered Nancy Twiss—"steadily, earnestly, and with great grace guided me through a process, grounded in a series of questions that helped me determine both my grand plan, and my next steps."[11] The questions, simply put, are: "Who am I? What do I care about? What kind of contribution do I want to make in this world? How am I going to get there?"

The third pertinent theory, *Experiential Learning Theory (ELT)*, offers a framework from which we can draw empirical evidence for the value added to our applicants who engage in the advising process. ELT, credited to psychologist and educational theorist David Kolb, suggests that people learn best by doing.[12] As fellowships advisors, we support student learning through several of the established experiential learning styles, including imagining, thinking, deciding, analyzing, and reflecting. According to the Association for Experiential Education, "Throughout the experiential learning process, the learner is actively engaged in posing questions, investigating, experimenting, being curious, solving problems, assuming responsibility, being creative, and constructing meaning."[13] Fellowship experiences are among the many opportunities for experiential learning in higher education, but the process of applying—regardless of outcome and participation in the experience—engages applicants in many of these same processes with similar benefits, including clarified values and skill development.

These theories are just a small selection that posit how our students' learning and development may be best supported. For us, they provide a framework for how we consider the advising process as it relates to our students' growth through the challenging and rewarding experience of applying to nationally competitive awards. Incorporating these theories into practice is an opportunity for fellow advisors to further investigate and provide evidence for how our work is advancing students' development and preparedness to be the leaders and changemakers they aspire to be.

Skill and Competency Frameworks

The centering of skill acquisition and competency building within learning and development theory is reflected in higher education institutions' focus on developing college graduates who are equipped to transition to and find success in career and life. A result of this focus is a greater emphasis on the concept of employability and the impact that universities have on preparing graduates. Centering fellowships advising and process management within career and professional development frameworks can provide grounding for measuring student growth, evaluating process success, and encouraging broader engagement with fellowships processes because of the skill development they offer. College and university career development associations have researched the integral skills and competencies expected of college graduates by employers and universities. The National Association for Colleges and Employers (NACE) outlines eight career readiness competencies that "broadly prepare the college educated for success in the workplace and lifelong career management."[14] Originally introduced in 2015, the NACE Career Readiness Competencies are a result of the shifting relationship between universities and the labor market. Refined in 2024, the eight competencies are Career and Self-Development, Leadership, Communication, Professionalism, Critical Thinking, Teamwork, Equity and Inclusion, and Technology. Each of the competencies is further broken down into greater detail; for example, Communication is described as "demonstrating verbal, written, and non-verbal/body language abilities."[15] Fellowships activities, particularly the student's engagement with a fellowship's application process, offers growth opportunities in many—if not all—of these competency areas.

Figure 2.1 shows the results of Villanova University's 2023 Fulbright Post-Submission Survey. The skills, competencies, and perceptions surveyed were structured to broadly connect to the larger competencies identified by NACE. For example, "articulating your research/study/career goals to people outside your field," "ability to write clearly," and "ability to write applications" connected to the Communication competency. "Ability to build relationships with professionals in your field" and "Self Confidence" were tied to the Career and Self-Development and Professionalism competencies. This structure offered the opportunity to ground fellowships' development outcomes in broader conceptual frameworks already

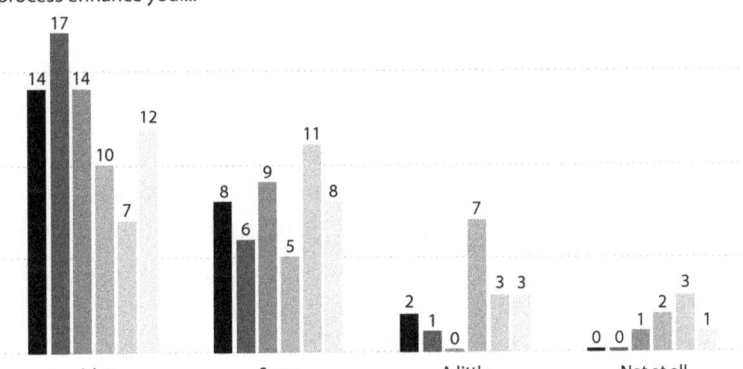

Figure 2.1. Villanova University Fulbright Post-Submission Survey, October 2023

understood and recognized by universities, while also providing an opportunity to examine whether Villanova's Fulbright applicants perceived any growth in these skill and competency areas.

In addition to the Villanova survey, Gallup also conducted research on college experiences that students felt prepared them to graduate with an undergraduate degree in four years and find success in post-college life. These "Big Six" included experiences such as "I had a mentor who encouraged me to pursue my goals."[16] Gallop's research was further supported by the American Association of Colleges and Universities' (AAC&U), which found that among the experiences most valued by employers "involved working with a mentor or individual advisor" and "working with people from different backgrounds."[17] Individual advising, encouragement of self-reflection, and student mentorship are daily tasks of fellowships advising, and those relationships between advisor and student can last months or years depending on the student and application timeline. Fellowships advisors are heavily engaged in preparing college graduates for a successful post-college life, and fellowships offices can point to Gallup and the AAC&U frameworks to showcase how their work and the experiences they offer students engaged in the fellowships process are directly tied to student development.

As the fellowships field continues to professionalize, using similar frameworks and tailoring advising approaches that reflect the existing research on developing career and life-ready graduates can provide insight to advisors in how to create a fellowships advising system on their campuses and potentially lead to a foundation-wide understanding within the National Association of Fellowships Advisors of what skills and developmental experiences fellowships offices offer to students who engage in any stage of the fellowships process. Using a skills and learning development approach also provides a clearer understanding of how fellowships offices and advisors support their institution's critical mission of preparing career and life-ready graduates.

Institutional Background

To develop these core career readiness competencies, our institutions have created purposeful opportunities for students that connect to fellowship application processes. These workshops and classes are most connected to NACE's Career and Self-Development, Communication, Leadership, and Professionalism competencies.[18]

Villanova University, Rutgers University–Camden, and the University of Delaware represent three different types of institutions and student populations along with distinct histories of fellowships advising.

Villanova University is a private Augustian-Catholic doctoral-granting university serving approximately 10,000 undergraduate and graduate students. Villanova students hail from over fifty-five countries and every US state. Fellowships are managed by the Center for Research and Fellowships (CRF), a three-function unit established in 2001. CRF supports undergraduate and graduate research programs and fellowships and manages the university's merit scholarship program. CRF has one staff member dedicated to fellowships, with additional advising support provided by the other four advisors when possible.

Rutgers University–Camden is a Public R2 institution serving approximately 6,000 total enrolled students. In 2017, the Office of Scholar Development and Fellowship Advising (OSDFA) was founded, initially as a part-time endeavor. In 2022, OSDFA became a full-time office with two dedicated staff serving undergraduates, graduates, and alumni. Rutgers-Camden is a Minority Serving Institution (MSI), with additional designations as an Asian American and Native American Pacific Islander-Serving Institution (AANAPISI) and an Emerging Hispanic-Serving Institutions (HSI). More than half (54 percent) of students are the first in their families to attend college and more than half (54 percent) are Pell eligible, while an overwhelming majority (88.9 percent) receive financial aid. Nearly half (46.8 percent) of incoming students arrive as transfers, with about 40 percent having earned an associate's degree. In the most recent World News rankings, Rutgers-Camden was recognized as a Top Performer for Social Mobility (fifteenth, of 433 ranked national universities).

The University of Delaware (UD) is a public, mid-size major research university with approximately 19,000 undergraduate students and 4,300 graduate students. The majority of students are not from the state of Delaware, but rather from a variety of neighboring states such as New York, New Jersey, Pennsylvania, and Maryland. Fellowships advising has mostly been housed within the Honors College as part of one staff member's responsibilities. Currently, UD is in the process of creating a new Office of National Fellowships.

Each of the institutions has worked on leveraging, cementing, and celebrating student development in the fellowships advising processes.

Fellowships Courses and Workshops: Leveraging the Process

One strategy for supporting student learning outcomes and gaining recognition as an important institutional unit is leveraging student development as a focus within fellowships work. Increasing awareness of fellowships opportunities is a preliminary step in getting applicants and prospective applicants to engage in the development work offered by fellowships processes. Incorporating fellowships skills and the developmental learning fellowships processes offer into an institution's academic offerings and curriculum can generate wider awareness of and access to the opportunities and growth available through fellowships.

In the early stages of establishing a fellowships office, UD offered personal statement writing workshops to all students at the university—not only those pursuing national fellowships, but also students in any year who were thinking about applying to graduate school, a summer Research Experience for Undergraduates (REU), or competitive internships. Open workshops that serve the entire university community are useful if a unit needs more visibility and if fellowships advisors want to meet potential applicants. Hosting workshops also allows connection with other key partner units if the events are advertised.

Furthermore, formal courses that explain the mechanics of applying to fellowships or courses that focus on wider but relevant skills, such as writing and goal-setting, can help fellowships advisors leverage the transferability and relevance of fellowships skills and translate it to a wider audience. This approach has benefits in that it provides a chance for fellowships advisors to connect with students who may be outside their normal recruitment pool, it delivers content and lessons focused on student development and skill acquisition in formalized classroom settings, it highlights the applicability of fellowship skills, and it affirms the status of fellowships advisors as instructors and professionals in student development realms.

At Villanova University, the first fellowships-focused course launched in January 2023 as part of the university's Arts and Sciences Professional Development program, a one-credit range of courses that are geared toward preparing students for post-graduation success. Fellowships at Villanova are considered part of the professional development offices, but this course was the first to identify fellowships opportunities and the application process as a professional development activity that would help students grow and prepare for post-university endeavors. One course, for example,

Global and Post-Graduate Opportunities and Fellowships, walked students through the process of researching, selecting, and preparing application materials for a fellowship or post-graduate opportunity. Students engaged in future planning and goal-setting exercises, conducted information interviews with past fellowship recipients, learned how to conduct self and peer reviews, and wrote and edited multiple personal statement drafts. The stated course outcomes included increasing writing and oral communication skills, learning about goal-setting, building critical thinking skills, and developing other skills and competencies that connect to NAFA's learning value and NACE's career competencies. Course feedback surveys indicated a 4.9/5.0 overall score with responses from ten of the sixteen course participants. Following the course, over half of the students have applied for a fellowship opportunity, and the course has been renewed for future semesters.

The University of Delaware also taught a fellowships/leadership development course starting in 2013 through the Honors College. The one-credit course, Intellect and the Good Life, was intended as a pipeline for identifying potential leaders and change agents among second-semester sophomores. In the course, students were asked to reflect on the connection between intellect and the good life, to evaluate the role of diversity in problem-solving and creative thinking, and to think about what comes after they finish their undergraduate degree. In addition, students developed the oral and written communication skills required for creative participation in intellectual, professional, and civic communities; discussed their goals and future plans; and prepared themselves for graduate school, scholarship, and employment applications. Through assignments, students explored the state of their fields and disciplines, ideas about leadership, the significance of "failures," and how to conduct informational interviews. The final assignment was writing a personal statement, which could be used for fellowship and graduate school applications and future cover letters. Between 2013 and 2022, ninety-six students completed this course, producing written materials and honing career-ready skills that supported their future endeavors, including fellowship, graduate school, and job applications.[19] Ultimately, 27 percent of students enrolled in this course have been applicants and finalists for some of the most distinguished fellowship awards supported by the institution.

Recently, Rutgers University–Camden began utilizing a learning management system to offer a course site with informational modules for all interested students to enroll in to learn more about award opportunities and their associated application processes. The university is also following the lead of several other institutions in offering a cohort, volunteer program that is intended to expose students to these awards from their first year and encourage their meaningful engagement in opportunities that will support their eventual applications. While data for these initiatives are not yet available, early indications suggest that these are positive additions to increasing awareness of fellowships and educating the campus population about the value of applying.

Assessment and Reporting: Cementing the Process

When we think about these processes in terms of assessment, we are setting intentions for how we communicate our services and what we offer our students through the ability to measure our effectiveness in delivering those services. Using assessment allows advisors to bolster storytelling and illustrate the benefits of the application process to all stakeholders, from campus leadership to foundations.

As advisors, we utilize data to inform and define for ourselves the experiences and outcomes that our students value most and that we are capable of providing through the advising process. This chapter has identified accessible experiences and outcomes that can become the foundation for what will be a defined scope of learning that all individuals who engage in the fellowship application process can successfully achieve. These proposed learning outcomes will serve as the evidence from which we can tell the story of how fellowships advising benefits our applicants' development.

At Rutgers University–Camden, learning outcomes and assessment are used to guide every aspect of our work, whether that is in programming or advising. In all our interactions, identifying the need—or what brought the applicant to us—and establishing clear learning goals enable us to determine whether we have moved the needle in supporting students' development. After identifying applicant need(s) and intentions, or learning goals, we can clearly articulate the learning objectives we want students to meet. For example, for each of our programs, we can say, "As a result of participating in this process, students will be able to . . ." Examples of those objectives might include "articulate associated career options," "identify personal values, goals, attitudes, and beliefs," or "identify attainable goals that yield confidence in one's ability to achieve them." At the conclusion of a program, workshop, or application cycle, we are then able to assess whether or not learning outcomes were achieved by surveying participants.

In 2023 Villanova University curated a new end-of-award survey that focuses on understanding student growth In terms of the skills and competencies identified by NACE, NAFA, and AAC&U. Figure 2.1 reflects responses to one question about student perception of skill growth throughout the Fulbright award process.

This assessment approach grounded Villanova's fellowships processes in development, rather than award outcomes, and it was continued in the reporting process. In all outward-facing reporting and presentations, including to the University's Board of Trustees, the focus was on the growth and skill gain experienced by participating in the fellowship application process and working with Villanova's CRF. Basing its work on student development, skill acquisition, and competency building provides CRF with the opportunity to detangle fellowships from "winning" and expand the understanding of the center's work—namely, engaging students in developmental processes that will prepare them to build and hone skills that will help them succeed after Villanova. This application-as-development approach provides a robust reporting framework that encapsulated the entirety of the fellowships advising and management process. It is a shift from previous reporting approaches, which centered outcomes in award recipient numbers. Challenges brought on by focusing on recipient outcome—such as low recipient years, the minimizing of advisors' work to producing winners, and the erasure of the non-winning applicants' work—were mitigated by the development focused-reporting approach.

In the absence of formal reporting requirements, there is still value in understanding the impact these processes have on fellowship applicants. For example, at the University of Delaware, tracking the long-term outcomes for applicants, including graduate education acceptances and career paths of all applicants, not just those who were selected as finalists and/or received awards. At UD, non-recipients have received full funding for law school at University of Virginia, a PhD in Chemistry at Harvard, a position with Teach for America in Hawaii followed by graduate school at University of Chicago, a professional staff member role on the US Senate Appropriations Committee, and a mission manager position with Nanoracks (private aerospace industry). Multiple fellowship applicant graduates went on to fully funded PhDs at Stanford, the University of Pennsylvania, and MIT. These accomplishments speak to the quality of UD's applicants and the application process, regardless of whether they received a fellowship.

Celebrating the Process

As advisors and institutional members of NAFA, we emphasize the value of students' intellectual and personal development through the fellowship process and use techniques that attempt to measure the value of the process of applying for fellowships.[20]

Rutgers–Camden is building a culture of awareness of fellowship awards and supporting students through the application process. For the largely first-generation population, presenting these awards as accessible has been the focus of the work since the formation of the office in 2017. As part of the effort to tell the story of how applying for awards can benefit their development—regardless of outcome—the university has established a few key processes.

First, Rutgers-Camden advisors focus on "success" as our applicants define it. Student success has no shortage of definitions within higher education, but we find often that our applicants define success by their willingness to try and learn from new experiences. Those who engage in the fellowship application process emerge having done just that. When we began surveying our applicants after they hit submit, we ended the survey with this final question: "Given your experience applying to Fellowships and Scholarships, what does 'success' mean to you now?" Here are some examples of the responses:

- "The application process allowed me to better understand my goals and aspirations and brought me closer to achieving them." S.F., DAAD Scholarship recipient
- "Applying for awards has not only helped me grow professionally, but also personally. These processes have been the hardest and most rewarding thing I have done." S.J., Fulbright & Schwarzman finalist
- "Through the application process, I had the chance to reflect upon and articulate who I am as a person and aspiring professional." J. B., Udall applicant

In each of these examples, applicants place emphasis on the process—not the outcome.

Another signature event at Rutgers-Camden is the "You Hit Submit" annual celebration. Late in the spring semester each year, we host an event that welcomes every applicant who "hit submit" on an award for that academic year, regardless of outcome. Campus leadership, faculty mentors, staff supporters, and applicant loved ones are invited to gather for an evening gala-style event. With a selection of speeches that celebrate and thank our applicants for their bravery and persistence in completing the application, along with hors devours, a photo booth, music, and a slideshow, this event is always one of the highlights of our year.

Finally, Rutgers-Camden celebrates applicants who complete the application cycle by awarding each a customized digital badge. These badges reflect the award they have applied for and recognize the effort required to successfully move through the application cycle to submission. Applicants can link their digital badges to their LinkedIn pages to signal to their peers and the larger community their commitment to the reflective and developmental processes that are inherent in fellowship applications.

Conclusion

Advisors set an intention with each applicant that the process of applying to fellowships is a developmental activity that offers applicants the chance to gain or hone skills and competencies. This idea allows both applicants and advisors to manage expectations in competitive selection processes over which we have no control. Communicating clearly to applicants that the process of applying is a worthwhile use of time and important to personal and professional development is an essential part of advising conversations.

There are efforts across our profession to collect and publish empirical research providing evidence for the inherent value of fellowships advising and applying, regardless of outcome—something to which we, as advisors, can all readily attest. It is our hope that this evidence will be used to standardize a set of learning outcomes that emphasize the value of the process. These standards will be useful not only to new fellowships advisors but also to advisors seeking ways to assess their work, demonstrate their value to student success, and/or establish a central unit for fellowships advising if one does not exist at their institution.

Empirical evidence is useful, but as advisors we see firsthand the growth in our fellowship applicants. We observe our NAFA values of Learning, Inclusion, and Collaboration at work. Fellowships advisors build relationships and provide guidance that has an impact beyond fellowship applications, and that is the true win.

Notes

1. National Association of Fellowships Advisors (NAFA), Values and Code of Ethics, May 6, 2024, https://www.nafadvisors.org/about-us/values-and-code-of-ethics/.
2. NAFA, Values.
3. Terri Flateby and Tara Rose, "From College to Career Success: How Educators and Employers Talk About Skills," *Liberal Education*, July 16, 2021, https://www.aacu.org/liberaleducation/articles/from-college-to-career-success-how-educators-and-employers-talk-about-skills.
4. NAFA, Values.
5. NAFA, Values.

6. Erik Erikson, *Identity: Youth and Crisis* (New York: W. W. Norton, 1994).
7. See Susan Branje, Elizabeth De Moore, Jenna Spitzer, and Andrik Becht, "Dynamics of Identity Development in Adolescence: A Decade in Review," *Journal of Research on Adolescence* 31, no. 4 (November 24, 2021): 908–27, https://doi.org/10.1111/jora.12678.
8. Kazumi Sugimura, Jan-Ole Gmelin, Mandy van der Gaag, and E. Saskia Kunnen, "Exploring Exploration: Identity Exploration in Real-Time Interactions among Peers," *Identity* 22, no. 1 (July 15, 2021): 17–34, https://doi.org/10.1080/15283488.2021.1947819.
9. Lisa Boes, Marcia Baxter Magolda, and Jennifer Buckley, "Foundational Assumptions and Constructive Developmental Theory: Self Authorship Narratives," in *Development and Assessment of Self-Authorship*, ed. Marcia B. Baxter Magolda, Elizabeth G. Creamer, and Peggy S. Meszaros (New York: Routledge, 2010), 3–24.
10. Marcia Baxter Magolda, *Making Their Own Way Narratives for Transforming Higher Education to Promote Self-Development* (Sterling, VA: Stylus Publishing, 2001).
11. Mary Hale Tolar, "A Path Revealed: Reflections of a Former Scholarship Advisor," in *Nationally Competitive Scholarships: Serving Students and the Public Good*, ed. Suzanne McCray (Fayetteville: University of Arkansas Press, 2007), 87–90.
12. Institute for Experiential Learning, "What Is Experiential Learning?" December 27, 2023, https://experientiallearninginstitute.org/what-is-experiential-learning/. For more on David Kolb's theory on experiential learning, see David Kolb, Richard Boyatzis, and Charalampos Mainemelis, "Experiential Learning Theory: Previous Research and New Directions," in *Perspectives on Thinking, Learning, and Cognitive Styles*, ed. Robert J. Sternberg and Li-fang Zhang (New York: Routledge, 2001), 227–48.
13. "What Is Experiential Education?," Association for Experiential Education, n.d., accessed August 28, 2024, https://www.aee.org/what-is-experiential-education.
14. National Association of Colleges and Employers (NACE), *Competencies for a Career-Ready Workforce*, 2024, www.naceweb.org/docs/default-source/default-document-library/2024/resources/nace-career-readiness-competencies-revised-apr-2024.pdf?sfvrsn=1e695024_3.
15. NACE, *Competencies*.
16. Gallup, *Great Jobs, Great Lives: The 2014 Gallup-Purdue Index Report*, accessed April 11, 2025, https://www.gallup.com/services/176768/2014-gallup-purdue-index-report.aspx.
17. Flateby and Rose, "From College to Career Success."

18. NACE, *Competencies*.
19. From 2013 to 2022, the class produced twelve Truman-endorsed applicants including two Truman Scholars, four Fulbright awardees, one Schwarzman Scholar, six endorsed Marshall/Rhodes applicants of whom one was a Rhodes finalist, two Gates Cambridge finalists, of whom one was a Gates Cambridge recipient, and one Critical Language Scholar.
20. Villanova and UD celebrate fellowships in various ways, including campus-wide recognition events, certificates, and photoshoots. This article focuses on one institution's approach, Rutgers-Camden's, for brevity.

3

Writing the Future in Fulbright Applications

PAUL FOGLEMAN

Many nationally competitive scholarship and award applications ask applicants to write about future plans.[1] Examples include questions twelve and thirteen on the Truman scholarship application: "What do you hope to do and what position do you hope to have upon completing your graduate studies?" "What do you hope to do and what position do you hope to have five to seven years later?" In the case of the Boren scholarship application (as of January 2025), applicants are asked to "make a specific, detailed, and focused argument specific to your academic interests and professional goals." The personal statement section of the Critical Language Scholarship (CLS) asks applicants to answer "What are your academic and professional goals? How will you make the most of your CLS experience to reach these goals?" The Program Information section of the Fall 2024 Fulbright US Student Program application asked applicants to write about their "plans upon return to the US. The applicant's career and/or educational plans after completing the Fulbright grant."

After advising undergraduate Fulbright applicants for several years, I started sensing "senior angst" among some undergraduate applicants when they were asked to write about their future plans. For the past seven years, starting with their first year in high school, these students have generally known what they will be doing the following year—as in "I am a fourteen-year-old freshman in high school this year, and next year I will be a fifteen-year-old sophomore." They repeat the sequence on starting college, but after reaching their senior year and thinking about their post-baccalaureate future, things can get murky. Factoring in comparisons with classmates, friends, and roommates, broader societal expectations à la "What are you doing after you graduate?" and economic expectations that they start earning a living and making student loan payments, anxiety is an understandable response. Further, previous research has concluded that "most traditional-age undergraduate students will not navigate a path to self-authorship by the end of their undergraduate careers."[2] Further still, neurotypical twenty-one- and twenty-two-year-olds are developing their prefrontal cortex, which is part of a "core network" in the brain that integrates information from the past to construct "possible future events."[3]

As advisors, we need to ask, "What is helpful guidance for these applicants in writing about their future selves at this stage in their lives?" Ideally, we serve as competent mentors, calmly encouraging them to take some time to think about what they would like to be doing during their "defining decade"[4] and how the scholarship or fellowship they are applying for fits into that plan. Many people have taken "right turns" in their lives, unexpectedly ending up in a profession, job, or graduate program they had not imagined themselves in. Such anecdotes provide paradoxical evidence that on the one hand, the future is uncertain, but on the other, students do steer their own course.[5] Among past applicants whom I advised, two Fulbright English Teaching Assistant (ETA) applicants stand out as examples of the two ends of a spectrum where one side is defined by a post-Fulbright life trajectory matching what they foresaw and planned for themselves (Student A) and the other represented by a trajectory that did not match those plans (Student B). Advising applicants like these two over the course of over a decade led to the central motivating question of this essay: "To what extent do Fulbright applicants end up fulfilling the plans they proposed for themselves?" Secondarily, would it be helpful if advisors were able to cite a study centered on this question when advising Fulbright (and other) applicants? This essay continues with an introduction about writing about the future and the concept of uncertainty before analyzing our survey results. Since humans expressing themselves through writing is involved in this study, we put AI to the test of writing about the future in the context of the Fulbright application prompt.

Writing the Future

One practical bit of writing and editing advice often conveyed in introductory composition classes is to apply individual lenses to what the student has written. The proofreading lens is one example—students may wish to read through an essay and focus solely on grammar or on citations and notes. In a similar vein, I have started advising applicants to apply a time and verb tense–oriented lens to their statements, to interrogate any sentence in the past tense, and to question how or whether that sentence is contributing to the overarching aim to convince the reader of the applicant's ability to carry out the proposed objectives. One of the unintentional outcomes for students who do not have the confidence and clarity of a "Student A" is that, when faced with writing about themselves teaching, studying, or carrying out their research in another country and their plans on return to the United States, they fall back on writing about what they have done rather than what they anticipate doing or hope to do. Moreover, application reviewers will have other materials (professional experience, awards and extracurricular activities, recommendation letters) that are fundamentally past-tense oriented, in essence relating: "Here are things I have done; places I have traveled; languages I have learned; and letters from people who can attest to my abilities and amiable personality." Students want to explain and impress simultaneously. When that understandable impulse carries through to personal statements and applicants encounter this easier-said-than-done aspect of applying for a Fulbright (and most other scholarships and fellowships), part of the advisor's job is to explain the need to contend with the boundaries of time and space and "be comfortable with ambiguity and complexity."[6] The wording of the Fulbright application prompt can result in this being especially intimidating to undergraduate seniors as it asks them to make a psychological leap of approximately two years from the time of the application and to hazard a number of presumptions: (1) in August or September they have successfully completed and submitted an application due in early October; (2) they will have advanced through the stages of the competitive process over the ensuing six to seven months; (3) they were selected in the spring of the following year; (4) they embarked on their Fulbright roughly one year in the future; (5) they had a significant and memorable experience as a Fulbright grantee.

Perhaps the most common comment our campus review committees share with applicants regarding writing about their plans is to assure them that no one is going to contact them in five, seven, or ten years after their return from a Fulbright experience to confirm that they actually adhered to the plans they had for themselves at the time of preparing the application. And when I am advising students who are familiar with the nuances of different genres of writing, I will explain that the genre they are aiming for in writing about their future is "plausible fiction."[7] This fiction does need to be based in their best understanding of their future at that moment of writing that they do plan to pursue a career in service or with the environment or connected to research, but it is understood that the actual outcomes will be affected by various circumstances ("right turns") that come along the student's career path.

An Aside About Uncertainty

At a recognition ceremony some years ago, a student recipient thanked staff and faculty in attendance for guiding her during her undergraduate career. She specifically called out one professor for assuring her that "uncertainty is okay!" This comment prompted me to start thinking more deeply about uncertainty and eventually led to the creation of a class activity about the difference between uncertainty and indecision. To help lighten the atmosphere, I displayed a *Bloom County* comic strip in which five of the characters are on the end of a wooden plank over a swimming hole.[8] They are hesitant to jump in because they think they see a snake. Right before the plank breaks in the last panel, the last one on the plank (Binkley) states: "Ya know, Voltaire once said that there's a certain inevitable futility in indecision." During the class discussion about nuanced differences between the two words, *indecision* was associated with phrases like "spinning one's wheels" or words like *inertia*; whereas, *uncertainty*, though a familiar word, was harder to pin down—veiled and suspenseful—and applicable in various contexts. The type of uncertainty that students most often experience is "operational uncertainty," which "relates to unpredictability in human actions and decisions." (There are five other types of uncertainty: aleatory, epistemic, parameter, model, deep.)[9]

Later in the discussion, I link this comic strip and the "uncertainty/indecision" discussion to scholarship and fellowship applications, noting to students that if they do not commit to a decision to apply, they certainly would not be successful in that context. But if they make a good faith, focused effort in preparing an application, there is uncertainty in whether or not it will be successful, but the hope is that they will have achieved something less quantifiable but also important—namely, that they will have learned something about themselves and their goals and will have gone through the process of articulating these goals in writing and discussing them with others. Perhaps they will have developed a degree of confidence and agency when responding to the "What are you doing after you graduate?" type questions. On a more practical level, advisors hope that the work an applicant puts into preparing a Fulbright application can be applied toward other post-baccalaureate pursuits, especially for those seeking ETA positions.

The Study and Findings

Having served as the primary advisor to Fulbright applicants for the past fourteen years at a large public university, I have access to hundreds of written responses to the "Plans upon return to the U.S." prompt in the Fulbright application. With the assistance of an undergraduate student, we invited approximately 200 past applicants to take part in the study. In the email invitation, we informed potential participants that if they agreed to take part in the study, we would retrieve the response they wrote to the "future plans" prompt and send it to them via email with a link to a survey. Participants were instructed to read their response and then answer two questions. The first question was, "Which one of the following statements most accurately describes the future plans you wrote about?" We provided four options:

1. The description of my plans matches what I have done since then and am doing now.
2. Some of the details are different, but my life has proceeded according to those plans.
3. About half of what I expected has occurred.
4. The plans I had for myself at that time are different from what I am doing today.

The second question was open-ended, asking participants if they recalled what motivated them to write those plans. We solicited graduate and undergraduate applicants who had completed applications in the fall semesters of 2013 through and including 2018 (six falls total) and did not distinguish between applicants who received a Fulbright award and those who did not. Thirty-two participants completed the survey, and Figure 3.1 displays the distribution of their answers to the first question. In addition, several respondents provided text entries.

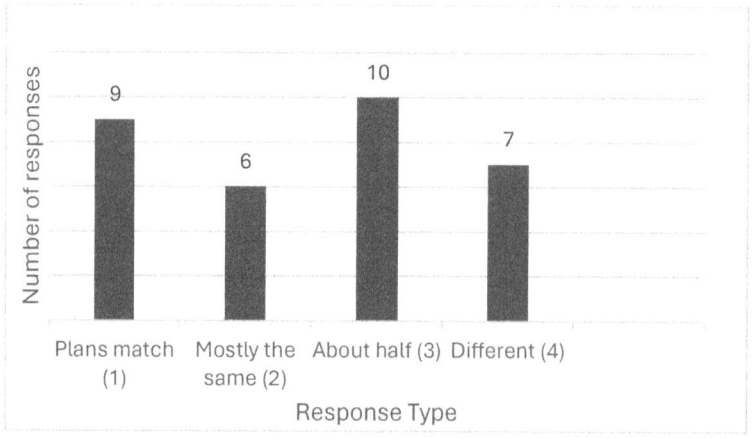

Figure 3.1. Survey responses

An initial observation is the relatively similar distribution across the four response types. One explanation for this outcome could be that the majority of Fulbright applicants from our university are in the social and behavioral sciences and humanities rather than field-specific disciplines such as nursing or accounting—with the exception of students completing degrees in education—so it would follow that they would have less of an ability to forecast their longer-term work and graduate study plans and goals.[10]

This aligns with a 2008 study by the National Center for Education Statistics, which found that one year after completing their bachelor's degrees, 39 percent of the social and behavioral science majors and 54 percent of the humanities majors answered that they were not working in a field related to their degree.[11] More recently, in his 2023 *New Yorker* essay, Nathan Heller reports on an interview with Jeffrey Cohen, Arizona State University's Dean of Humanities. Cohen had 826 undergraduates surveyed, and one of the conclusions was that students "had no idea which careers humanities study led to."[12]

The Written Responses

There were twenty-seven written responses to the open-ended prompt asking participants if they recall what motivated them to write these specific plans. Written responses were anonymized and were not analyzed alongside what the respondent wrote at the time of the Fulbright application. Most of the written responses (sixteen) expressed being motivated for academic and professional reasons—nine describing wanting to eventually work or study in an international context and seven specified plans to attend graduate school or continuing their graduate school education as motivating factors. Six responses included the phrase "at the time," suggesting that these applicants were reflecting on a period of their life when they had plans and goals that later did not come to fruition. None of those six respondents selected option one in the first survey question (plans match outcome). Of the remaining five responses, three did not recall what had motivated them to write those future plans at the time of the application, and two of the written responses were too short and general to categorize.

Three respondents related that they were motivated by what their parents, professors, or mentors had done and aimed to follow their academic and career path. Two respondents recalled being unsure or uncertain about their plans, and three recalled writing something that was plausible.

AI and Future Plans in Fellowship Applications

The use of AI in the preparation of scholarship and fellowship applications and review of them seems inevitable. As fellowship advisors, we can, at a minimum, warn students about presenting the writing AI generates as if it were their own and caution them about the inevitable pitfalls, including the lack of specificity and originality and that it will not help to distinguish them from other candidates. Here is the prompt and response from Anthropic's AI program Claude:

> **Prompt:** I need a short paragraph that describes my future plans after teaching in Colombia with a Fulbright ETA grant.
>
> **Response:** After completing my Fulbright English Teaching Assistantship in Colombia, I plan to leverage this international education experience to pursue a career in international development and education policy. Building on my Spanish language skills and firsthand understanding of Colombian educational systems, I aim to work with organizations like USAID or education-focused NGOs that promote educational access in Latin America. My experience teaching English and collaborating with Colombian educators has inspired me to pursue a master's in international education policy, which will equip me with the expertise needed to develop and implement programs that bridge educational gaps in the region. Long-term, I aspire to work at the intersection of education policy and cultural exchange, creating sustainable partnerships between U.S. and Latin American educational institutions.[13]

If a student submitted this to a committee during the campus review stage, members would not have major issues with it (if they thought the prose was the student's). After all, it is a *plausible* trajectory. However, the committee would likely ask the applicant who submitted this response about what they know and understand about the United States Agency for International Development (USAID) or for more specifics about what area of international education policy interests them. AI can be useful here—if an applicant did not previously know about USAID or the possibility to study international education policy, and this prompted them to learn more and provide more specifics about those plans in the Fulbright statement of grant purpose or personal statement, this would be a positive. But applicants would be shortchanging themselves (and the process) if they used AI to represent ideas about their future career path.

In advising students about using AI, I encourage them to read Laura Hartenberger's essay on "What AI Teaches Us About Good Writing" and share this excerpt with them:

> How we measure successful writing changes depending on what the writer is trying to accomplish, and good writers are flexible enough to adapt to different scenarios. They make intentional decisions around three elements: audience, purpose and context. Who am I writing for, to what end and in what circumstance?[14]

As fellowships advisors, we are in a position to help applicants understand those three elements. In terms of preparing a response to the Fulbright "future plans" prompt, advisors who have observed Fulbright National Selection Committee meetings or attended events hosted by the Institute of International Education that included host country staff are well-positioned to describe the audience. As the "future plans" response is one that reviewers ostensibly read toward the beginning of an application and before reading an applicant's statements, one goal of the response is that it coheres with other parts of the application. Regarding the circumstances, applicants who exhibit a naivete about their future prospects (e.g., "I want to be a Foreign Service officer") are best served by receiving guidance and advice on how to realistically assess possible outcomes.

Concluding Observations

Given the distribution of the survey question responses and the variety of motivating factors shared in the written responses, our applicants in the social and behavioral sciences and humanities are, at some level, aware of a degree of uncertainty about their future plans, or that there are "known unknowns" in their future. They could glean this from talking to parents, faculty, advisors, older siblings, and friends, whose life trajectories veered from an expected one and who, despite the unanticipated turn, ended up on a rewarding path.

After getting survey results and going back through the applications to note the academic degrees of Fulbright applicants we solicited, we found that almost half of them (49 percent) were pursuing degrees in language and area studies, indicating a willingness to devote several semesters of study to learning another language—this, despite research that shows there is a small amount of financial return on learning another language for college students in the United States.[15] So it also seems that there is a degree of self-selection among our applicant pool in that they are motivated by the intangible benefits and enhanced "meaning, understanding and perspective"[16] they expect from a long-term stay in a host country.

While I was researching the topic of post-baccalaureate outcomes, some directions of inquiry were, at times, difficult to avoid. Chief among them was the impulse to explore earning potential and outcomes of students who study social and behavioral sciences and humanities versus those in profession-specific disciplines or potential outcomes for students who were awarded a Fulbright versus those not awarded one. The most intriguing responses of this study were from those whose plans differed from what they are currently doing and might also be considered in a broader project. Did their lives, in terms of academic and professional goals, take a hard right turn or left turn? What circumstances motivated the change? How did they cope with it? Who and what helped them? As we feed more and more quantifiable data via surveys and other data-gathering tools and continue quantifying social aspects of life (friend requests, followers, connections, and so on) and using AI, advisors should strive to maintain time and space for honest, candid, and calm discussions with students about their academic and professional plans and aspirations.

Notes

1. Micah Pence is an undergraduate and Cox Legacy Scholar at Indiana University, Bloomington pursuing degrees in Biochemistry and Neuroscience. He assisted in designing and distributing the survey, communicating with respondents, gathering data, and anaylzing responses.
2. Marcia Baxter Magolda, *Making their Own Way: Narratives for Transforming Higher Education to Promote Self-Development* (Sterling, VA: Stylus, 2001) quoted in Richelle Bernazzoli, Joanna Dickert, Anne Moore, and Jason Kelly Roberts, "Excellent Sheep or Passionate Weirdos?," in *Bridging the Gap: Perspectives on Nationally Competitive Scholarships*, ed. Suzanne McCray and Dana Kuchem (Fayetteville: University of Arkansas Press, 2019), 43–64.
3. Thomas Suddendorf, Donna Rose Addis, and Michael C. Corballis, "Mental Time Travel and the Shaping of the Human Mind," *Philosophical Transactions of the Royal Society B* 364, no. 1521 (2009): 1317–24.
4. Meg Jay, *The Defining Decade: Why Your Twenties Matter and How to Make the Most of Them Now* (New York: Hachette, 2012).
5. There is a graphic illustration of this paradox in the form of a meme by Tim Urban. It is available via his Wait but Why? Facebook page: https://www.facebook.com/waitbutwhy/posts/forget-about-the-black-lines-cause-look-at-all-that-green/3758837247498482/.
6. John Warner, *Why They Can't Write: Killing the Five-Paragraph Essay and Other Necessities* (Baltimore: Johns Hopkins University Press, 2018).
7. This expression was shared with me several years ago during an advising meeting with a graduate student. His faculty advisor had related it to him.
8. Berke Breathed, *Bloom County Babylon* (Boston: Little, Brown and Company, 1986), 76.
9. Information generated by Claude AI, January 31, 2025, ClaudeAI, https://claude.ai.
10. We went back through the list of solicited applicants and twenty-three of the 210 (11 percent) indicated in their Fulbright application that they were pursuing a degree outside social/behavioral sciences and humanities. Of those twenty-three, nine were in education, nine in business fields, two in nursing, two in library science, and one in recreational therapy.
11. National Council for Education Statistics (NCES), "Relationship Between Job and Bachelor's Degree," n.d., accessed January 29, 2025, https://nces.ed.gov/datalab/table/library/detail/11822.

12. Nathan Heller, "The End of the English Major," *The New Yorker*, February 27, 2023. The article also describes relatively recent initiatives on US campuses to promote study of the humanities including the American Council on Learned Societies' Research University Consortium and the Humanities Indicator project sponsored by the American Academy of Arts and Sciences.
13. Information generated by Claude AI, January 14, 2025, ClaudAI, https://claude.ai. We also entered a revised prompt with more specifics: I need a short paragraph that describes my future plans after *completing bachelor's degrees in Spanish and Latino Studies and* teaching in Colombia with a Fulbright ETA grant. ClaudeAI generated the same response as the one in this essay.
14. Laura Hartenberger, "What AI Teaches Us About Good Writing," *Noema*, July 25, 2023.
15. Albert Saiz and Elena Zoido, "The Returns to Speaking a Second Language," *Working Papers, Federal Reserve Bank of Philadelphia*, no. 02–16 (2002).
16. Drew Faust, "The University's Crisis of Purpose," *New York Times*, September 1, 2009.

4

From Imagination to Reality

Leveraging the Fellowship Application Process as an Imaginative Tool

NICOLE GALANTE

When most think about the fellowship application process, their minds are naturally drawn toward its heart—the application itself. Advisors and others often focus on elements such as writing, revision, and all the transferable skills that result from the iterative nature of the application process. And for good reason—the application process holds significant transformative potential for applicants. However, by focusing too much on the application, advisors often overlook a critical component and benefit of the process that should be included in the first step in an advisors' work with applicants and that is *imagination*.

The application process ought to be understood as one beginning with and centering on imagination, which has the potential to impart tangible educational benefits to applicants. The National and International Fellowships Office (NIFO) at Elon University has taken great care to prioritize imagination in its approach to working with its applicants, and unpacking this approach can be helpful for conceptualizing how and why imagination is critical to the process of applying for fellowships.

The National and International Fellowships Office at Elon University: Our Process

At NIFO, we support applicants through three phases in the application process, as summarized by our maxim: "Envision, Apply, Embark." We believe that the first stage, envision, is a unique and critical first step in our work with applicants because it kickstarts the imaginative process.

The envision stage is a bit like a match-making process, and it almost never begins with a specific fellowship in mind on our part or the applicant's. Instead, there is one primary question that we as advisors are trying to get an answer to: Who are you? In fact, our meetings usually begin with some variation of that question: "Tell us a little bit about yourself." "What makes you who you are?" "Where have you been and where are you going?" We also ask the standard questions about academics, leadership, and service, but each question we ask is part of our quest to gain more insight about the student. We cannot advise applicants well without first having an overall understanding of them.

Only then, after we have spent thirty to forty-five minutes in this kind of exchange and we start to have a sense of what this applicant has done and who they are, do we turn our attention to the idea of fellowship applications. *This* is when the imagination process begins.[1] Equipped with our evolving knowledge of various fellowships, we prompt potential applicants to imagine what is possible:

- "You've participated in so much research. It's clearly something you enjoy. Did you know you can make a career out of this? There are awards like the National Science Foundation Graduate Research Fellowship Program (NSF GRFP) that can fund you to pursue a PhD, and from there you could apply for a job as a professor or even as a researcher for the government."
- "You've spent four years as a tutor and sports coach. You also participated in a unique study abroad experience. Have you ever thought about what it would be like to spend a year teaching English abroad after graduation?"

- "There are prestigious programs that can fund your master's degree *and* lead to employment with the federal government. Have you considered the Foreign Service?"

Applicants come to us with various levels of understanding about what is possible in general and what is likely for them specifically. For students who have a less clear picture of the possibilities, we ask them to imagine what their future could look like with each of these suggestions and to mentally commit to the possibility, if only for a few moments. The process of imaging this possibility is the first step toward making it real.

After we have done this imaginative work, we turn our attention to the second two phases of our process—apply and embark—which are much like they sound. The benefits of the apply stage—all the work that happens once the student has a fellowship in mind and begins to tackle the application through the writing and revision process—have been explored at length in NAFA publications, conferences, and online forums and thus are not covered in this chapter. Embark, the final phase, looks different for each applicant, and due to the competitive nature of these awards, most of the applicants we work with will not be embarking on a fellowship. As a result, we have been careful to design this phase to ensure that each applicant walks away with the knowledge to embark on their future journey, no matter what form it takes, with more purpose, direction, and confidence than before, all of which is far easier to do if they have previously done intentional work to leverage the process as an imaginative tool.

Imagining one's goals is necessary and critical to the process of achieving them, and imagining the future can help make it real. While the word *imagination* can mean many things, this chapter adopts a colloquial definition of the word and uses it to refer exclusively to the formation of new ideas, images, or concepts that *could conceivably come true* (as in an academically strong applicant imagining what it would be like to attend graduate school). *Fantasy*, by contrast, involves imagining something that could *not* conceivably come true (as in an applicant with no research experience imagining they will win the Goldwater Scholarship). Imaginations are necessary and useful, while fantasies are not.

It is important to clarify early on that when I say the imaginative process holds the potential to make something real, I am *not* arguing an applicant can simply imagine their future and "manifest their dreams"; in fact, I expressly reject that idea. There is no amount of manifestation that will land a student with a 3.5 GPA the Rhodes Scholarship or a student with no leadership record the Truman. For advisors to encourage these fantasies is both unethical and unhelpful to the applicant, foundations, and our profession. Instead, I am arguing that imagination should be leveraged as a tool, encouraging applicants to imagine their futures and begin the process of achieving their goals.

This chapter begins with a discussion of why imagination is critical for applicants and the process. Then, after establishing a shared understanding of the importance of imagination, I offer strategies for fellowship advisors to incorporate this approach into their practice and then discuss the ethics of imagination and the distinction between imagination and fantasy. Imagination holds incredible transformative power, especially for applicants from oppressed groups, but the line between imagination and fantasy is slim. Fellowships advisors encourage imagination while discouraging fantasy, because encouraging the latter breaks our ethical obligation to applicants (and foundations, too) to help them imagine while keeping one foot firmly planted in reality. The conclusion discusses our office context and limitations.

Central to this essay will be the voices and stories of Natalie T., Megan C., and Delyla M., who are three recent Elon graduates and seasoned fellowship applicants in our office. Over the course of their time working with us, Natalie, Megan, and Delyla submitted a combined total of seventeen fellowship applications. Imagination was critical for each of these women as they set off on the process of applying for fellowships and achieving their goals. They had different journeys, with varied successes and failures along the way, but each is (I hope) in a better place because of the process. Their stories speak for themselves, providing telling insights as well as concrete experiences that support those insights.

Natalie

I am from a suburb of Seattle, Washington and am a 2023 graduate of Elon University, where I majored in religious studies and international studies, concentrating on North Africa and the Middle East. Since my first year of college, I have been applying for fellowships with the support of NIFO, including the Critical Language Scholarship (twice), a Fulbright Study/Research Award, and the James C. Gaither Junior Fellows Program at the Carnegie Endowment for International Peace. I was rejected both times for CLS and accepted for Fulbright and Gaither. My relationships with mentors at Elon are what propelled me to apply for fellowships from the first to the last.

Megan

I am a graduate of Elon University, where I earned degrees in journalism and public health in 2023. During my time at Elon, I developed a strong passion for the intersection of storytelling and public health, which led me to begin researching fellowship opportunities that would support my exploration of these fields. This process led me to NIFO in the fall of my junior year, when I applied for the Truman Scholarship. Over the next two years, I applied for Princeton in Asia, the Marshall Scholarship, and twice each for Fulbright Study/Research (Norway, United Kingdom), the Luce Scholars Program, and a Rotary Global Grant (Iceland, Germany). I was named a finalist for Luce and Rotary in 2023. I ultimately received the Rotary in 2024 to fund an MPH at the Hamburg University of Applied Sciences. This yearslong cycle of applying and being rejected was not always encouraging, but I sincerely believe that each application served the purpose of making my next one stronger. As my education continued and my hopes evolved, so too did the types of programs I applied for and the confidence with which I applied.

Delyla

> I am an advocate, leader, researcher, and first-generation college student. Because of my identity as first-generation, I had no previous understanding of fellowships. In fact, I didn't know they existed and was unaware of the fact that there was a whole office dedicated to obtaining fellowships until I met its director. She shared with me the purpose of the fellowships office and the types of awards she thought would be fitting for me: Truman, National Institutes of Health Undergraduate Scholarship Program, Marshall, and Fulbright. I ultimately did not receive any of these fellowships. Now that I've graduated (2024), I am attending the University of North Carolina at Chapel Hill School of Social Work and the Gillings School of Global Public Health to obtain dual degrees: an MSW and MPH. Within the School of Social Work, I am concentrating on Community Management and Policy Practice, and at the Gillings School of Global Health, I am concentrating directly on my passion: health equity. My attendance at these programs was made possible by internal scholarships I received based on merit.

Why Is Imagination Critical?

Imagination is the necessary first step in the process of taking a thought, desire, or goal and making it real. But that must be followed by intentional planning and dedicated effort. If an applicant's mental work starts and ends with imagination, the likelihood of their dream becoming a reality is left to chance.

Educational theorists have both embraced and neglected the usefulness of imagination, partially because the definition of imagination is so evasive.[2] Those who neglect its usefulness often conceptualize imagination as playful or fantasizing. Those who embrace it generally think of imagination in a realistic context—as the mental ability to simulate what could realistically be—and argue that it plays a central role in meaning-making, well-being, and overall attainment of one's goals.[3] This latter philosophy is embraced in this chapter: Imagination is important to help applicants understand who they are, who they can become, and how to get there.

The imaginative process also has inherent educational benefits when applied to an academic context that can yield tangible, positive results for students. Psychology research finds that mental practice has significant positive effects on an individual's performance; the more one imagines doing something, such as scoring a goal while playing soccer or attending graduate school, the more likely they are to succeed when they really perform the action.[4] Within the context of education specifically, there is evidence to suggest that imagination can both enhance and deepen a student's overall learning.[5] Students will perform better and learn more if they incorporate imagination into their approach.

The fellowship application process presents a compelling opportunity for applicants to imagine themselves and the world as they could be, thereby increasing the likelihood that what they imagine is realized. Both Natalie and Delyla's stories perfectly illustrate the importance of imagination as a central part of the fellowship application process in different ways. In her junior year, Natalie was committed to the idea of law school, but she could not explain why. Natalie had spent the better part of her college career studying the Middle East and North Africa, learning Arabic, and conducting impressive religious studies research (she even won Elon's top undergraduate research prize), and she enjoyed it. She loved research so much that she could not bear the thought of attending law school before getting to do a bit more of it, so she decided that a Fulbright independent research grant made sense for her initial postgraduate work. She described it as her "last hurrah." But should someone be planning a "last hurrah" from research at twenty-two years old?

Here is how Nathalie recalls the application process:

> When I sat down for my initial meeting to discuss the possibility of Fulbright, [NIFO advisors] listened to me explain what my research interests were and why I wanted to apply. They told me that they saw me as a competitive candidate for Fulbright, but that to be truly competitive, I needed to figure out something: How was Fulbright necessary to my trajectory and future career? The answer in that moment and in the early drafts of my application evaded me, as truthfully, I did not know how Fulbright was essential to my future.

During the meetings as we discussed drafts, I was encouraged to let go of the assumption that I had to follow through with what I was writing about in my application to a tee; rather, I should think about what I could reasonably see myself doing and imagine myself in the future without commitment. In being able to imagine rather than feeling a complete sense of commitment, the pressure to have all my life choices figured out was alleviated.

While I was in Morocco on my Fulbright grant, I received an email from the office encouraging me to apply for the Gaither Junior Fellows Program, of which I had not previously known. Since I had the flexibility in my brain established from completing other applications, I felt comfortable to imagine and apply for Gaither without being certain if work at a think tank was absolutely what I wanted to do with my career. Applying for fellowships is just opening up to new opportunities, and imagination was a tool NIFO taught me to relieve stress and generate excitement for a future that could be.

Prior to applying for Fulbright, Natalie had imagined a future for herself that only involved attending law school. It was not until the application process helped her imagine a future in which she was a researcher that she began to fathom that it could come true. She imagined that she could conduct research in Morocco, then she imagined that she could be a Gaither Junior Fellow, and before she knew it, she was not just *imagining* about being a researcher—she *was* a researcher.

Natalie also raises an interesting point about imagining without commitment and feeling free in the process. Imagination and commitment are not mutually exclusive: One can imagine something but never actually believe it will come true. Natalie found freedom in this lack of commitment—detaching herself from the idea that she had to do everything she outlined in her application—but this is not necessarily the case for every applicant. For others, imagination might not feel freeing if their day-to-day reality is shaped by oppressive systems. Delyla's story illustrates this well.

When she started applying for fellowships, Delyla did not fully understand what was possible for her life. As a low-income, first-generation college student, she had not yet been introduced to opportunities such as research or graduate school. Students with her identities (she is also Black) are also less likely to participate in the high-impact experiences—research, study abroad, internships—that could help make them more qualified for many of the opportunities fellowships afford, not because they are less skilled or interested, but because of systemic barriers may make it difficult or impossible for them to participate.[6] Although participation in these high-impact experiences benefits all students, low-income and first-generation students often stand to gain the most.[7]

Delyla's positionality led her to believe that she was in some way "not worthy" to even consider these options as legitimate possibilities for herself. The process of applying for fellowships educated her about new options, encouraged her to imagine herself engaged in them, and instilled a confidence in her that those options were not just hypothetical. In the end, she did not receive any of the fellowships she applied for, but today she is living the exact reality she imagined for herself two years ago in her Truman application.

Here are her recollections:

When I applied for the Truman Scholarship, I was early in my college career and found it hard to think about my future post-grad. It was my first application, and it was hard to begin imagining so quickly and intently; so, I painted a picture of what I wanted if I stayed in North Carolina. I researched the top institutions in the state, found a program focused on health equity, and decided that attending the University of North Carolina at Chapel Hill would be one of the many futures I would consider.

For me as a low-income Black woman who is also a first-generation college student, the imaginative nature of the fellowship application process was my first experience of affirmative mentorship. Being first-generation, I couldn't explain the leadership or research I did on campus to my family. Although they were important to me, my family couldn't understand, so my achievements were often downplayed with an "Oh, that's great honey," which ended the conversation about whatever experience I was sharing with them. My advisor's affirmative mentorship helped me no longer question my worthiness of receiving any fellowship or scholarship.

Simultaneously, my marginalized identities restricted my imagination. Being a Black woman applying for fellowships abroad was intimidating. The intersection of my identities as low-income and first-generation also limited my sense of safety when applying for scholarships. My family has never traveled abroad; how would they know how to help me? Who could I lean on when everything feels overwhelming, but everyone around me seems to know what they're doing? Who could financially support me outside of the funding of the fellowship?

Although the imaginative process of applying for fellowships did not negate these worries, it did encourage me to consider taking the risk that comes with these experiences. I gained the confidence to believe I was worthy of receiving the scholarship, so then I finally believed I was worthy of the experiences I was applying for. I had faith that although I would be somewhere out of my comfort zone, I was still deserving of the experience.

After applying for Truman, Delyla went on to apply for the NIH UGSP, the Marshall Scholarship, and Fulbright. Imagining herself at UNC in her first application gave her the skills and confidence to imagine herself as a career researcher, and finally as a graduate student in the United Kingdom. While her fellowship applications were not successful, she herself was successful because she was able to leverage the process as a tool to make her imaginings real. The Truman application gave her the opportunity to outline a future goal and the steps she would need to take to get there; simultaneously, as her goals became clearer to me as her advisor, I had the opportunity to makes suggestions about how she could achieve them. With this knowledge acquired through the imaginative process—about herself, the world, and her goals within it—she was able to make the future she imagined in her Truman application all those years ago her reality. Perhaps most importantly, she began to believe she deserved it.

Imagination and Equity

For members of an oppressed group like Delyla, being asked to imagine the future can be a particularly difficult task, both practically and emotionally.[8] On a practical level, it is nearly impossible for students to imagine what they do not have a frame of reference for. If no one in Delyla's immediate life went to graduate school, let alone college, how could anyone expect her to know it was an option for her future?

Imagined realities are always situated in larger contexts that for some applicants can be characterized by racism, classism, sexism, and oppression.[9] Simple imagination in oppressive contexts is not enough. In these situations, advisors and applicants must employ what Black and Indigenous scholars and movements have called *radical imagination*—imagination that simulates the world not as it is but as it could be, a world where all are free from oppression.[10] In these instances, much of the responsibility to facilitate radical imagination lies with advisors: We are the ones equipped with knowledge about fellowships and the world and trained to help applicants make sense of themselves and their experiences.[11] Not only may we need to help some applicants understand the ways in which their realities have been shaped by oppressive systems, but we may also need to educate and encourage them to imagine a future free from them.

Radical imagination can lead to radical belief, which has the potential to be transformative. As Delyla explains, the fellowship application process not only encouraged her to imagine but also instilled in her a confidence that she was "worthy" of doing all that she imagined. It is important to reiterate that imagination and belief are not mutually exclusive; one can imagine something they might never believe will come true, as was the case with Natalie imagining what her life would be like as a Gaither Junior Fellow all while doubting that she would ever actually become one. Delyla had to see that getting into graduate school with her record of strong academics and leadership was both possible and probable if only she would take a chance on imagining it.

Imagination in Practice

Leveraging the process to center on imagination is not as difficult as it might sound. The first step for advisors is simple: Ensure that the primary goal when meeting a potential applicant is to discover who they are as a person and not as a fellowship applicant. The easiest way to do this is to ask questions that attempt to get at the core of who a person is beyond what they have done. Some questions to ask in meetings outside of the standard ones that get at an applicant's collegiate experiences include the following:

- Who are you now and who would you like to become?
- If the world was a perfect place, and money and geography were not barriers, what would you do after graduation? What would you be doing ten or twenty years from now?
- Why? (This is my favorite, the most underrated, and the easiest question to ask. A student tells the advisor they studied abroad in Taiwan. Why? Volunteered every week? Why?)

Due to the open-ended nature of these questions, students might reveal details that do not seem immediately relevant, such as where they are from or how many siblings they have, but advisors should trust that every detail learned is relevant to understanding who an applicant is. They would not have shared it if they did not feel it was important.

With nine applications under her belt, Megan might be the most prolific applicant in NIFO's history, and the best-positioned to reflect on this approach to learning about applicants. Here is her story.

> One of the most crucial aspects of NIFO's process to me is the intentionality behind getting to know students and their motivations. Early on, I was hesitant to share about myself yet quickly understood that the team asked me for information not to judge me, but to better understand how to support me in finding fellowships to pursue.
>
> As I continued to apply for awards throughout college and beyond, there were points where their support was truly the only thing I was motivated by. For example, in the spring of 2023, I learned that I did not receive a spot in the Luce Scholars Program after a successful finalist

weekend, so I decided to apply again in 2024. On the second attempt, I was not even offered an initial interview, which was by far the largest blow to my confidence in those three years. When I shared that news with the NIFO staff, they reacted as though the rejection happened to them personally. This bothered me at first; I felt like it was my loss alone to claim. After reflection, though, I came to appreciate this level of commitment and the fact that I had two people who understood how much my imagined future as a Luce Scholar meant to me.

Our strongest students often apply for several fellowships simultaneously or over the course of several years, and not all those fellowships will proliferate the same possibilities. For example, Megan simultaneously had to imagine what it would be like to earn a graduate degree in the United Kingdom *and* spend a year in Asia as a Luce Scholar. She had to commit to these different futures equally when writing the applications (speaking in active voice, making concrete and detailed plans, and so on) all while being ready to abandon one or more of them when something did not materialize. Simultaneously, she also had to retain a consistent sense of self that was not contingent on one or more of the imagined futures she outlined in her applications becoming reality.

Not every applicant will mediate the tension between imagined and actual self or leverage it as a source of empowerment. Sometimes applicants can become attached to their imagined futures and experience real distress when they do not work out. Advisors must be prepared to temper expectations by providing equal doses of encouragement and reality checks, frequently reminding students that one of the primary goals of the fellowship application process is to discover who they are as a person apart from the award. If the only thing an applicant walks away from the process with is a clearer sense of self, then they have succeeded.

Ethics: Imagination Versus Fantasy

Imagination as outlined in this essay is helpful, but fantasy is not, and the line between imagination and fantasy can be slim and difficult to navigate for applicants and advisors alike. To complicate matters further, the place where imagination ends and fantasy begins will be different for each applicant at different moments in time. Part of advisors' jobs is to help applicants identify that line and encourage their imaginations while discouraging fantasies. Encouraging fantasy is not only dangerous and unhelpful, but also breaks advisors' ethical obligations to applicants, to foundations, and to themselves and their profession.

Advisors' ethical obligation to the applicant should always be the priority. As such, they must help applicants to see what is possible and feasible and encourage these endeavors while explicitly discouraging fantasies. This requires that advisors both know applicants well and have an evolving knowledge of foundations and fellowships, as fit largely determines whether receiving an award is a feasible endeavor.[12]

The kicker, of course, is that none of these awards are particularly "feasible" to obtain. And because of that, it is very easy for both advisors and applicants to mistake imagination for fantasy. For example, the odds were never in Megan's favor when she applied for fellowships with acceptance rates as low as 5 percent. However, Megan had a stellar track record, as well as experiences and values that aligned with various awards, and seeing that she could benefit from the process of imagining her future into existence, I put the ball in her court by suggesting that she should apply for a fellowship. Luckily, she was better at towing the line between imagination and fantasy than most applicants and was mature and self-aware enough to know what was best for her when.

Supporting the applicant's autonomy at all times is important to fulfilling our ethical obligation to them, even if we as advisors disagree with their choices. That might mean that an applicant who is less mature than Megan chooses to fantasize even after their advisor has encouraged them toward imagination rooted in reality. For example, an applicant might choose to apply for a particular Fulbright grant they are not qualified for no matter what their advisor says. At that point, the advisor has fulfilled their ethical obligation to the student, and the best course of action at that stage is to put reservations aside and attempt to make the process as educational as possible.

Furthermore, what is a fantasy for an applicant today could turn into a legitimate possibility for them in the future with enough time, growth, and self-awareness.

Advisors' second ethical obligation is to foundations, whether or not the application includes a formal institutional endorsement. Foundation directors and application readers, many of whom are volunteering their time, have an enormous task with the selection process, and advisors owe it to them to encourage applications only from students for whom the opportunity is a good fit. This highlights the need for fellowships advisors to know applicants and individual fellowships well to aid with the initial process.

Finally, advisors have an ethical obligation to themselves and their profession. This relies on the integrity of the application process, which ultimately places student development, learning, and well-being above the acquisition of an award. To do right by the process, which inherently implies doing right by the applicant and by foundations, advisors must encourage applicants to engage in imaginative projections in a manner that is formative for them.

Context and Limitations

Contextualizing Elon University is important. Elon is a private, medium-sized liberal arts institution with a low student-to-staff ratio and a high emphasis on engaged, relationship-rich education. Faculty and staff are not only encouraged but also expected to know individual students and work with them in a personalized manner. Those of us who work at Elon tend to champion the assertion that positive relationships play an essential role in shaping a student's educational experience, and that attitude is usually reflected by our students.[13]

NIFO is housed within the Provost's Office, and we are fortunate to report to administrators who understand our process and believe in its transformative potential for students; they trust that the number of students interacting with our process is more important than the number of those students who receive awards. The model described in this essay works at Elon because NIFO has both the capacity and directive to enact it.

For different institution types, enacting this model fully might be hard or impossible due to realities such as understaffed fellowship offices and growing attitudes of higher education administrators that prioritize outcomes over process.[14] This model also requires close(r) relationships between staff and students, and the emotional toll that sustaining these relationships can take on staff, especially those from oppressed groups, cannot be understated. Putting this model into practice is not easy and might in some cases be impossible; therefore, the goal is not to discount other methods of conceptualizing the fellowship process that have been adapted to meet a school's individual needs.

Rather, the goal is for all fellowship advisors to both understand the role that imagination can play in the process and to reconceptualize "the process" itself as an imaginative educational tool that begins well before the application phase. There is not a one-size-fits-all model to achieve this goal, and advisors should feel empowered to adopt a model that works best for their institution, as this practice can be scalable. An advisor might not have time to talk with all applicants for forty-five minutes about their life stories, but that advisor might be able to send out a pre-meeting questionnaire with reflective prompts that generate the same sorts of self-discoveries for applicants. Just as there is no singular definition of imagination, there is no singular way to wield it as a tool. The important thing here is that imagination is conceptualized and implemented as a central component of the fellowship application process so all parties benefit.

Because when it is, students like Natalie realize that they are meant to be researchers instead of lawyers, a Megan can be empowered by the fact that they have multiple good options on the table, and a Delyla learns the most important lesson of all: to believe in herself. Her final remarks during our interview illustrate this perfectly: "Once I began to believe in myself through the process of applying, I became less disappointed when I didn't receive a fellowship and more confused about why they couldn't see that I was a worthy enough candidate to receive it. It was then that I realized that *I* was the prize, and that I wasn't just applying for a fellowship. I was giving these fellowships the opportunity to support the change that I was already making in this world."

She is, like Megan and Natalie, the prize indeed, and I struggle to imagine a more worthy endeavor than helping students like them come to this conclusion through the process of applying for fellowships.

Notes

1. For some students. Not every student we talk with is a good fit for fellowships. While we love meeting potential applicants, we consider forty-five minutes spent getting to know a student and discovering they are *not* a good fit for fellowships a productive use of our time, too.
2. Moira von Wright, "Imagination and Education," in *Oxford Research Encyclopedia of Education*, 2021, https://doi.org/10.1093/acrefore/9780190264093.013.1487.
3. Beau Gamble, Lynette Tippett, David Moreau, and Donna Rose Addis, "The Futures We Want: How Goal-Directed Imagination Relates to Mental Health," *Clinical Psychological Science* 9, no. 4 (2021): 732–51.
4. James E. Driskell, Carolyn Cooper, and Aidan Moran, "Does Mental Practice Enhance Performance?" *Journal of Applied Psychology* 79, no. 4 (1994): 481–92.
5. Hajer Mguidich, Bachir Zoudji, and Aïmen Khacharem, "Does Imagination Enhance Learning? A Systematic Review and Meta-Analysis," *European Journal of Psychology of Education*, no. 39 (2024): 1943–78.
6. Jayne E. Brownell and Lynne E. Swaner, "Five High-Impact Practices: Research on Learning Outcomes, Completion, and Quality," American Association of Colleges & Universities, 2010.
7. Ashley Finley and Tia Brown McNair, "Assessing Underserved Students' Engagement in High-Impact Practices," American Association of Colleges & Universities, 2013.
8. Moreover, imagining and achieving a new future are not always positive experiences. Jennifer Morton's book, *Moving Up Without Losing Your Way: The Ethical Costs of Upward Mobility* (Princeton, NJ: Princeton University Press, 2019) offers insights into why upward mobility is not always an easy choice or process for members of oppressed groups.
9. Erin Dyke, Eli Meyerhoff, and Keno Evol, "Radical Imagination as Pedagogy: Cultivating Collective Study from Within, on the Edge, and Beyond Education," *Transformations: The Journal of Inclusive Scholarship and Pedagogy* 28, no. 2 (2018): 160–80.
10. Robin D. G. Kelley, *Freedom Dreams: The Black Radical Imagination* (Boston: Beacon Press, 2002); Taiaiake Alfred, "What Is Radical

Imagination? Indigenous Struggles in Canada," *Affinities* 4, no. 2 (2010): 5–8.

11. I was a first-generation college student. In too many cases, my own scope of knowledge does not feel much broader than my applicants.' For example, the first time I learned about the Foreign Service was when a student came to me wanting to apply for Rangel and Pickering. There is such a quick and interesting shift in power that occurs when people with marginalized identities assume advisory roles, and it can too often lead us to question our place in this profession.

12. Another reason we do not start with a specific fellowship in mind at NIFO is that applicants are often not the best judge of which fellowships they are well-suited. It is *our* job as advisors to attend trainings, conferences, and webinars so that we may facilitate a good fit between applicant and award. In addition, I often need to do the most work to convince my most qualified students that they should apply for prestigious awards. The students who walk through the door shouting they want to apply for the Rhodes Scholarship are rarely the best fit.

13. Peter Felten and Leo M. Lambert, *Relationship-Rich Education: How Human Connections Drive Success in College* (Baltimore: Johns Hopkins University Press, 2020).

14. Malcolm Tight, "The Neoliberal Turn in Higher Education," *Higher Education Quarterly* 78, no. 3 (July 2019): 273–84.

5

Advising for Knowledge Transfer

Building Better Writers for Life

CLAIRE KERVIN

Fellowships advisors often express a desire to understand advising in developmental terms, as a practice with a focus that goes beyond winning, to use Suzanne McCray's phrase, toward learning and growth.[1] Advisors most value the process, not the prize, and hope that our efforts with applicants will help them develop skills with lifelong relevance. While advisors do not typically articulate their goals using the term *transfer*, we hope that is what we are doing: advising in such a way that promotes applicants' ability to apply prior knowledge or abilities to a new context. As the Yale Poorvu Center for Teaching and Learning suggests, "Because transfer signals that a learner's comprehension allows them to recognize how their knowledge can be relevant and to apply it effectively outside original learning conditions, transfer is often considered a hallmark of true learning."[2]

Transfer is a significant concept in the field of writing studies, and "teaching for transfer" has been an active area of inquiry since the 1980s.[3] Scholarship on transfer rarely addresses advising, yet the relevance of knowledge transfer to advising practices is compelling. When I think about transfer, I think about those applicants who take what I teach them and run with it. I recall a Fulbright applicant whose personal statement draft started with that dreaded phrase, "Ever since I was a child...." With support, the applicant was able to rework the opening to be much more effective, and when writing a personal statement for graduate school applications a few years later, the applicant drew on previous knowledge about how to begin an essay with a compelling, vividly told personal story rather than a cliché. There was also a Goldwater applicant who initially struggled in an essay to clearly explain technically complex research; after learning principles of effective science writing related to clarity and cohesion, the applicant formulated scientific presentations that conveyed the research findings to nonexperts.

Despite the happy outcomes in the above examples, there are good reasons not to be overly optimistic about the ease of knowledge transfer: Research suggests that learners often fail to apply knowledge and skills from one context to another. Transfer is far from guaranteed, especially in certain learning situations, such as when the initial learning was not particularly deep, when the learner was narrowly focused on the specific task in front of them, or when the new context in which the learning might be applied is quite different from the initial context in which the learning took place.[4] These learning situations likely sound familiar to advisors, who have seen the lack of deep learning that comes from a rushed application process or the applicant who conceives of the personal statement as an entirely unique and self-contained genre of writing.

While it is critical that the skills and insights applicants develop be useful in novel contexts, this outcome cannot be assumed. What advising practices can help maximize an applicant's abilities to transfer what they learn from the application process to other contexts? This chapter considers some possible answers to that question, drawing on research findings about classroom teaching practices that support transfer and suggesting how those findings might be translated into fellowships advising practices. The primary focus will be on writing skills, but contemplating the importance of advising for writing transfer might lead to further work exploring how other kinds of transfer can be supported by fellowships advisors.

Preventing Negative Transfer

For the most advanced transfer to occur *out of* fellowships advising, it is important to maximize the successful transfer of skills and knowledge *into* the fellowships advising process. Prior knowledge about writing can be a solid foundation on which to build if it is accurate and pertinent, but it can be detrimental if that knowledge is unreliable or irrelevant. As King Beach posits, "Transfer most frequently occurs without anyone thinking about how to apply prior learning or reason by analogy on a new problem or situation."[5] Accordingly, an applicant making an unconscious, unacknowledged analogy between a fellowship essay and prior writing tasks might import ineffective approaches into their fellowship writing process. This is called "negative transfer."[6] Negative transfer occurs regularly in fellowships advising—think, for instance, of the applicant who has concluded that effective personal writing must involve an adversity and redemption arc or even the applicant who writes in passive voice because they have been told by prior writing instructors to avoid using the personal pronoun "I."

To minimize negative transfer, advisors need to gauge not only advisees' knowledge but also their attitude: "Some dispositions seem to better afford engaged rhetorical problem-solving [than others]," suggests a statement on writing transfer from Elon University.[7] Thus, for example, Neil Baird and Bradley Dilger emphasize the importance of a disposition involving "ownership" of writing, "the extent to which writers invest in, identify with, and seek to maintain control of their writing."[8] While some fellowship applicants are eager writers who readily take ownership of their writing, others are not. Writing is fraught with anxiety for many people, and writing that is personal or vulnerable in nature can be especially difficult. Bringing a negative disposition toward writing to the application writing process can be considered a form of negative transfer.[9]

Advisors, therefore, should consider asking applicants to reflect on what existing knowledge and skills *and* previous experiences and beliefs about writing they are bringing with them to the writing process. This can occur through a preliminary conversation and/or an intake sheet. Advisors can consider asking applicants questions such as

- What aspects of writing do you feel confident about?
- What aspects of writing do you think you could improve?
- What are three things you believe make a good piece of writing? What are three things you believe make a good writer?

- Do you consider yourself a writer? Why or why not?
- Complete the following sentence: "The opportunity to write about myself on this application makes me feel _____."

In conversation, the advisor can ask illuminating follow-up questions and, if necessary, challenge the advisee's thinking. For instance, an advisee who articulates a belief that they do their best writing under the pressure of an impending deadline raises alarm bells about procrastination habits and invites a longer discussion about the importance of prewriting and revision. In dialogue with applicants, advisors can also articulate their own beliefs about writing and build mutual understanding to facilitate a better relationship with applicants and encourage their progress. In sum, because negative transfer causes trouble in the initial stages of learning a new domain,[10] taking some time at the outset to gauge an applicant's prior knowledge, self-assessed skills, and beliefs and attitudes is worth doing early in the process.

Facilitate Developmental Goal-Setting

As a new advisor, I earnestly believed in the developmental benefits of applying for fellowships—greater introspection, increased communication skills, clearer writing—but I did not necessarily explicitly discuss these benefits with applicants in a deliberate way. Starting my position in early September, as students were already in the midst of applying for major awards, I had so much to learn about the logistics of the job (all those different online portals!) that I could not fathom having time to do anything else. Over time I realized that applicant learning (including various skill sets necessary to submit a competitive application) and the transfer of that knowledge to other settings would likely be increased if I actively discussed transfer and engaged applicants in reflecting on their learning processes. Indeed, research on transfer suggests that transfer is fundamentally caught up with metacognition, the practice of being aware of one's own thinking. As a 2015 essay synthesizing existing scholarship on transfer concluded, "Students' meta-awareness often plays a key role in transfer."[11]

Metacognition can occur at many points during the fellowship application process. In fact, it can occur even before the application process begins. When I give presentations about fellowships, I ask audience members what they imagine would be most challenging about the application process and what they think they would get out of wrestling with that challenge. During the first one-on-one meeting with an applicant, advisors can discuss what they believe to be the potential developmental benefits of the application process and, further, ask applicants to articulate specific goals for themselves. Do they want to solidify a sense of their values and life goals so they can clarify a career path? Are they looking to improve the clarity and authority of their written voice? Do they hope to come away with a succinct way to summarize their research?

According to Elon University's "Statement on Writing Transfer," "Reflective writing promotes preparation for transfer and transfer-focused thinking."[12] Moreover, having a written record of the applicant's goals can allow the advisor to reinforce them by returning to them regularly and discussing progress toward them, so it is ideal to assign developmental (intentional learning and skill acquisition) goal-setting as a task to accomplish before the next meeting. Since applicants might not realize how many potential developmental benefits exist or what they are, advisors can assist applicants by giving them a goal-setting handout that lists potential goals and provides a structure for the goal-setting process.

Advisors can increase advisee engagement in this process by emphasizing that setting goals is a way to ensure that the application process will be helpful no matter the outcome. While applicants cannot control what decisions selection committees make, they can exert control over their own learning. Accordingly, this approach may help an applicant maintain motivation by locating the locus of control within themselves rather than externalizing it to others.

Reinforce a Few Key Concepts Using Shared Vocabulary

Knowing an applicant's developmental goals can also assist advisors in their advising approach: Advisors can adjust their feedback on written materials to actively remind applicants of their goals and help progress toward them. For example, if an applicant wants to use the application process to help them learn how to synthesize their academic, co-curricular, and extracurricular activities into a coherent narrative, the advisor can zero in on the places in a personal statement where the applicant is missing opportunities to show connections between intellectual interests and personal experiences. Once the applicant revises enough to achieve the synthesis they seek, the advisor can then remind them that these synthesis skills can be applicable to other writing tasks—such as a research abstract or policy proposal. Reinforcement of knowledge, along with opportunities for the writer to conduct repeated practice and reflection, is likely to lead to deeper learning and therefore better transfer.[13]

Effective reinforcement of writing goals, however, might require greater clarity and specificity in the applicant's self-articulated goals. For instance, if an applicant says that they want their writing to flow better, the advisor will need to discern whether they are focused primarily on local cohesion (how one sentence connects to the next) or on more global coherence (fitting the different pieces of the application materials together into a consistent story). By providing applicants with a more precise vocabulary, advisors can help them further hone their writing goals and skills. A good practice is to collect a central set of resources to share with applicants, such as *Style: Lessons in Clarity and Grace* by Joseph Williams and Joseph Bizup, which focuses on principles for writing clearly and effectively with an audience in mind.[14] Other helpful works include *They Say/I Say* by Gerald Graff and Cathy Birkenstein and *Student's Guide to Writing College Papers* by Kate L. Turabian, both of which provide useful strategies for writing research essays that situate one's viewpoint in the larger discourse on the topic.[15] Regardless of which handbook(s) or other resources advisors use, the key for advisors is to intentionally articulate essential writing concepts and develop clear, consistent ways to talk about those concepts with advisees.

Promote Deeper Learning

If transfer is less likely to happen when initial learning is superficial, then maximizing transfer requires learning on a deeper level. Toward that end, fellowships advisors can adapt teaching strategies from the writing classroom, such as role-playing, peer engagement, and modeling.

- **Role-playing:** Inviting the writer to act as their own reviewer can be an effective way of role-playing. This works best if the applicant's draft sits unread for a period before the advisor returns it to them, along with the essay prompt and a summary of the fellowship selection criteria (or perhaps, to make it more manageable, a few specific criteria selected for them to assess). The advisor can then ask the applicant to play selection committee and evaluate their own writing as if they had never seen it before.
- **Peer engagement:** Peer review can be a terrific tool for deepening applicant learning, as we remember better what we have taught to others. When possible, consider pairing up applicants to review each other's statements or do practice interviews (ideally, of course, these would be candidates who are not directly competing with each other; they could be two Fulbright applicants to different countries, for example). A "peer feedback" handout, on which an advisee is prompted to assess the strengths and weaknesses of their peer's current draft, can be a helpful tool to guide them.
- **Modeling:** Modeling can aid learning and retention.[16] As Muriel Harris puts it, "Seeing how something is done can indeed be interesting and demystify processes too long considered arcane."[17] During conferences, I frequently model how I would approach a task that is similar to the one I am asking the student to do. For example, I might say, "If I was asked to discuss my capacities as a cultural ambassador, I would start by doing free writing on what I consider to be cultural

aspects of my identity. Some of my ideas might be deep and profound, but others might be less so, like my love for cheese curds and the Brewers."

It can also be productive to perform a task alongside an applicant. For instance, when an applicant is struggling to generate essay ideas, the advisor might break down the prompt to a more focused topic—say, intellectual and academic interests and development—and then invite the writer to take five minutes to write down every relevant idea that occurs to them. During that time, the advisor can also write about their own intellectual development and model for the student how to start to move toward making decisions about what ideas seem most promising.

Modeling can also be used to help further explain and apply specific feedback on applicant writing. For instance, if a writer is struggling with wordiness, the advisor can select a characteristic sentence and show them how they might edit it for concision. The advisor could also provide the applicant with a few brief written examples of successful editing for concision—"befores" and "afters"—drawn from other applicants' drafts.

Be Explicit About Transfer as Advising Continues

While transfer is often done unconsciously, assisted metacognition—conscious and deliberate discussion of what an advisee is learning and the potential applications of that learning—can increase the likelihood of transfer in the future.[18] In addition to discussing transfer during the initial stages of working with a candidate, advisors can also reinforce transfer by inviting them to engage in metacognition. There are various ways to do so:

- Point out and provide positive reinforcement when applicants are already doing transfer during the application process. If during a practice interview, a candidate is using the kind of assertive, confident voice that they have practiced in their

writing, commend them for successfully applying this skill to a new task. If a Udall applicant drafts an application essay with strong topic sentences, a skill they learned from writing a Critical Language Scholarship application the year before, congratulate them on this successful transfer of knowledge.
- Discuss how they might transfer the skills they are acquiring. If a Goldwater applicant wants to be a chemistry professor, discuss with them how learning to convey their scientific research to the Goldwater selection committee will prepare them for an academic career in which they will regularly need to discuss science with a broad audience. If a Gilman applicant is writing a personal statement for the first time, talk about how their work on developing a personal voice in their writing applies to future writing projects in their college classes. And so on.
- Use assessment as a learning tool for applicants. Exit evaluations, for example, can do more than document how applicants assess fellowships advising; they can help writers solidify and transfer their learning. Ask questions such as
  ○ What is the one piece of advice you received that you will never forget?
  ○ What is one skill that you improved through the fellowships advising process that you think you can apply in the future? When will it be useful to you?
  ○ Did the advisor assist you in meeting your developmental goals? If so, how?

Consider Facilitating Future Transfer Directly

Applicants sometimes return to a fellowships advisor with requests for help on other applications that are not, strictly speaking, fellowships, or at least not the kind of awards fellowships advisors typically support. Graduate school applications are a good example. While I could not possibly accommodate every student who would like feedback on their application essays for graduate school, I do offer one round of graduate essay review for individuals with whom I have already worked on a fellowship application. Schedule permitting, I also work with fellowship alumni on a wide range of applications.

I initially agreed to these activities primarily out of a sense of responsibility to the individuals and a desire to be of assistance during a key career stage. But viewed through the lens of transfer, the decision to offer fellowship applicant alumni further assistance in other contexts means that an advisor can directly facilitate transfer of skills and knowledge from the fellowship application process to fresh contexts. Continued contact with an advisor may enable transfer, as the advisor can help the writer see how what they have already learned from the fellowship application process can be applied to this new task. At the same time, the advisor can reasonably expect to be less intensely involved and to see higher levels of ownership from these applicants, given what they have already learned through the process of applying for fellowships. In other words, continuing to work with a past applicant acts as a more longstanding form of scaffolding—adaptive support by a knowledgeable teacher (whose support will no longer be needed with time), a teaching practice that can support deeper learning.[19]

Although extending the advising process to other contexts can help further assist with learning transfer, there is a downside of doing so: It requires advisors to take on additional work outside core job duties and so may not be feasible for all advisors or advising offices. Fellowships advisors who cannot offer ongoing support to fellowship alumni might instead partner with other offices on campus, such as a career center or writing center, to bolster the support for transfer on campus. In addition to simply referring former applicants to such campus partners, fellowship offices might consider instigating direct communication with those partners about how, specifically, their services can serve an important role in facilitating transfer, building on the skills emphasized in fellowships advising.

Conclusion

This chapter has suggested how insights from research on transfer might usefully apply to fellowships advising. The implication, of course, is that the field of fellowships advising stands to benefit from writing studies and other disciplines in which transfer is being examined. However, I want to close by suggesting that it might also be the other way around—it might well be that research on transfer would benefit from considering fellowships advising. In writing studies, one finds regular calls for colleges to design curricula that facilitate transfer of writing skills by asking students to write in a way that is integrated with real-world outcomes and aimed at specific audiences. For instance, Anne Beaufort calls on university writing instruction to "acknowledge and exemplify to students 'real' rhetorical problem-solving in multiple discourse communities," while Paula Rosinski argues that "students gain more experience making rhetorical writing decisions based on audience awareness when they are actually writing for real audiences."[20] A fellowships application nicely checks these boxes: it is "rhetorical problem-solving" done for a specific, pragmatic purpose, aimed at a particular audience. In addition, a fellowships application is inherently metacognitive; it *automatically* compels writers to contemplate their own learning and articulate the applicability of that learning. Fellowships writing might fulfill many similar purposes to curricular interventions often proposed to assist with transfer, such as e-portfolios that include reflective writing or metacognition exercises. Perhaps, then, fellowships might comprise a neglected subject within research on transfer.

Contemplating fellowships in light of transfer could have payoff for college instructors and administrators. Beyond providing even more reason to encourage students to apply for fellowships, one can imagine that fellowships essays could serve as inspiration for curricular interventions in writing courses. Indeed, completing the research for this article has compelled me to alter an assignment in a writing-intensive course I am teaching this upcoming year. Rather than a traditional academic essay, I will ask students to write a short grant proposal. Will this improve transfer? We will see.

Notes

1. Suzanne McCray, *Beyond Winning: National Scholarship Competitions and the Student Experience* (Fayetteville: University of Arkansas Press, 2005).

2. "Transfer of Knowledge to New Contexts," Yale Poorvu Center for Teaching and Learning, n.d., accessed August 29, 2024, https://poorvucenter.yale.edu/TransferKnowledge/.
3. David N. Perkins and Gavriel Salomon, "Teaching for Transfer," *Educational Leadership* 46, no. 1 (1988): 22–32.
4. Susan M. Barnett and Stephen J. Ceci, "When and Where Do We Apply What We Learn? Taxonomy for Far Transfer," *Psychological Bulletin* 128, no. 4 (2002): 612–37; David N. Perkins and Gavriel Salomon, "Transfer of Learning," in *International Encyclopedia of Education*, 2nd ed., ed. Torsten Husen and T. Nevill Postlethwaite (Oxford: Pergamon Press, 1992), 1–13; Keith J. Holyoak and Kyunghee Koh, "Surface and Structural Similarity in Analogical Transfer," *Memory and Cognition* 15, no. 4 (1987): 332–40; T. J. Nokes-Malach and J. P. Mestre, "Toward a Model of Transfer as Sense-Making," *Educational Psychologist* 48, no. 3 (2013): 184–207.
5. King Beach, "Consequential Transitions: A Sociocultural Expedition Beyond Transfer in Education," *Review of Research in Education* 24, no. 1 (1991): 111.
6. Perkins and Salomon, "Teaching for Transfer," 23.
7. "Elon Statement on Writing Transfer," Elon University Center for Engaged Learning, 2015, http://www.centerforengagedlearning.org/elon-statement-on-writing-transfer/.
8. Neil Baird and Bradley Dilger, "How Students Perceive Transitions: Dispositions and Transfer in Internships," *College Composition and Communication* 68, no. 4 (2017): 690.
9. Dana Lynn Driscoll and Jennifer Wells, "Beyond Knowledge and Skills: Writing Transfer and the Role of Student Dispositions," *Composition Forum* 26 (Fall 2012), http://compositionforum.com/issue/26/.
10. Perkins and Salomon, "Teaching for Transfer," 22.
11. "Elon Statement."
12. "Elon Statement."
13. Anne Beaufort, "Reflection: The Metacognitive Move Towards Transfer of Learning," in *A Rhetoric of Reflection*, ed. Kathleen Blake Yancey (Logan: Utah State University Press, 2016), 36.
14. Joseph M. Williams and Joseph Bizup, *Style: Lessons in Clarity and Grace*, 13th ed. (Hoboken, NJ: Pearson, 2021).
15. Gerald Graff and Cathy Birkenstein, *"They Say/I Say": The Moves That Matter in Academic Writing*, 5th ed. (New York: W.W. Norton, 2021); Kate L. Turabian, *Student's Guide to Writing College Papers*, 5th ed. (Chicago: University of Chicago Press, 2019).

16. Muriel Harris, "Modeling: A Process Method of Teaching," *College English* 45, no. 1 (January 1983): 74–84.
17. Harris, "Modeling," 81.
18. Samuel B. Day and Robert L. Goldstone, "The Import of Knowledge Export: Connecting Findings and Theories of Transfer of Learning," *Educational Psychologist* 47, no. 3 (2012): 153–76.
19. Janneke Van de Pol, Monique Volman, Frans Oort, and Jos Beishuizen, "The Effects of Scaffolding in the Classroom: Support Contingency and Student Independent Working Time in Relation to Student Achievement, Task Effort and Appreciation of Support," *Instructional Science* 43, no. 5 (2015): 615–41.
20. Anne Beaufort, *College Writing and Beyond: A New Framework for University Writing Instruction* (Logan: Utah State University Press, 2007), 152; Paula Rosinski, "Students' Perceptions of the Transfer of Rhetorical Knowledge Between Digital Self-Sponsored Writing and Academic Writing: The Importance of Authentic Contexts and Reflection," in *Critical Transitions: Writing and the Question of Transfer*, ed. Chris M. Anson and Jessie L. Moore (Denver: University Press of Colorado, 2017), 259.

6

What Do We Get Out of This?

Helping Students (Re)Examine Purpose and Positionality in Study Abroad Fellowships

MEGAN BRUENING

Introduction: The Stakes

Many higher education institutions promote study abroad as essential to the college experience, especially for undergraduate students. For many students, fellowships are necessary to access international education, and so the fellowship application provides students the chance to convey their enthusiasm for pursuing education abroad. This enthusiasm can stutter, however, when applicants are asked to talk about why a fellowship foundation or host community would want them to go abroad.[1] Initial responses to these questions often revolve around personal motivations or individual development. Perhaps engaging with a host community is a means to that growth, but conceiving and articulating motives beyond individual growth for international education can be difficult.[2] Individual purpose in pursuing study abroad is closely tied to the identity of an applicant. Whether the applicant is a first-generation college student planning to be the first in their family to travel outside the United States or someone who hopes to be a foreign service officer dedicated to promoting US interests, the identities applicants bring to the application deeply affect how they view their purpose overseas. Having conversations about the purpose of international education also means having discussions about identity and positionality or how identities change or interact in different contexts overseas.

Why is it important to have these personal, and often difficult, conversations with fellowship advisees? First, because as members of the fellowships advising profession, we promote the values of equity and inclusion.[3] Efforts to create equitable practices and inclusive relationships among fellowship stakeholders (the applicant, the advisor, the domestic institution, the fellowship foundation, and the host country) are integral to these values. We must consider whether we are being equitable and inclusive in our advising *and* how our advisees treat their hosts—ideally with respectful curiosity and cultural sensitivity. Second, applicants benefit from having these tough conversations. They will certainly create more thoughtful applications, but they will also have a more transformative experience abroad than if advisors gloss over the complexities of purpose and positionality in study-abroad fellowships. Carly Womack-Wynne argues that "challenging students to critically analyze concepts [such as purpose and positionality] from a variety of perspectives, especially those that differ from their personal system of beliefs, is essential" to empower students to effectively and respectfully engage with new environments overseas.[4]

The current cultural climate increases the urgency of discussing these topics with advisees. Scholars in international education have argued that we are operating in a context of rising nationalism, xenophobia, and exclusionism that discourages potential fellows from critically thinking about identity and equitable international collaboration.[5] At the same time, scholars of neocolonialism point to the neoliberal ideology dominating society, which defines everything (including human beings) in terms of market value.[6] Rhia Moreno remarks, "Focus on economic, social, and political success dominates the rhetoric used to promote study abroad where it is positioned as a competitive tool to advance the nation-state, the academic institution, and personhood."[7] Or, as Talya Zemach-Bersin more bluntly puts it, "A long-held assumption that U.S. students who study abroad will actively endorse and advance U.S. interests (both 'abroad' and when back 'home') has gripped the hopes and imaginations of the U.S. government and nongovernmental organizations alike."[8] In sum, fellowship applicants are constantly told (explicitly or indirectly) to view study abroad as a way to enhance personal economic value and to contribute to vague US political goals (such as fostering goodwill between nations) without considering the motives of or cost to other international stakeholders.[9] Fellowships can be avenues to form reciprocal, equitable partnerships between individuals and communities, but only if applicants start the experience with a critical eye informed by their purpose and positionality. This essay offers three reflective exercises to help fellowship applicants develop this critical lens.

Key Terms and Literature

First, however, it is important to define the key terms and framework informing these exercises. *Identity* is defined in this chapter as the constructed, intersecting meanings or traits we ascribe to ourselves, both as unique individuals and members of specific groups.[10] Identity is not static, as Kalwart Bhopal and John Preston explain, but rather "changes through different times in history and transforms through different spaces."[11] International education and social justice scholar Malaika Marable Serrano uses the word *saliency* to describe how certain aspects of identity have a larger impact on daily life in a given context.[12] I recall my own surprise as an undergraduate overseas that my identity as a US American was much more salient (and publicly commented on) than my identity as a woman, for example, when I studied at Oxford. *Positionality*, then, is the shifting saliency of our identities based on our current spatial and temporal context.

Looking at this framework, some advisors may raise concerns: "What if I am working with an advisee who does not agree that identity is constructed? Or balks at the word 'intersectional'?" To be transparent, I do not introduce these exercises by saying, "Let's deconstruct neoliberalism and neocolonialism through reflections on positionality." These are the terms and theories that inform the exercises below. The practice is simply, but significantly, to get applicants to think critically (e.g., considering other perspectives) about who they are and why they travel. The goal of these exercises is to set advisees on the path of critically reconsidering simplified and narrow approaches to study abroad.

International education scholars have noted with increasing concern the need for study-abroad participants to discuss purpose and identity before, during, and after a program. As David Wick and Tasha Willis remind educators, "International education [programs do not] automatically or inherently lead to critical self-reflection, intercultural competence, critical empathy, or the betterment of humanity."[13] Unfortunately, there is little research explicitly discussing fellowships or the fellowship application process in terms of preparing for or reflecting on study abroad. One goal of this chapter is to begin filling this gap, acknowledging the opportunities for self-reflection and broader trajectory considerations a fellowship application provides. Fellowships advisors have the opportunity to work extensively with students before they are even accepted into a study-abroad program, which is unique among some international education professionals, who can only meet and advise students briefly before departure. Much scholarship focuses on what international education professionals can do in pre-departure workshops or activities, but fellowships advisors can begin this work in the earlier phase of application writing. Because fellowships advisors have this unique access point, the exercises described below are framed by process composition pedagogy. Championed by composition scholars such as Peter Elbow, process pedagogy views the practice of writing as more important than creating a perfect product or essay. Writing can thus be a means for study-abroad applicants to critically examine their sense of purpose and positionality, and advisors have an important role helping them do so in the drafting or revision stages of a fellowship application. The three exercises below are tailored to this process and possibly to a pre-departure orientation or course.

Exercises

The first exercise is the "Rhetorical Triangle Revised." It is a way to visually break down the purposes that motivate a study-abroad fellowship (see Figure 6.1). In the traditional composition model of a rhetorical triangle, each corner is labeled with one of the three classic rhetorical appeals (logos = argument, ethos = writer, and pathos =

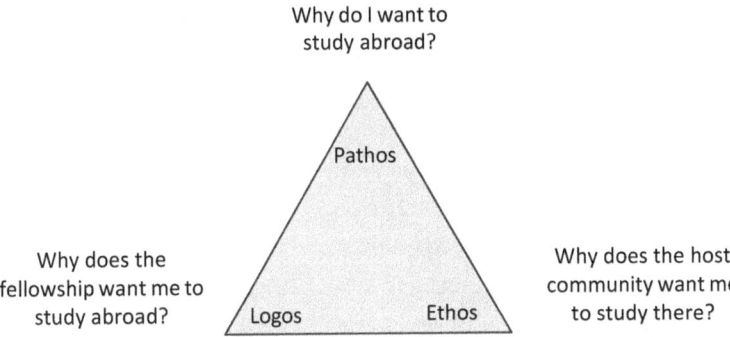

Figure 6.1. Rhetorical triangle revised.

audience). Persuasive writers successfully consider all three appeals to create an argument to which the audience will positively respond.

In the revised triangle, each corner is labeled with a person or group whom the applicant must address in their argument for why they need to study abroad. The writer must address themselves (ethos, or their own reason for studying abroad), the fellowship foundation (logos, or why the sponsor is promoting study abroad), and the host community (pathos, or how the community will emotionally respond to the writer's presence). This exercise can be used in a brainstorming setting or in a revision context if the applicant needs assistance expanding on why they should receive the fellowship. In the composition classroom, students are regularly asked to fill out the rhetorical triangle to ensure they address all parts of an argument. The revised triangle offers college students a familiar visual to spark conversation and, if needed, additional research to complete the triangle. Asking applicants "How could the community respond to my presence?" (the pathos corner) can catalyze especially fruitful discussion.

It is important to discuss the applicant's answers (and not just have the applicant fill out the visual), because initial responses may be under-developed. For example, in the "pathos" corner, an initial response could be narrowly US-centric (for example, the host community will respond only with enthusiasm) or promote a culturally parasitic relationship that "positions the host community as a place to be consumed or discovered by the student for personal benefit" (as in the host community wants to share its resources with me so I can grow professionally).[14] If advisees struggle with completing the triangle, I recommend using Tara Yosso's model of cultural capital to have students generate a list of what they bring to a fellowship and how these internal resources can connect to the foundation's goals, the host community's needs, and their personal motives for going abroad.[15] If an advisee needs help expanding on the ethos corner, students can perform research on their intended destination to get a general sense of the host's relationship with the United States and examine examples of previous fellowship projects to see how fellows responded to community needs. Overall, the exercise requires applicants to step outside of their personal identity and goals to consider the perspectives and goals of other fellowship stakeholders.

The second exercise, "Pebble in the Pond," is an excellent way to get applicants thinking about the short- and long-term impacts of their goals (see Figure 6.2). It can be used in a brainstorming or revision context, and it is especially useful for generating conclusion paragraph content. Like the revised triangle, this exercise offers applicants a visual to break down how the fellowship will impact others: students can work backward to reflect on what their goals are or how they will achieve the outcome they identified. It is usually easy for applicants to set goals and intended outcomes for themselves. They want to learn a language, gain research experience, or boost their resume. The struggle begins when applicants consider how they will impact various communities (not just US ones) during and after the fellowship.

First, applicants imagine the fellowship as a pebble that they drop into a calm pond. Each ripple that expands out from the pebble is an impact on a specific person or community. In Figure 6.2, the ripples are labeled according to the degree of closeness to the applicant. The ripples expand across time as well as space; applicants should consider their impact on multiple communities *during and after* the fellowship. Before applicants begin writing, encourage them to consider how their purpose for study abroad can have tangible as well as more abstract outcomes. For example, one outcome may be to publish a research paper with a mentor from the host community. Another outcome can be to share their experience with their local

What Do We Get Out of This? | 105

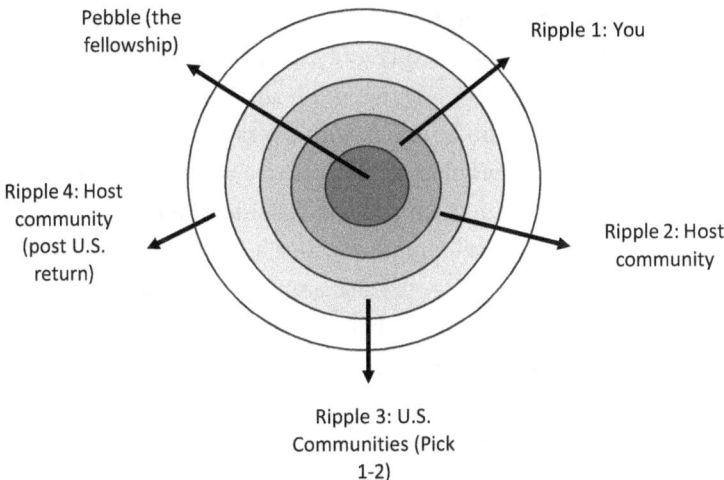

Prompt: Write down how your fellowship experience will affect the subject of each ripple. The impact could be a product, or something more abstract.

For the "U.S. Communities" ripple, think of at least one group of people that you interact with (e.g.: family, friends, co-workers).

Figure 6.2. Pebble in the Pond.

high school to help teens understand the importance of international education. Both outcomes are valuable, but challenge advisees to think of concrete results and not only vague goals such as "increasing cultural awareness." Addressing the ripple of "US communities" is often a new avenue of thought for many advisees and encourages them to consider what communities they engage with as a result of their identities.

After giving applicants a few moments to write and reflect, start the conversation by asking which ripples were easy to fill in and which were difficult. Acknowledging the degree of difficulty is an opportunity to engage in further self-reflection (e.g., "Why was thinking about the impact on myself easier than the impact on a US community?"). After this initial conversation, students work backward to state a goal and plan that will lead to the outcome described in one ripple or more. This backward goal-setting process is a good opportunity for applicants to evaluate the feasibility of their purpose. For example, grand plans of spreading US democracy often get broken down in this process, turning into realistic and reciprocal plans of exchanging music and movies with peers to talk about cultural values. This exercise requires applicants to engage in self-reflection and step outside of their own goals to consider the needs of others, which is a means to developing sophisticated goal-setting skills.[16]

The third exercise is a group discussion of study-abroad scenarios. The two example scenarios below were written by international educator and scholar LaNitra Berger, and we have used them in our presentations on allyship and cultural ambassadorship during the Boren awardee pre-departure convocation for several years.[17] These two scenarios represent a spectrum of challenges a fellow may face while studying overseas. The stakes are different in each, but both require the discussants to consider their positionality and how their identity as US students would impact their behavior in a host community. This exercise could be implemented in a pre-departure activity or in a workshop setting to help applicants generate responses for questions about how they will react to challenges overseas.[18]

The first scenario asks participants to navigate both a safety concern and an obvious case of identity-based violence. Scholars note that many pre-departure programs focus on safety concerns, and this scenario helps participants grapple with the way that identity impacts safety in different cultural contexts.[19] The second scenario requires participants to navigate a socially awkward conversation; while less "serious" than scenario 1, the second is still likely to happen in a study-abroad setting.

> **Scenario 1:** An African American woman is studying Czech at a university one hour outside of Prague. She met another Boren scholar at orientation who is also studying Czech, and they agree to meet in Prague for the weekend. After a long night out, they board a bus to go to their hotel, and a group of aggressive Neo-Nazis boards the bus. They approach her and tell her that "all black dogs need to go back to Africa."

Scenario 2: Aisha is Somali-American studying in the Middle East. She is in a café with a few other Boren scholars and a few local students in her Arabic class. A student mentions that she is from Minnesota and makes negative comments about Somali American congresswoman Ilhan Omar. She believes that Omar should be grateful to be in the United States and should stop complaining. There is silence in the room, but everyone is looking at Aisha.

After reading the scenarios, direct groups to discuss the following questions:

- What do you think the different actors (people) in the story are feeling? What emotions would you experience and why?
- What would you do in this scenario to be an ally to your friend? How would a cultural ambassador respond?
- What would you do a week after this scenario occurred?

The first question requires participants to engage in sympathetic or empathetic reflection and to consider how their identities impact the way they experience an emotional challenge. It is also an opportunity to discuss the salience of identities (e.g., my identity as a US American, a woman, a person of color informs the way I would feel about this situation). The second question requires participants to problem-solve within the scenario's specific context. The language of allyship and cultural ambassadorship is specific to the Boren convocation context, but students can also just discuss how they would support the central party in the scenario. This question also opens up the possibility of discussing purpose while overseas: How is supporting others part of our goals for studying abroad? The third question encourages participants to (1) identify appropriate resources for immediate response (such as campus safety officials) and later support (like a fellowship helpline to find local mental health resources) and to (2) reflect on how the emotional impacts of being in a new, challenging environment do not end immediately. It also demonstrates that post-challenge reflection and sharing is crucial to growing through a study-abroad experience.

Conclusion: A Call to Action

These three exercises encourage fellowship applicants to begin grappling with broad discussions of identity, purpose, and international collaboration. The key word is "begin." International educators report that students who experienced the most significant growth during study-abroad programs participated in reflective activities before, during, and after their time overseas.[20] Fellowships advisors, especially if they are working alone or with limited resources, may not have the ability to guide this kind of reflection while a fellow is abroad or when they return to the United States. How do we continue the growth that these application exercises can spark?

An internal institutional option is to partner with study-abroad offices, finding ways to include fellowship recipients in any initiatives for reflection before, during, and after the program. This partnership could also represent a new avenue for research by comparing the experiences and learning outcomes of fellowship recipients versus those of university-led study-abroad program participants. On a professional level, as fellowships advisors we can leverage our collective strength to (1) ask fellowship foundations what practices they implement to encourage self-reflection before, during, and after the fellowship; (2) if none, to advocate for the inclusion of guided discussions; and (3) to advocate for fellowship foundations to collect and publish data on the experiences of host communities.[21] Every year, fellowship recipients returning to the United States speak about the power of their experiences abroad. Fellowships advisors have the opportunity to make these experiences even more significant for everyone (students, host communities, and domestic communities) by sparking conversations of identity, purpose, and equitable international collaboration.

Notes

1. Students are not alone in the struggle to expand their goal for study abroad beyond personal development: "The goal of enhancing students' global perspectives and other dimensions of development can lead us to overlook or underexamine the impact of student mobility on host

communities" (David Wick and Tasha Willis, "International Education's Potential for Advancing Social Justice," in *Social Justice and International Education: Research, Practice, and Perspectives*, ed. LaNitra Berger [Washington, DC: NAFSA, 2020], 27). The *we* in asking "What do we get out of this?" includes not only the students but also their homes and host communities.

2. Talya Zemach-Bersin connects the individual using a host country as means to a personal end to a larger, imperial project: "Through study abroad, global citizens are expected to enact a similar process by harvesting the resource of international knowledge to strengthen and benefit America" ("Entitled to the World: The Rhetoric of U.S. Global Citizenship Education and Study Abroad," in *Postcolonial Perspectives on Global Citizenship Education*, ed. Vanessa de Oliveira Andreotti, Lynn Mario, and T. M. de Souza [New York: Routledge, 2012], 97).

3. "Values and Codes of Ethics," NAFA, accessed August 28, 2024, https://www.nafadvisors.org/about-us/values-and-code-of-ethics/.

4. Carly Womack-Wynne, "Global Citizenship 2.0: Supporting a New Breed of Stewards to Confront a Changing Reality," *International Educator* 27, no. 3 (2018): 23.

5. Supriya Bailey, "Equity Education in a Time of Rising Nationalism: Challenges and Complexities," in *Social Justice and International Education: Research, Practice, and Perspectives*, ed. LaNitra Berger (Washington, DC: NAFSA, 2020), 43–62. See Marcel Coenders and Peer Sheepers for an interesting discussion of how education can counteract exclusionist discourse by promoting sophisticated cognitive processes: "The Effect of Education on Nationalism and Ethnic Exclusionism: An International Comparison," *Political Psychology* 24, no. 2 (2003): 313–43.

6. As Wick and Willis have pointed out, neoliberal ideologies present in contemporary rhetoric of higher education internationalization are also inherently colonial ("International Education's Potential," 15).

7. Rhia Moreno, "Disrupting Neoliberal and Neocolonial Ideologies in Study Abroad: From Discourse to Intervention," *Frontiers: The Interdisciplinary Journal of Study Abroad* 33, no. 2 (2021): 96.

8. Zemach-Bersin, "Entitled to the World," 91.

9. Moreno remarks that "study abroad has become—and is promoted as such—a very individual-centered concept of personal investment" but only for those "who have the means, time, and capital to participate in study abroad" ("Disrupting Neoliberal and Neocolonial Ideologies," 98).

10. I am drawing on the works of Judith Butler and Kimberlé Crenshaw in this definition. See Butler, *Gender Trouble* (London: Routledge, 2006)

and *Bodies That Matter: On the Discursive Limits of "Sex"* (New York: Routledge, 1993); and Crenshaw, "Demarginalizing the Intersection of Race and Sex: A Black Feminist Critique of Anti-discrimination Doctrine Feminist Theory and Antiracist Politics," *University of Chicago Legal Forum*, no. 1 (1989): 139–67.

11. Kalwart Bhopal and John Preston, "Introduction: Intersectionality and 'Race' in Education: Theorising Difference," in *Intersectionality and Race in Education* (Taylor and Francis, 2011), 1–10.

12. Malaika Marable Serrano. "Social Justice-Centered Education Abroad Programming," in *Social Justice and International Education: Research, Practice, and Perspectives*, ed. LaNitra Berger (Washington, DC: NAFSA, 2020), 155–72.

13. Wick and Willis, "International Education's Potential," 12.

14. Heather Haeger, John E. Banks, Roman Christiaens, and Lily Amador, "Steps Towards Decolonizing Study Abroad: Host Communities' Perceptions of Change, Benefits, and Harms from Study Abroad," *Frontiers: The Interdisciplinary Journal of Study Abroad* 36, no. 1 (2024): 84–85

15. Examples of cultural capital include "aspirational capital," or "the ability to maintain hopes and dreams for the future, even in the face of real and perceived barriers," and "navigational capital," or the "skills of maneuvering through social institutions. Historically, this infers the ability to maneuver through institutions not created with Communities of Color in mind" (Tara J. Yosso, "Whose Culture Has Capital? A Critical Race Theory Discussion of Community Cultural Wealth," *Race Ethnicity and Education* 8, no. 1 [2006]: 77). Yosso's model also prevents advisors from ignoring or downplaying the cross-culturual skills students may possess. As Zemach-Bersin explains, "The idea that Americans are not already, but must be transformed into, individuals with international knowledge and cross-cultural skills renders invisible those Americans who have already developed such skills and experiences as an everyday necessity, such as immigrants, those with multicultural backgrounds, or the many Americans who do not have membership in dominant cultures and thus have no choice but to be 'cross-culturally literate' on a daily basis" ("Entitled to the World," 95–96).

16. Kelly K. Lemmons, "Study Abroad Academic Pre-Departure Course: Increasing Student's Intercultural Competence Pre-Sojourns," *Frontiers: The Interdisciplinary Journal of Study Abroad* 35, no. 3 (2023): 128–50.

17. At Boren convocations, we defined allyship as "partnering with a marginalized community you are not a member of to advocate for the rights and needs of that group." We defined cultural ambassadorship as "facilitating

the reciprocal exchange of cultural values and practices with the goal of learning from one another." Megan Bruening, "Becoming an Ally and Cultural Ambassador," oral presentation, Boren Awardee Convocation, Washington, DC, June 2, 2023.
18. Womack-Wynne confirms that "students need a curated predeparture experience that models self-reflection" ("Global Citizenship 2.0," 23).
19. From Wick and Willis: "When preparing students for international experiences, international educators often focus on issues of health and safety and emphasize cross-cultural differences. Abes, Jones, and McEwan's (2007) model, however, stresses preparing students for the many ways in which they will experience all aspects of their identity differently in the international context" ("International Education's Potential," 24). See also Lemmons, "Study Abroad Academic Pre-Departure Course," 129.
20. Shari Galiardi and Jenny Koehn, "Strategies to Mitigate the Negative and Accentuate the Positive Impacts of International Service-Learning on Host Communities," *Partnerships: A Journal of Service Learning & Civic Engagement* 2, no. 1 (2011): 1–12.
21. We can partner with international educators and scholars in this call: "The vast majority of research on educational travel and international study experiences has focused on student outcomes, and more research is needed that takes into account the perspective of host community members." Heather Haeger, John E. Banks, Roman Christiaens, and Lily Amador, "Steps Towards Decolonizing Study Abroad: Host Communities' Perceptions of Change, Benefits, and Harms from Study Abroad," *Frontiers: The Interdisciplinary Journal of Study Abroad* 36, no. 1 (2024): 82.

7

English Belongs to "Those Who Use It"

Cultivating Authentic Voices with Inclusive Writing Pedagogies and Linguistic Pluralism

ELENA REISS, MITCH HOBZA, AND JULIA GOLDBERG

In 1974, the Conference on College Composition and Communication (CCCC) responded to growing anxiety about English literacy and non-standard dialects in college classrooms by adopting a resolution entitled "Students' Right to Their Own Language,"[1] which asked, "What should... schools do about the language habits of students who come from a wide variety of social, economic, and cultural backgrounds?"[2] While the 1974 resolution was situated within a context of a growing number of economically and racially diverse students gaining access to higher education, the authors of the resolution note that "the question is not new."[3] Today, fifty years after the passing of the resolution, the impetus behind the resolution has spawned the development of inclusive writing pedagogies to address different varieties and dialects of English in college writing. Moreover, as we continue to work with an increasing number of international students and other students from linguistically diverse backgrounds, how we address the issue has particular urgency for fellowship advising. As more foundations increasingly make calls to diversify their scholar cohorts and espouse the desire for applications that reflect the author's "authentic voice," how can fellowships advisors, foundation representations, and scholarship selection committees make room for diverse dialects and Englishes in students' applications?

For many fellowships advisors, writing instruction is part of our everyday labor, while the assessment of the submitted writing is part of any review process. In turn, reviewers' assessments shape how advisors instruct the writing of fellowship applications. Insofar as the CCCC's 1974 resolution on how college-level composition is taught has implications for how writing is assessed in the context of a fellowship application, it is notable that the resolution stands in contrast to the commonly-held belief in writing instruction that "there existed somewhere a single American 'standard English' which could be isolated, identified, and accurately defined" and that the standard "'English of educated speakers,' the language used by those in power in the community, had an inherent advantage over other dialects as a means of expressing thought or emotion, conveying information, or analyzing concepts."[4] The resolution asks writing instructors to question if "our attitudes toward 'educated English' are based on some superiority of the dialect itself *or the social prestige of those who use it*" or if "our rejection of students who do not adopt the dialect most familiar to us is based on any real merit in our dialect or whether we are actually rejecting the students themselves, rejecting them because of their racial, social, and cultural origins."[5] This kind of rejection can occur when an applicant's writing is being assessed for not aligning with the expectations of "Edited American English" (EAE) or "Standard American Written English" (SAWE) during the drafting process and/or review and selection process. How might these attitudes about English usage affect an applicant's ability to use their own variety or dialect of English in their application?

The questions posed by the CCCC's resolution are difficult, and we offer no easy answers. Every person who teaches and assesses writing, including fellowships advisors and reviewers, will arrive at their own conclusions about how they teach and correct written English. That is, in many ways, one of our central arguments: English belongs to those who use it. Everyone uses it, and subsequently teaches it, differently. The fundamental question then becomes, How do we account for linguistic diversity in our work with applicants and assist applicants with meeting their audience's expectations without diminishing their experiences and authentic voices? How can we respect the varieties of English that belong to our applicants and still advise on composing a competitive application?

The resolution's legacy has been far-reaching for the field of composition studies, and its ramifications are still present in the teaching of writing in postsecondary education across the United States. We chose to use this resolution as a starting point for the discussion because its questions about the values society places on certain dialects, registers, and varieties and the consequential constraints on students' voices are perennial issues and still haunt the teaching of writing today.

Indeed, since the initial publication of the "Students' Right to their Own Language," many composition scholars and instructors have extended the 1974 resolution's argument about SAWE. The authors of the 2021 "CCCC Statement on White Language Supremacy" note that the 1974 resolution was "forged in the political backdrop of the Civil Rights, Black Power, and other liberation movements worldwide to provide 'open access' for racially and linguistically oppressed groups."[6] The authors build on the 1974 resolution to argue against pedagogical approaches that position SAWE within a "stance of neutrality, objectivity, and apoliticality," which "shapes aesthetics, epistemologies, attitudes, ideologies, and discourses that structure social arrangements" and thereby diminishes many writers' access to their own language at the peril of silencing or hamstringing their ability to express themselves. Advocating for a broader understanding of our applicants' modes of writing is increasingly a topic of concern that is driven by foundations' calls for application essays that are reflective of the applicant's "authentic voice," particularly as our applicant pools are representative of greater linguistic, cultural, and other intersectional aspects of diversity. This desire for authenticity and a writer's linguistic right to their own language are interrelated because many students are negotiating the possible tensions between their dialects and languages, the expectations of SAWE, and the specific rhetorical objectives of a fellowship application.

The writing entailed by scholarship and fellowship applications is complex and falls at the nexus of the conventional "academic" paradigm and the creative in asking applicants to authentically and personally convey who they are, how they meet the desired selection criteria, and to do so often within highly constrained word or character limits. Their writing must be compelling, succinct, and intended for highly subjective review processes by unknown selection panels who are themselves tasked with making difficult decisions regarding the merits of an individual's application over those of another's, and often doing so quickly. In essence, scholarship application writing is its own genre and one that may be unfamiliar to many applicants because the conventions and expectations for each award are markedly different from adjacent genres such as college admissions essays. While personal statements are their own genre just as research plans are another, how these genres are defined by each individual award is what is known as a "genre instance."[7] For example, a one-page Fulbright personal statement is a "genre instance" that differs from the three-page personal statement required for the National Science Foundation Graduate Research Fellowship Program. Both documents will follow the genre conventions of a personal statement, such as communicating one's experiences through narrative, articulating one's career goals and the desired impact of achieving such goals, and demonstrating how one's values and motivations align with an award's mission. However, how these conventions are addressed in each genre instance will vary because of an award's stated mission, the essay's prompt, reviewers' expectations, and an advisor's knowledge of what has and has not succeeded in previous cycles.

In essence, each genre, and more importantly, each genre instance, is socially and disciplinarily mediated by writers, advisors, foundations, and reviewers. Bill Hart-Davidson[8] argues that "the stabilization of formal elements by which we recognize genres is seen as the visible effects of human action.... Genres are constructions of groups, over time, usually with the implicit or explicit sanction of organizational or institutional power."[9] Hart-Davidson's discussion of power is significant in the context of fellowships in that the genre instances of fellowship applications are an enactment of institutional power: Reviewers and foundations determine who receives an award, and once there are enough recipients, their essays begin to establish a genre that other applicants follow through samples and advisement.

Hart-Davidson describes the "textual structure" of genres as the "fossil record left behind, evidence that writers have employed familiar discursive moves in accordance with reader expectations, institutional norms, market forces, and other social influences."[10] Advising students on the genre conventions of any essay is another site for negotiation, as an applicant should demonstrate an understanding of a genre instance's conventions without their voice and content sounding so generic that the essay appears to have been written by ChatGPT for at least a hundred other applicants. While applicants' success in their application essays often determines the conventions of a genre instance, such as how to structure a paragraph on a research experience, the other "fossil record" created by winning applications is the variety of English used in the document. If applicants continue to win by using SAWE (or having their voices edited to conform to SAWE by services such as ChatGPT), then SAWE may emerge as the language of prestige in an application at the risk of applicants' not using a voice that more accurately represents their lived experiences or backgrounds. Paradigms that promote linguistic pluralism, such as translingualism's methods of utilizing all of one's linguistic resources rather than treating languages as discrete entities, may offer alternative means for understanding language that can be used to facilitate some applicants' ability to compose their application essays in a more "authentic voice."

As fellowships advisors who recognize the highly nuanced nature of how applications are read, how do we empower scholarship applicants to convey who they are, while recognizing that what and how they write is indicative of their "promise" in terms of the scholarship's mission and scholar expectations? The answer to that question will vary depending on the scholarship itself as well as the applicant.

Insights derived from a variety of inclusive writing pedagogies combined with the overarching importance of selection criteria and audience expectations inform our work, walking a delicate line between an overly processed, homogenous voice and that of the applicant's authentic voice. Of course, as advisors, we must nevertheless recognize and honor the rhetorical sovereignty of our applicants to ensure that they still have, and should have, the latitude and the agency to determine what and how much to incorporate into those final application products.

Translanguaging, translingualism, and code-meshing and code-switching are terms all used to describe moving between languages, dialects, and codes in writing and speaking and were originally employed in bilingual educational programs or when working with students whose first or preferred language was not the linguistic variety employed in the classroom.[11] "Code-meshing" and "code-switching" describe moving between languages or dialects and can be used interchangeably in some of the scholarship; however, Juan C. Guerra provides clear distinctions between the two concepts.[12] Guerra outlines three approaches to "language and cultural difference," which he labels "Monolingual/Monocultural," "Multilingual/Multicultural," and "Translingual/Transcultural." The "monolingual" approach is aligned with "code segregation," or keeping certain languages and codes separate for different rhetorical occasions and audiences and is aligned with assimilative practices such as "English-only" contexts. Code-switching is aligned with the "multilingual approach," which he characterizes as "tolerant and accommodationist"—the latter because the manner of switching between codes (or languages) still needs to be appropriate to an audience or context.[13] For example, a student needs to consider whether to use a certain language or variety in a specific context, such as using some Spanish mixed with English in an essay. Since the "monolingual" and "multilingual" approaches often establish a false binary, Guerra proposes a third approach: the "translingual" approach, which can be enacted through code-meshing and is "fluid and in constant revision" because the translingual approach focuses on "mutual intelligibility rather than fluency."[14] This focus on "mutual intelligibility" and fluidity is key to our advocating for cultivating student's authentic voices: Even if an applicant is moving between languages and dialects that may not belong to their reader, their goal as a writer is to communicate their experience to their readers.

What bridges various inclusive writing pedagogies (translanguaging, code meshing, code switching, and so on) is the idea that language does not operate in a vacuum; instead, it is driven by culture, politics, geography, climate, health, and other human factors. Thus, language choice (grammar, word selection, dialect, variety) is not a fixed communication medium; just as it is influenced by the intricacies of human interaction in a given space and time, so are these interactions influenced by the rhetorical choices people make in communication. According to Paul J. Thibault, we do not use a predefined and fixed language code; rather, we construct communication in real time.[15] In that process, we inevitably switch between different fluid literacies as we communicate and re-negotiate meanings. In that sense, translanguaging empowers individuals to use resources and structural features of acquired languages (including dialects and registers) for "sense- and meaning-making."[16]

Essentially, scholarship applicants are tasked with using lexical and grammatical structures of the language to provide their readers with an "accurate" impression of who they are for the purposes of that scholarship. In this rather daunting task, they are further limited by the conventions of standard academic English and the perceived expectations from scholarship foundations and review committees. Imagine an artist who is asked to paint a self-portrait using only a prescribed color palette and medium. A skillful painter might be able to complete the task, but the portrait would most likely feel flat and somewhat lacking in authenticity and of limited creativity and self-expression. Similarly, when we ask the applicants to only use predefined language conventions, we limit their voice and, with that, their ability to create an authentic, vivid image of who they are as individuals, leaders, change agents, intellectuals, and scholars worthy of serious consideration.

Many scholarship applicants already experience anxiety associated with writing "perfect" applications. Often, it is exacerbated by what Stephen Krashen calls "affective filters" created by negative writing experiences that applicants might have had in the past.[17] Given the diverse backgrounds of our applicant pool, we may be working with applicants who come from less than privileged and often resource-poor pre-collegiate backgrounds and/or with those who have had limited or vastly divergent experiences engaging in collegiate-level intensive academic writing coursework. As such, it is not uncommon for them to have encountered experiences that make them question their writing ability. Just as a dirty lens can inhibit a person's vision, so affective filters that are created during negative experiences inhibit a writer's ability to create a clear vision of what their final product should look like, which restricts their writing process and writing outcome.

Often, this conflict is further complicated by the "identity crisis" that many of our applicants experience as they begin to explore who they are and how they want to present themselves in their essays. This tension is particularly true for nontraditional, non-majority students negotiating their identities on college campuses. A sense of "otherness" inevitably leads to further self-doubt and struggles with determining which aspects of their identity they want to or should share as well as questioning their self-integrity and their voice.

Even assuming confidence with standard academic English, few applicants have experience with the scholarship genre itself, especially when it comes to writing personal statements outside of limited contexts such as college admissions essays, which is why many students may default to writing personal statements that read like cover letters as that is a genre they understand better. Coupled with writing anxiety and other affective filters, these candidates then struggle with the content of their scholarship applications as well, not because they do not have anything to write about, but because the task of putting their experiences on paper is paralyzing.

One advisor shared that she recently had a fascinating conversation with a Filipino American Gilman Scholarship candidate who grew up speaking Cantonese and Tagalog. When discussing his personal statement, he felt as though he was unable to express his sense of humor and his resilience in English the same way he would in Tagalog. Multilingual students who are often judged for their accent or familiarity with cultural inferences (such as references to TV shows in humor) often feel the disconnect between their native cultural identity and the one they are forced to construct when communicating in English. This is not a rare occurrence.

On the other end of the spectrum, fellowship advisors might work with multilingual applicants who fully assimilated into American culture and are not aware of the influence of their heritage languages on their identity development. One example is a recent scholarship candidate whose father and grandmother are Japanese, and the candidate was initially unaware of the extent to which her heritage influenced her personality, values, beliefs, and aspirations.

In this context, translanguaging, code-meshing and other inclusive pedagogies become a powerful advising tool that serves a dual purpose. First, by tapping into applicants' linguistic resources, advisors help them to arrive at a better understanding of their "selves" and thereby empower them to draw a unique and accurate portrait of who they are as a scholar and a unique human being, while also eliminating writing anxiety associated with the application process.

The Filipino student, was asked to brainstorm and create outlines of his essays in whatever language he was most comfortable with, and his initial outlines became a true mix of Cantonese, Tagalog, and English. Having created that authentic context, he was then able to shift his focus to the "form," shaping his essay in a way that was comprehensible and acceptable to his audience. In later stages, the student worked to polish essay organization and language use, making sure to abide by the academic standards appropriate for the audience. Here is an example from the student's final draft:

> In Tagalog, there is a phrase, "Utang na loob," meaning "debt to one's blood," which I use to describe my deep gratitude and duty to family. Growing up distant from both my Filipino and Chinese roots, my grasp of Tagalog and Cantonese felt fractured, and I often felt alienated from my own culture. Yet, this experience illuminated the unique power language has in bridging cultures, particularly for those raised in communities distinct from their heritage.

Regarding the student with Japanese heritage who she was struggling with identifying how it influenced her identity—when asked to recall any words or phrases that her Japanese relatives would use, and almost without hesitation she said: "makeru ga kachi—to lose is to win, which means that we often learn more from the process itself, rather than the result, and that the greatest learning often comes from losing." Interestingly (but perhaps not surprisingly), saying this phrase activated something in her memory, a realization that she holds this value that stems directly from her Japanese heritage. Through further discussion, she came to the realization that this phrase and the associated value have a direct correlation with her academic interests. Her goal is to design athletic equipment for people with physical disabilities to participate in winter sports. Because of this value, she puts more emphasis on the process of engaging with the sport rather than winning, and she wants to make it accessible to others. As a result of using translanguaging during the advising process, this candidate, who previously had not seen the impact of her Japanese heritage, arrived at a very important self-discovery, suddenly making sense of the reasons she is drawn to a particular career path. Here's how she incorporated her cultural identity into her Fulbright personal statement:

> Growing up in a Japanese-American household instilled in me a deep desire to pursue opportunities and also help create opportunities for others. Shinto, Japan's most populous religion, emphasizes the idea of "michi"—a principle I grew up with, which can be interpreted as a path, process, or journey. This principle encourages individuals to seek personal growth, self-improvement, and the pursuit of opportunities aligned with their purpose or calling. I sought opportunities for personal growth through snowboarding professionally for Team USA in competitions across the world. Snowboarding has taught me how to welcome competition and challenges, appreciate losing and have humble winnings, learn from cultures around the world, and bridge the connection between body and mind. My grandmother, a fourth-degree black belt in judo, used to tell me "Makeru ga kachi" or "to lose is to win"; I carry this mentality with me every time I compete. I have always interpreted this saying as losing can teach you more than winning, and one should be grateful for the opportunity to compete against victors. I didn't know it then, but my "purpose" or "calling" was to empower people to seek personal growth through the help of technology. All of these products I dreamt about as a kid had one thing in common: accessibility. Accessible products play a vital role

in fostering opportunities for individuals by breaking down barriers and creating a more inclusive environment.

The second purpose of using translanguaging is to create more vivid imagery in the output and even an "accent" in writing. Here is one example of a recent applicant with a Cuban and Polish heritage, who describes her Cuban *abuelos* trying *halupki* and arguing about *solidarność*. In it, one can almost hear her accent while reading the essays. The meaning of individual words becomes unimportant since the general meaning can be understood from the context; yet, they make the essay more vibrant, creating a visual, almost tangible image of the applicant:

> My Thanksgiving dinner seldom consisted of traditional American staples. Plates of Cuban arroz con frijoles nestled against *halupki* and *babci's bigos*—a mixed feast of Polish and Cuban cultural fare. Our Thanksgiving table represented the cultural crossroads of global migration, as both my Polish and Cuban grandparents fled their home countries. My Cuban great-grandparents were born in Galicia, the Gallego language never leaving their tongues. With three different languages being thrown around the conversation, I garnered the political meanings behind words like *exilio* and *solidarność*, when referring to the effects of the communist regimes that impacted both Cuba and Poland. The connection between learning a new language and acquiring a global awareness became clear to me.

As noted earlier, scholarship applications are a unique genre, a hybrid that is largely both narrative and expository in nature but may also include elements of the argumentative and descriptive. The genre has its variations with a slew of delimiting features: combinations of short and longer answers to specific prompts, divergent unknown audiences (from campus to US to even international, including combinations thereof), reader/selection committee constraints and "scoring" criteria, and an increasing desire for applicant voice authenticity and fresh rather than "over processed" prose. The need for understanding the rhetorical situation is ultimately a fundamental problem that impacts the shape of the message (word choice, sentence structures, and so on). According to Charles Bazerman, "Bringing such things to reflective attention through the concepts of rhetorical situation, genre, and activity systems is a necessary step to understanding their writing and making deeper choices."[18] Speaking to the efficacy of translingual writing pedagogies, Horner, Lu, Royster and Trimbur note that "a translingual approach proclaims that writers can, do, and must negotiate standardized rules in light of the contexts of specific instances of writing. [However,] against the common argument that students must learn 'the standards' to meet demands by the dominant, a translingual approach recognizes that, to survive and thrive as active writers, students must understand how such demands are contingent and negotiable."[19] By using translingual pedagogies in fellowship advising, students can continue to develop their rhetorical awareness of when to deploy their different languages and dialects instead of assuming that SAWE is the standard for every rhetorical occasion. As shown in the previous examples, when writers do so, readers stand to learn more about an applicant and their background than could be expressed in a strictly monolingual style.

Beyond providing applicants with an understanding of the application's unique rhetorical demands and constraints, accompanying letters of recommendation as well as nomination or endorsement letters can contribute to the entextualizing process by providing readers with insights into the applicant's discursive presentations of self. These insights can do much to encourage readers to engage in the co-construction of meaning and intent and to tolerate divergences from the conventional or dominant (preferred) standard use of academic English. Sharing this context can be particularly useful for supporting writers who use different codes, dialects, or languages, but it can also be useful for educating readers, selection committees, and foundations to enact their receptivity for diversifying who they recognize as scholars.

While we have discussed how inclusive writing pedagogies can capture aspects of an applicant's "authentic voice," they can be just as revelatory when it comes to what is not said. Here is where letters of recommendation and endorsement are equally beneficial, particularly for applicants whose cultural backgrounds and rules for communicative engagement diverge from stereotypical US cultural norms. For example, years ago when working with a Japanese American Truman applicant and subsequent finalist, our campus committee was bemused and frustrated by her reluctance to discuss her accomplishments and leadership experiences even when directly asked about them, preferring, instead, to demure and deflect. It was not until her academic mentor shared with us the cultural influence of her paternal Japanese heritage that we were able to make the connection. Unfortunately, by then it was too late to share that information with the national selection interviewing committee, who shared with us similar frustrations with the finalist's seeming reluctance to engage with her committee.

Similarly, when working with non-native speakers and writers of English, letters of recommendation and endorsement can serve to alert readers to culturally mediated rhetorical structures. These culturally mediated variations were originally investigated by linguist Robert B. Kaplan, albeit rather superficially and simplistically. According to Kaplan, standard American discourse was considered linear, while Asian cultures employed a more circular pattern and those from Slavic, Semitic, and some Romance languages employed different degrees of almost a zig-zagging pattern.[20] Today, the study of culturally mediated discourse and rhetorical patterns is considerably more nuanced.[21] Information about an applicant's rhetorical traditions can provide additional insight into the choices an applicant has made; however, it is important to position these choices as a difference rather than a deficit.

Inclusive linguistic paradigms such as translingualism and translanguaging can provide advisors and applicants with tools and methods for developing an "authentic voice" in their application documents. A translingual approach, as characterized by Guerra,[22] that focuses more on mutual intelligibility and fluidity rather than rigid cohesion to a monolithic standard of language usage offers opportunities for applicants to more holistically represent themselves and establish mutual understanding with reviewers. In all, the role of a fellowships advisors is not limited to helping students win the scholarships.

Instead, we also act as storytellers, career and academic advisors, and life coaches, all to help our students discover their authentic voice. Our hope is that we become an overall support system that can help every voice be heard and welcomed.

Notes

1. Committee on CCCC Language Statement, "Students' Right to Their Own Language," *College English* 36, no. 6 (1974): 709–26.
2. Committee on CCCC Language Statement, p. 709.
3. Committee on CCCC Language Statement, p. 709.
4. Committee on CCCC Language Statement, p. 710.
5. Committee on CCCC Language Statement, p. 710.
6. Conference on College Composition & Communication, "CCCC Statement on White Language Supremacy," June 2021, https://cccc.ncte.org/cccc/white-language-supremacy.
7. Ryan Ozimo and Bill Hart-Davidson, "Finding Genre Signals in Academic Writing," *Journal of Writing Research* 7, no. 3 (2016): 485–509.
8. Bill Hart-Davidson, "Genres Are Enacted by Writers and Readers," in *Naming What We Know: Threshold Concepts of Writing Studies*, ed. Linda Adler-Kassner and Elizabeth Wardle (Denver: University Press of Colorado, 2015), 39–40.
9. Hart-Davidson, 39.
10. Hart-Davidson, 39.
11. Ofelia Garcia and Angel M. Y. Lin, "Translanguaging in Bilingual Education," in *Bilingual and Multilingual Education*, ed. Ofelia Garcia (New York: Springer, 2016), 117–30.
12. Juan C. Guerra, *Language, Culture, Identity and Citizenship in College Classrooms and Communities* (New York: Routledge, 2015).
13. Guerra, 14.
14. Guerra, 12.
15. Paul J. Thibault, "The Reflexivity of Human Languaging and Nigel Love's Two Orders of Language," *Acuity: Journal of English Language Pedagogy, Literature, and Culture* 8, no. 1 (2017): 74–85.
16. Wei, Li. "Translanguaging as a Practical Theory of Language," *Applied Linguistics* 39, no. 1 (2018): 22.
17. Stephen D. Krashen, "Applications of Psycholinguistic Research to the Classroom," in *Methodology in TESOL*, ed. Michael H. Long and Jack C. Richards (New York: Newbury House Publishers, 1987), 33–44.

18. Charles Bazerman, "Writing Speaks to Situations Through Recognizable Forms," in *Naming What We Know: Threshold Concepts of Writing Studies,* ed. Linda Adler-Kassner and Elizabeth Wardle (Denver: University Press of Colorado, 2015), 37.
19. Bruce Horner, Min-Zhan Lu, Jacqueline Jones Royster, and John Trimbur, "Opinion: Language Difference in Writing: Toward a Translingual Approach," *College English* 73, no. 3 (2011): 305.
20. Robert B. Kaplan, "Cultural Thought Patterns in Intercultural Education." *Language Learning* 16, no 1 (1966): 1–20.
21. John R. Baker, "Exploring How Rhetorical Organization Contributes to the Readability of Essays," *Journal of Language and Education* 7, no. 2 (2021): 78–92.
22. Guerra, *Language, Culture, Identity and Citizenship,* 12–14.

8

That's Going to Leave a Mark

Writing About Trauma in Fellowship Applications

TARA YGLESIAS, KRISTIN JANKA, MATHILDA NASSAR, ELISE RUDT-MOORTHY, AND MELISSA VERT

High academic and extracurricular achievement sometimes masks serious trauma. Being busy is a convenient way to avoid internal examination, and external validation can act as a balm for internal turmoil. That is not to say that well-adjusted, successful people do not exist—but they may not always find their way into fellowship offices.[1]

For those who do, the process itself can often revive old traumas or intrude into well-established personal boundaries. Applicants feel pressure to share events and details that they may not have processed themselves, while advisors are asked to deal with the emotional fallout. Fellowship providers sometimes find themself the guardians of personal information they are not sure how to handle. While the process may prove beneficial—a successful application or a better understanding of how to craft their personal narrative—it is often emotionally fraught.

In this chapter, we put forward strategies for working with applicants who have traumatic experiences that may or may not make their way onto the application page. We also examine the impact the current cultural moment has on how students craft their essays. Next, we provide suggestions for working with applicants and how to assess various approaches to writing personal narratives. We conclude with some perspectives from application readers and advice on when and how best to refer to traumatic experiences in applications.

In Context

Emotion, or pathos, has been a crucial component of rhetoric since its beginnings as a field.[2] Aristotle categorized logos, ethos, and pathos in the 300s BCE, noting that pathos was least reliable, but crucial to a complete argument.[3] Emotional appeal to an audience has been a practice for centuries and evolved recently to merge with modern psychology. Alexander Bain, one of the first to apply the scientific method to the field of psychology, contributed heavily to the fields of composition and rhetoric in the late 1800s, often stressing the importance of understanding the way one's writing will affect the audience's emotions.[4] As psychology has grown and spread in popular awareness, modern writers are ever more cognizant of the power that narratives hold for both persuasion *and* manipulation. Our applicants now sit at a crossroads, where one direction points to using emotional appeal as the entire content of their application to coax reviewers into offering the award and the other direction points in the opposite direction in order to either guard the personal narratives of applicants or to protect the narratives of more privileged applicants who do not have an emotional appeal to begin with. Both directions are wrong. Perhaps unsurprisingly, the best path is a moderated use of pathos in service of the applicant's goals.

"The other day, I spoke to one of my seniors about their college application experience and they told me about how they had to watch both their parents die due to Covid. The first thing that came to mind was 'damn, I bet those made good essays.'"[5] Though this quotation from a high school counselor is disconcerting, the notion itself that trauma yields success did not come out of the ether; nor was it the result of a nefarious plot by fellowships advisors or admissions officers or high school counselors. The public—and this includes fellowships reviewers—also loves a "poor kid makes good" story. Charles Dickens and Horatio Alger made careers out of the rags-to-riches motif. But until very recently, in competitive applications, students tended to put a genteel veneer over these stories. Committees welcomed accounts of hard work; but did not seem to warm as much to admissions of being poor; and it was certainly not okay to bring intractable issues like racism into the narrative.

Starting in the early 2000s, however, there was a movement to reclaim personal narratives in applications and tell the less-varnished truth.[6] Admitting to being the first in a family to go to college or to struggling with dyslexia was now acceptable. The openness of these narratives was a welcome change—assessing an application with the understanding of the background of the applicant was much easier—but sometimes the candor was too much.

Pre-pandemic years saw the release of some bestsellers of the trauma-to-ivy-league narrative, including J. D. Vance's *Hillbilly Elegy* (2016) and Tara Westover's *Educated* (2018). If Truman Scholarship interview mentions are any indication, these narratives were foundational for a lot of applicants who experienced similar types of trauma. They easily outpaced the previous applicant touchstone, Tracy Kidder's *Mountains Beyond Mountains* (2003)—perhaps a kind of meta-narrative of trauma itself.

There was, of course, a backlash. In the wake of the unrelenting trauma of the COVID-19 pandemic, both sharing and evoking emotion has become criticized, as evidenced by phrases such as "trauma-dumping" or "poverty porn." Google Trends data show that "trauma dumping," the oversharing of traumatic narratives with no clear aim, had almost no searches until the pandemic, but interest surged during the pandemic and has stayed constant since.

Young adults in high school and college have been posting TikToks, Reels, and Snaps about trauma dumping for a grade or for college admissions since the pandemic, when most of our current students were among this age group or applying for college themselves.[7] Even a cursory browse of various social media channels suggests a consensus of sorts that it is lucky to have trauma because it helps with admission to a good school. Meanwhile, various reputable publications such as *The New Yorker*, *Forbes*, and *The Chronicle of Higher Education* run stories about the manufacturing of authenticity through traumatic experiences, resisting the urge to share traumas in application essays, and not "selling your pain" to admissions committees.[8]

Many of the critiques of trauma narratives come from either a place of concern (applicants should not have to plumb their worst experiences to grab the attention of an admissions professional) or cynicism (applicants are manipulating admissions professionals with experiences that are not traumatic at best and untrue at worst). Recently, a new critique has emerged—namely, antipathy for diversity, equity, and inclusion initiatives that may ultimately lead students to rethink the value of revealing traumatic experiences that might place them within one of these groups.

In the Fellowship Office

The initial focus concerning trauma-infused applications was placed on the college admission process because it is the first time in most students' lives when they engage in self-sponsorship—that is, writing about themselves for a persuasive aim. They then tend to carry what they learned from the college application process into all self-sponsorship in the future, including fellowships, cover letters, and graduate school applications. If an essay that focused on the student's significant challenges was successful at the early stage of college admission, then the student has a model that will be tempting to replicate.

Thus, such students arrive not only with their trauma, but also the baggage that surrounds writing about trauma. The shift from "emotion is a valid part of persuasion" to "emotion is a sad attempt to manipulate readers" only serves to invalidate narratives of those who have struggled in favor of elevating those who have not. This messaging can erode the confidence of people who have experienced trauma when they write applications—they feel part of their life stories are off limits because including it may be perceived as a ploy to gain sympathy. This feeling makes it even harder to write about something that is difficult to process and share with others in the first place.

Meanwhile students who have never experienced trauma may try to mimic the experiences of students who have by co-opting the narratives of those around them (parents, siblings, friends) to meet what some still seem to presume is a trauma quota for essays. A parent's immigration story before the writer was born, a sibling's mental health struggles, a friend losing a parent—such experiences likely have a bearing on the writer's life, but they are usually vestigial to the application itself, and if they are used, it becomes clear to reviewers that the writer is trying to co-opt another person's most difficult life experiences because they do not have something of their own to share.

In many ways, fellowship application prompts invite this issue. While they may not include the word "trauma," many applications make clear what they are looking for with words such as "difficulties," "hurdles," "personal circumstances," "lack of opportunities," "obstacles or challenges overcome," and "setbacks" and "failures." Below are examples from college admission and fellowship applications that are overtly soliciting such responses:

- "Please describe how and when any unusual family or personal circumstances have affected your achievement in school, your work experience, or your participation in school and community activities" (Obama-Chesky Voyager Scholarship for Public Service scholarship application).
- "The lessons we take from obstacles we encounter can be fundamental to later success" (The Common App 2024–2025).
- "Please tell us when you: a) made someone particularly proud of you, b) were most challenged, and c) fell short of expectations" (Knight-Hennessey scholars application).
- "It [your statement] should deal with your personal history, family background, influences on your intellectual development, the educational, professional, and cultural opportunities (or lack of them) to which you have been exposed, and the ways in which these experiences have affected you and your personal growth" (Fulbright scholarship application).

These prompts emphasize overcoming challenges, which can be a helpful metric when evaluating a candidate. But students often interpret these questions as seeking a certain type of response. Applicants are now in risky territory—either reliving traumatic experiences for the purpose of an application or mining the experience of another for less than admirable purposes.

Even the generic language of the phrase "personal statements" can be difficult for students to interpret. Several scholars who have discussed advising first-generation students or students from under-resourced backgrounds have noted the misconceptions they can have when it comes to writing about themselves, along with the need for genre-based guidance when no one in the household can provide it.[9] The terminology of *personal statement* itself implies a personal relationship between the student and reviewer when they are actually writing for a highly judgmental audience.[10] Applicants not only risk reliving their own traumatic experiences, but they also risk misinterpreting the tone and content of the question itself.

Recommendations for Advisors

Given the potential risk in the rhetoric of competitive applications, advisors may want to explore a trauma-informed approach to composition pedagogy. While advisors are not licensed therapists, they can incorporate facets of trauma-informed practices developed by the Substance Abuse and Mental Health Services Administration (SAMHSA). Doing so would better support students who have experienced trauma, shift the national narrative around emotion as a manipulation, and honestly address the pressures to manufacture trauma on the part of students who have not experienced it. Adapting SAMHSA's four Rs would look something like this:

1. **Realize**—the widespread impact of trauma and understand potential paths for recovery
2. **Recognize**—the signs and symptoms of trauma in yourself and students
3. **Respond**—by fully integrating knowledge about trauma into policies, procedures, and practices
4. **Resist**—re-traumatization of the student.[11]

The potential for re-traumatization is particularly high in the application process because revisiting, discussing, writing, editing, sanitizing, and/or sharing a traumatic experience can in and of themselves have that effect. Furthermore, the success or failure of the application opens up the writer to judge their trauma as deserving (or not) of support.[12] To avoid re-traumatization in fellowship applications, students need time for self-care or reflection.[13] They may also have to meet with counseling to process the negative emotions and experiences that applications can trigger. As SAMHSA notes—and this applies to fellowships advising as well—"Creating a safe environment, for both physical and emotional safety, requires intentionally and comprehensively incorporating trauma-informed principles and practices into an organization's structure, service delivery, and culture. It is important that agencies and organizations evaluate their current practices and procedures and take actionable steps to incorporate [trauma-informed] strategies within their policies and practices."[14]

Part of creating the safe environment includes getting feedback from students. To better understand the experiences of students who applied for scholarships, Kristin Janka of Michigan State University and Melissa Vert of the University of Michigan have created a pilot survey that focuses on whether college students felt pressure to write about their personal experiences and trauma in their applications for competitive scholarships and post-graduate opportunities. The survey has institutional review board approval and is currently being administered to graduating seniors and alumni who apply for competitive awards such as Beinecke, Churchill, Marshall, Rhodes, Truman, and Voyager Scholarships, among others. Survey questions include the following:

1. How many applications have you completed?
2. In the application(s) did you feel pressured to share a difficult experience (e.g., hardship, struggle, challenge, trauma)?
3. If you felt pressured to share a difficult time, what was the source?
4. Did this experience affect your approach to other applications?
5. Do you have any additional comments regarding your experience?
6. Are there any additional comments you would like to share?

The goal of implementing such a survey is to help identify whether there are gaps in service or there are unintentional advising practices that need to be addressed. A university that is concerned about a trend in application essays that focus on trauma, especially those that include events that do not connect to a student's trajectory, may also want to conduct such a survey.

The Writing Process

There is an opportunity to strike a balance between the lived experience of the student and protecting that student from feeling pressure to share what they wish to keep private. Encouraging a student to allow their application-writing experience to be cathartic but reminding them that they are in control of their own story and with whom they share it can be an empowering method for application composition, especially for applicants who are underrepresented and feel increased pressure to adhere to the prompts. The following principles help achieve that balance:

- Students are allowed to address their trauma, and their story is valid.
- Sharing an experience should be cathartic, not damaging.
- Students need to feel empowered to decide whether and how much they want to share.
- Students and advisors should consider unconscious bias and the hidden meaning behind questions and prompts that are asked.

While writing to process traumatic experiences can improve short-term health and long-term psychological well-being,[15] the process of justifying a request for resources by expounding on one's traumas can easily spiral into re-traumatization.[16] While the process of writing to process trauma can have benefits, advisors should keep in mind that the scholarship arena is not necessarily a safe place to do so. Scholarship advisors and foundation representatives are not therapists, and do not have the capacity to provide the security a person may need to address their deepest difficulties.[17] In fact, many advisors may find themselves in the position of trying to coach an applicant on how to best present their story, which necessarily involves debating the literary elements of one's experiences. A successful essay may need to be more sanitized and palatable, and this can subject an applicant to having their lived reality erased in front of their eyes.[18] Advisors may unintentionally minimize the value of a traumatic experience because of an applicant's lack of narrative ability.[19]

Writing of this kind requires a safety net—which could mean trauma-informed advising, an inclusion of trained personnel in the process, or the opportunities for applicant feedback. But as the advising process shifts to writing and editing, so must the focus change to the intention of the application. Applicants might be asked about hurdles and overcoming obstacles not to elicit trauma, but to better understand the depth of their commitment to their work and their research. The intimate understanding of a problem that comes from personal experience might impress a reviewer as being authentic.[20]

The struggle then becomes how best to frame the experience to achieve application goals without creating additional stress for the student. The following examples help to illustrate different scenarios.

- **Truman Applicant:** Annie faced discrimination when entering STEM. She was frequently told by her teachers and others in her community that having women pursue STEM careers was silly and wasteful. She is now the top student in the chemistry department and runs her own nonprofit to improve STEM access for girls in her hometown and has made it her mission to ensure others do not face the same challenges and discouragement that she did.
    - *This is a good example of pathos at work. Annie's experiences are an emotional connection to her work and they further her argument and connection to the future goal.*
- **National Science Foundation Graduate Research Fellowship Program (NSF GRFP) Applicant:** Mark's mother emigrated from Mexico to the United States, where she was subject to hate crimes and had an extremely difficult citizenship process. Mark often reflects on his mother's experience, which he sees as motivation for his success in

the United States. He loves soft robotics and wants to design more efficient and comfortable prosthetic devices.
    - *Mark's mother's experience took place before his lifetime, and this narrative notably omits his father and his own experiences. While his mother is inspiring, this narrative distracts from his mission in prosthetics, and it would not be an effective use of pathos.*
- **Fulbright English Teaching Assistantship (ETA)**
  Applicant: Susan hopes to become a culturally competent teacher and promote multilingual education in the United States. She speaks four languages at a B2 level and has received funding to study abroad several times. When she was in high school, she and her brother were involved in a car accident in which she fractured her wrist and had to miss her junior year softball season. As a result, she lost the chance to play at a collegiate level and this was a very difficult experience for her emotionally, physically, and mentally.
    - *Susan has an impressive and broad record, but her traumatic experience is completely unrelated and prompted a change in her life that is much earlier than her current trajectory. Given the space limitations of a Fulbright ETA, there will not be room for such extraneous material.*

In each of these scenarios, the applicant was motivated by trauma—either their own or someone else's. The distinction comes from thinking through how that experience relates to their current trajectory and the goals of the program. Not all situations are quite this neat, however. The NSF GRFP and Fulbright examples above would likely require the same sort of care for the student's experience as the Truman example. Just because an experience does not "make the cut" for the application does not make it any less valid.

Once a student begins to develop their essay, they may find it helpful to return to the program goals to better understand what is needed. Fellowship organizations develop their applications with care and intention; applicants should use that same approach in crafting their essays. A narrative that worked for undergraduate admission may not be as helpful in a Rhodes application. Likewise, emphasizing determination, while generally a favorable characteristic, might not be as helpful for a program that values collaboration and empathy.

The Foundation Perspective

The use and misuse of trauma in applications is a frequent topic of discussion among foundations, fellowship providers, and other admissions professionals. These discussions are motivated by concern for the students who are being encouraged to write about these traumatic events, as well for the readers and interviewers who are then expected to absorb these experiences and then evaluate the application.

When looking toward program goals and helping students to craft narratives, reviewers suggest asking a few preliminary questions:[21]

1. *Is this necessary to understanding the application?*
   Applicants should have a clear idea of why they want to tell their trauma story. Is the story intended to underscore an important criterion of the award? Does it explain an interest or commitment? Or does it answer a question readers might have about issues or gaps in the application? If the story is particularly significant to the student's, elements should appear throughout the application. For example, if a student is interested in immigration because of their own immigration experience, that information should appear in various parts of the application, including supporting letters. When and how to discuss the trauma in the application should be determined by how best this information fits within the student's interests and goals. Reviewers should never be put in a position to ask, "What am I supposed to do with this information?"

2. *Does the applicant want to talk about it? Could someone else talk about it?*
   Some students are just not able or willing to discuss a traumatic experience, but they may feel it is important for

reviewers to know about it. In those cases, it might be possible to have other recommenders or advisors discuss the issue. From the Truman Foundation perspective, it would be fine to reference a student's experience in the nomination letter along with information on whether they are able to talk about the issue in person. Every applicant is different—some feel writing is easier; others are more inclined to talk—but if knowing the information is important, there are other avenues, apart from self-disclosure.

3. *Are there downsides to not disclosing?*
   Any discussion with a student prior to submission of the application should include downsides to not disclosing particular details or information. If not disclosed, serious medical issues can be a barrier to participation in some programs, and even more concerning, students may not be able to receive the care they need while in the program if the award takes them to a country that does not provide that care to international students. Also, if there is a reasonable chance that the student will bring the challenging experiences up in an interview, it is better to prepare interviewers about a traumatic event or ongoing significant concerns on paper rather than for the first time at the interview. However, which details need to be disclosed, when, and to whom are likely different for every student and every program. One helpful piece of advice provided by a recent Truman scholar: "Most of us are way too young for appropriate boundaries."[22] Helping them to develop these boundaries would be an excellent result no matter the outcome.

4. *Are there downsides to disclosing?*
   There are, of course, some areas where disclosure might set up a dangerous legal situation for a student. Students with these types of considerations may wish to seek expert advice. They should also be aware that if they disclose an issue, they may be asked about it during an interview. If they are uncomfortable discussing the issue, they may wish to reconsider. Students have sometimes cried in interviews

when discussing such issues, making for a difficult interview for the student and for the committee alike. If students have difficulty discussing the experience with the advisor, then they will also likely have difficulty discussing it with an interview panel.

In addition, foundations should ensure that readers and interviewers are prepared for these narratives. Not everyone is capable of or amenable to sifting through harrowing accounts.

Foundations should also be mindful of the prompts they are developing and whether eliciting these kinds of stories is within program goals. For the Truman application, we have adapted questions and guidance over the years to try to discourage students from feeling as if they had to discuss trauma to win.[23] While it is important to understand an applicant's motivations and distance traveled, it is also important to make the process of applying worthwhile.

Conclusion

Some students arrive at fellowship offices and foundation interview rooms having several lifetimes worth of experience. In no way should this chapter be interpreted to be suggesting that a student choosing to share that information is not worthy and valid. But being prepared for the advising process when a student chooses to write about trauma is a vital skill for any advisor. The best result might be allowing a student to realize that their experience and identity are not static, but that the skills they developed by surviving can never be taken from them.

Notes

1. This essay was developed from the authors' presentation "Tenacity or Trauma: Personal Experiences in Fellowship Applications," which was delivered at the 2023 NAFA Conference in New Orleans.
2. In *Rhetoric,* Aristotle further writes about how to evoke certain emotions and which emotions are most powerful and which ones to avoid. He also indicates how difficult it is to fully assess the attitudes of others and that trying to evoke a particular emotion from them without a full knowledge

of the passions that drive them is likely to have limited success. See William M. A. Grimaldi, *Aristotle, Rhetoric I: A Commentary* (New York: Fordham University Press, 1980).

3. Patricia Bizzell, Bruce Herzberg, and Robin Reames, *The Rhetorical Tradition: Readings from Classical Times to the Present*, 3rd ed. (Boston: Bedford, St. Martin's, 2020).

4. See Alexander Bain, *Mental and Moral Science: A Compendium of Psychology and Ethics* (London: Longmans, Green, and Company, 1883).

5. U/netheritenub15, "trauma = good essays," Reddit, April 18, 2021, https://www.reddit.com/r/ApplyingToCollege/comments/mt859t/trauma_good_essays.

6. Who among us can forget the 2003 Lifetime classic *From Homeless to Harvard: The Liz Murray Story* (Peter Levin, director; Barnet Films and Magic Rock Productions) or the somewhat more prestigious 2004 retelling of the life of Vivien Thomas in *Something the Lord Made* (Joseph Sargent, director; HBO Films).

7. For two examples of the many that can be found on social media, see @1tashadotcom, "I got accepted tho [sic]" TikTok, 2023, https://www.tiktok.com/@1tashadotcom/video/7220091526108515627; @renhinkey, "My essay was full of defrosted trauma," TikTok, 2021, https://www.tiktok.com/@ren_hinkey/video/6938239251934940421.

8. Christopher Rim, "Are You Oversharing in Your College Admissions Essay?," *Forbes*, May 10, 2023, https://www.forbes.com/sites/christopherrim/2023/05/10/are-you-oversharing-in-your-college-admissions-essay/; Claire Wu, "Trauma Dumping: The Ethics of College Essay," *Wellesley News*, September 17, 2024, https://thewellesleynews.com/2024/09/17/trauma-dumping-the-ethics-of-college-essays/; Ethan Sawyer, "Why You Don't Have to Write About Trauma in Your College Essay to Stand Out—and What You Can Do Instead," College Essay Guy, accessed April 3, 2025, https://www.collegeessayguy.com/blog/trauma-in-college-essays; Anne Trubek, "The Ethics of Trauma Dramas," *The Chronicle of Higher Education*, January 12, 2007, https://www.chronicle.com/article/the-ethics-of-trauma-dramas/; Elijah Megginson, "When I Applied to College, I Didn't Want to 'Sell My Pain,'" *New York Times*, May 9, 2021, https://www.nytimes.com/2021/05/09/opinion/college-admissions-essays-trauma.html.

9. Jessica Early and Meredith De Costa-Smith, "Making a Case for College: A Genre-Based College Admission Essay Intervention for Underserved High School Students," *Journal of Writing Research* 2, no. 3 (2010): 299–329; Steven Alvarez, "Arguing Academic Merit: Meritocracy and

the Rhetoric of the Personal Statement," *Journal of Basic Writing* 31, no. 2 (2012): 32–56; J. Warren, "The Rhetoric of College Application Essays: Removing Obstacles for Low Income and Minority Students," *American Secondary Education* 42, no. 1 (2013): 43–56.

10. "Most prompts ask applicants for personal narratives, but the essays function as arguments that make a case for the applicant's potential as a college student.... College essay prompts ask for a type of discourse that rhetoricians, following Aristotle, call 'epideictic,' which means the writer or speaker celebrates an individual for a sympathetic audience. In reality, however, college essays function as 'deliberative' rhetoric, meaning the writer/speaker must garner the vote of an audience that is at best indifferent and, at worst, skeptical" (Warren, "The Rhetoric of College Application Essays," 44).

11. Substance Abuse and Mental Health Services, "SAMHSA's Concept of Trauma and Guidance for a Trauma-Informed Approach," prepared by SAMHSA's Trauma and Justice Strategic Initiative, July 14, 2014, 1–18, https://library.samhsa.gov/sites/default/files/sma14-4884.pdf.

12. The SAMHSA manual (2014) discusses implementing this approach in a government setting, and Self-Healing Communities, an NGO based in South Bend, Indiana, has a helpful manual for implementing it in an NGO setting. See Kate Brown, Karina Duffy, Carey Gaudern, Aysha Givson, and Nancy Michael, *Becoming a Trauma-Informed Organization*, Self-Healing Communities, 2022.

13. In the original conference presentation (see n1), this text linked to a gif in which a crying boy is told to "Stop crying! It won't do any good. And anyway, you have a lot of work to do. Starting right now."

14. SAMHSA manual, 2023.

15. James Pennebaker and Sandra Beall, "Confronting a Traumatic Event: Toward an Understanding of Inhibition and Disease," *Journal of Abnormal Psychology* 95, no. 3 (1986): 274–81.

16. Tina Yong, "The Rise of the Trauma Essay in College Applications," TEDxUBCStudio, March 2020, https://ted.com/talks/tina_yong_the_rise_of_the_trauma_essay_in_college_applications?language=en.

17. Elijah Meffinson, "When I Applied to College, I Didn't Want to 'Sell My Pain,'" *New York Times*, May 9, 2021, https://www.nytimes.com/2021/05/09/opinion/college-admissions-essays-trauma.html.

18. Alexa Leon, "I Regret Trauma Dumping in My Admissions Essay," *Daily Texan*, November 8, 2022, https://thedailytexan.com/2022/11/08/i-regret-trauma-dumping-in-my-admissions-essay/.

19. Aya M. Waller-Bey, "The T Word: Resisting Expectations to share Trauma in College Essays," *Forbes*, April 21, 2022, https://www.forbes

.com/sites/civicnation/2021/12/10/the-t-word-resisting-expectations-to-share-trauma-in-college-essays/?sh=66f897c266a4.
20. u/ScholarGrade, "Trauma in Essays: Why it Can Work and When it Doesn't," Reddit, May 2021, https://www.reddit.com/r/ApplyingToCollege/comments/n413dc/trauma_in_essays_why_it_can_work_and_when_it/.
21. These were developed primarily through conversations with readers for the Truman finalist selection committee as well as a number of readers and interviewers for other awards.
22. We had conversations with recent Truman scholars about their experiences writing for the award.
23. Adjustments made to Truman's Question 14 are discussed in detail in Tara Yglesias, "When the Abyss Stares Back: The Eldritch Horror of the 'Additional Information' Prompt," in *Wild About Harry: Everything You Have Ever Wanted to Know About the Truman Scholarship*, ed. Suzanne McCray and Tara Yglesias (Fayetteville: University of Arkansas Press, 2021), 75–90.

PART II

On the Profession

9

You May Ask Yourself "Well, How Did I Get Here?"

Advisors as Application Reviewers for Foundations

SARAH CHOW, KURT DAVIES, LINDSAY LAWTON, AND TARA YGLESIAS

For every competitive fellowship, a panel of reviewers reads applications and plays some role in selecting recipients. Fellowships advisors have likely encountered (or at some point held) the belief that these reviewers hail from the upper echelons of whatever the foundation purports to do, moving in those elite circles that applicants hope to someday join. In fact, reviewers come from a wide range of backgrounds beyond the foundations and include community and university leaders, as well as fellowships advisors. The role of advisors who serve on these review panels is not always clear, even for members of the National Association of Fellowships Advisors (NAFA).[1] In this chapter, four authors give insight into how this relationship works, how both foundations and advisors can benefit from it, and how advisors can get more involved.

Advisor Perspective: Reading for the Boren Awards

Lindsay Lawton, University of Denver

Whether the email calls them "selection panelists," "reviewers," or "external readers," the notices calling for advisors to serve at some stage of the selection process tend to come at inconvenient times. Whether it is weak boundaries, poor memory, or a sincere commitment to the value of this process, I often volunteer.

Among the longest-standing reader commitments is my role as a panelist for Boren Awards. As a new fellowships advisor, I was excited to participate, and what I saw was deeply affirming. I met dozens of academics who were taking time from their busy lives to discuss applications and to work out which lucky few to advance. Of course, it was also challenging to be a part of this culling. Knowing how much effort went into these applications and what hopes were riding on the competition made it difficult to move one application forward instead of another, only slightly less amazing, proposal. The challenge was complicated by the need to make those final, impossible decisions within the time available, which limited the depth and length of our debates.

The opportunity to review made my work as a new advisor easier in many ways. I had more credibility and a clearer sense of how to help students prepare applications that would be easy on reviewers. After being a part of so many discussions trying to understand why someone had applied for Boren, I was also in a better position to help some applicants find other opportunities that better fit their goals. Working through disagreements to select top candidates was an important reminder that reviewers can respond in wildly different ways to the same narrative, a fact that can help applicants avoid focusing on what they think reviewers want to read. Fellow panelists wondered aloud about gaps or inconsistencies, and I have become much more comfortable in pushing applicants to address these in their own work.

Here I offer several strategies for participating as a reviewer on a national panel.

Practical strategy #1: Identify competitions of interest and ask colleagues what a typical reviewer timeline is. As with a fellowship application, it helps to plan and to estimate the hours it will take.

Reviewing as a new advisor can make fitting in tricky. I was not proactive in reaching out about competitions that interested me; instead, I waited for a call to go out and then scrambled to make time to participate. As with the publicize-advise-apply-celebrate cycle of a fellowship application, it took me a few tries to get a handle on the call for reviewers-volunteer-read-meet cycle of a fellowship review panel and to develop realistic expectations for myself about how long it would take.[2] Understanding reviewer timelines early is important.

Practical strategy #2: Make the case to the supervisor that reviewing for an award is professional development and should be done during regular work hours.

At various points along the journey from NAFA's new advisor workshop to my fourth NAFA conference, I promised myself I would not review for Boren the next time around. I was too busy, and I already had good insight into the selection process. The few cycles that I did not review, I learned new lessons about the value of this service: I missed the perspective shift, wondered about the trends in national security essay topics, and found it more difficult to gracefully accept the outcome of the selection process.

In those years when I did not review for any competitions, the absence of this work also helped me recognize that without it, finding balance in my job was a bit more challenging. Because reading for foundations helps me balance service to students with service to awards and to the institution that employs me, and since my work as a reviewer was uncompensated, I was able to advocate for including this work as professional development hours.

Practical strategy #3: Compare the learning curve and the number of cycles it would take to develop a selection-panelist level of insight with reviewing one's own campus applications only. Serving as a panelist is more efficient.

As professional development, reading for Boren has made me a more discerning advisor. This is due primarily to volume: Even a robust Boren pool at a single institution will not give an advisor the quantity of applications to read as serving on a selection panel. Moreover, the conversations that take place during panelist meetings provide a greater range of perspectives. Boren is very transparent about its criteria, but the experience of applying those criteria to actual applications—and debating with fellow panelists about them—has helped me show students how the criteria may be applied to their own essays. Another benefit to serving as a reviewer has been the deeper understanding I have gained about other institutional contexts and practices, as well as the different paths students take to (and out of) Boren. As with national security, I am now more aware of the range of federal career paths because of the interesting plans some students propose.

Perhaps the greatest impact on my advising has come from the specific examples I have been able to draw on. I can emphasize to applicants that Boren does not define national security for them, but I will still get a dozen generic draft essays about the same issue-of-the-week. This changes when I tell stories of applications from review panels that have stuck with me over the years and why. I still remember an essay from several years ago about dairy exports to Japan because it was detailed, focused, and provided such a unique perspective on national security. Review panels have also helped me persuade students to write more clearly. Panelists should not connect the dots of a student's plan on their behalf. Forcing myself to avoid this as a reviewer has helped me do more to point out gaps to applicants that I might have otherwise overlooked.

That said, it is important to note that serving as a selection panelist includes certain terms and conditions. Advisors can use what they learn as panelists but should also use professional judgment in how they frame the information that they share. It is helpful to give students and colleagues generalized insight into who is reviewing applications, what typically stands out to those reviewers, and common missteps to avoid. But advisors have a responsibility to keep student development and learning outcomes in mind in these conversations. A prescriptive approach is harmful, and advisors will not be invited back if they undermine the integrity of the selection process.

Practical strategy #4: If selected to be a reviewer, advisors should read application as they want their own student applications to be read.

Although serving as a panelist benefits me and my students, I believe (and Boren confirms) that my service benefits the program as well as other advisors and applicants. I have worked in several institutional contexts and worked with a huge range of students. This experience informs my review. Equally important is that I have been a NAFA member for many years, and this organization has shaped my attitude about the value of the application process. I want my applicants to be reviewed in a thoughtful and humane way in any competition; I bring this golden rule to my work with Boren and all fellowships for which I have reviewed. Panelists have an opportunity to provide feedback to Boren about the experience and to suggest others who might do well in the role, so advisors can shape the process in more ways than selection. Finally, for large scale competitions such as Boren (Gilman, Critical Language Scholarships, and so on), the more volunteer panelists, the smaller the number of assigned applications. I know that working as a reviewer reduces the load for fellow panelists, which also increases the odds that every applicant will have a fair and thoughtful review.

Foundation Perspective: Advisors as Boren Awards Panelists

Sarah Chow, Program Officer, Boren Awards,
Institute of International Education

The Boren Awards were created to support U.S. undergraduate and graduate students as they study less commonly taught languages in world regions that are deemed critical to U.S. national security. It is the signature program of the National Security Education Programs (NSEP) overseen by the Defense Language and National Security Education Office within the U.S. Department of Defense and is administered by the Institute of International Education. U.S. students who receive a Boren Award will receive funding to immerse themselves in intensive language study for up to one year. In exchange for funding, Boren Award recipients commit to working in the federal government for at least one year after graduation, with preference given to individuals that demonstrate interest in long-term federal service. NSEP's mission, through programs like the Boren Awards, is to develop a pipeline of foreign language and culture expertise for the U.S. federal government workforce.[3]

The Boren Awards are unique in that they are both nationally competitive academic awards that give students the opportunity to study language and culture overseas long term and a pathway to a federal career through the service requirement. To further Boren's mission, our program depends on reviewers' expertise and experience to select candidates who will both (1) benefit from the language training and cultural understanding the experience offers and (2) become future leaders in the federal government. As with other awards, the Boren selection process requires specific academic credentials from its reviewers. However, due to Boren's focus on language acquisition, coupled with its federal service commitment, Boren places as much value on its reviewers' advising experience and related expertise as on their academic credentials. The overall Boren program benefits significantly when advisors participate in the selection process, and we specifically seek them out as reviewers.

As Lawton outlines above, advisors also benefit from participating in the selection process. Advisors who have reviewed for Boren in the past are exposed to the varying national security arguments put forward in the applications, as well as different pathways to complete the federal service commitment. This exposure to the particulars of the program, as well as both common and uncommon application mistakes, allows advisors to help their students create stronger applications. In addition, both our sponsor, the Defense Language and National Security Education Office (DLNSEO), and the Institute of International Education (IIE) leadership observe the panels and can communicate their vision for Boren's overall goals directly to reviewers.

Selection Process

The selection process for the Boren Awards entails two rounds of selection panels. Each round has specific requirements for the makeup of the panels, and advisors are involved in both rounds. Because the second round is a much smaller group of panelists who have several years of previous experience reviewing for Boren, I will focus on the first round here.

Since 2020, the Boren panels have been held virtually. When panels were held in person, each panel of three could read up to sixty applications, but since we have implemented virtual panels, we increased the number of panels to reduce the number of applications per panel to between thirty and fifty. At the start of the review period, reviewers participate in training on the selection criteria and Boren program goals. The review period spans two full weeks, including two full weekends, and culminates in a virtual meeting during which all three reviewers discuss each application and, as a panel, make a final recommendation guided by a Boren facilitator. In their role as observers, DLNSEO and IIE leadership are available to answer specific questions about fulfilling the federal service requirement, although they do not weigh in on specific applications.

The panels are held the at the end of February and in early March. This timeframe can be a very busy time for reviewers, and Boren has requirements about the expertise, experience, and/or credentials for different panels (see Boren Appendix for details), so Boren starts recruiting reviewers in late November. Recruitment continues through early February, although the time commitment does not actually start until applications are ready to review in early February.

Benefits

In the first round of review, Boren benefits from including advisors in a few practical ways. Advisors represent a range of academic backgrounds and regional expertise, which helps the program meet Boren's guidelines for panelists. For example, Boren would not have three political science professors serving on a single panel; rather, a strong panel should consist of one professor of political science, a fellowships advisor (perhaps with a doctorate in linguistics), and one area studies professor. With Boren's focus on US national security, language study, and federal service commitment, reviewers with a political science, policy, or language background are a natural fit. However, since applicants from all academic backgrounds are encouraged to apply, we also recruit reviewers from all academic backgrounds. We have found that reviewers with differing backgrounds create a more insightful and thorough panel.

Advisors also provide different perspectives on the central questions applicants answer. Boren's first essay asks the applicant to explain the significance of the proposed country, region, and language to US national security. It is the applicant's responsibility to make a specific argument and to make the relevance of their topic to US national security clear throughout. One successful applicant's essay connected wilderness and public land to the wildlife trade in their overseas location to US national security. This kind of unique and specific national security example benefited from having multiple academic viewpoints represented on the panel. Advisors benefit from reading this kind of essay because it demonstrates the broader challenges of global issues that fall under US national security.

Boren strives to include a wide range of institutions as well, both within each panel and among the overall pool of reviewers. Boren makes a point to recruit reviewers from both large and small public universities, private universities, community colleges, Historically Black Colleges and Universities, and Minority and Hispanic-Serving Institutions. Advisors help us meet this goal, and they are sensitive to how different institutional contexts may influence applicants' overseas program choices.

Boren Awards are nationally competitive academic fellowships with a specific focus on language acquisition with the goal of creating a pool of students with language and cultural skills committed to federal service. Due to the academic and professional nature of the Boren Awards, reviewers with experience in both the teaching and the professional sides of academia, as well as reviewers with experience in the federal government have typically been excellent Boren reviewers. Advisors take many paths to fellowships advising and offer unique opportunities to expand the reviewer pool.

As a group, advisors tend to be dedicated volunteers who meet our deadlines and engage in discussions with other panelists about the merits of applications. We are pleased to include them and know they benefit as well. Advisors know how people write essays for other competitions, but Boren is very specific to the individual applicant; reviewers do not necessarily understand this until they read dozens of applications. Reviewing applications increases advisors' awareness of how applicants define national security, which may differ from what they encounter on their campuses. This also applies to the connections between an applicant's plan for overseas study and their future federal career. Panelists are instructed not to connect the dots for applicants during review. Advisors with this experience can help students ensure their connections are clear in their applications. In addition, having both DLNSEO and IIE leadership observe the panels allows reviewers to communicate directly with them about the program's vision and goals. Including advisors in selection panels presents a few practical challenges. Those who work more actively to recruit and advise candidates are also likely to have more conflicts in the review process. Because the reading period may overlap with other important work, the timing of the review can be challenging for advisors. While we encourage advisors to participate in the review process, Boren also offers them the opportunity to observe panels, although observers do not read individual applications.

Advisor Perspective: Reading for the Truman Scholarship

Kurt Davies, New York University

I started working in fellowships advising in 2014 as assistant director of the Center for Undergraduate Research and Fellowships at Villanova University, a role I held for three years. I spent a year and a half as the director of Prestigious Scholarships at James Madison University. Since early 2019, I have been the director of Global Awards at New York University's New York City campus. Throughout this tenure, I have found great value in participating in and observing selection processes for both campus-level and nationally competitive awards. Here I discuss some of the benefits that I have gained from participating and share some specific insights from my service on the 2022 Finalist Selection Committee for the Truman Scholarship.

Practical Considerations

Participating in selection processes has provided significant benefits to my practice as a fellowships advisor. Finding the time, however, to participate in these processes can be a significant challenge. Many advisors are offices of one or have positions in which fellowships advising is only a fraction. I have been fortunate that each of my professional advising roles has been wholly or primarily dedicated to fellowships advising. Even so, finding the time to contribute to selection processes can feel like an additional set of responsibilities that may compete with on-campus responsibilities.

Some foundations provide compensation to selectors; others rely on volunteer service. In the former case, advisors considering serving on a review panel should understand their institutional policies on external compensation. Many institutions will prohibit employees from using work time to engage in external service for which they are compensated. If this is their policy, an advisor should determine how much discretionary time can be dedicated to external service. In situations where foundations do not provide compensation to reviewers, advisors should check with their supervisors as to whether the institution's policies allow them to participate at all. I have found that framing such participation as professional development and being able to articulate the value to practice at the home institution can help supervisors buy into incorporating service into the workday. For faculty members with fellowships advising responsibilities, volunteering for selection processes can be considered as service for tenure review or other performance evaluation processes. Advisors should also look at the overall time commitment required for service and see how the opportunity aligns with their other responsibilities.

Benefits

Over the last decade, I have participated in and observed a wide range of selection processes. I have served as a reader for Boren, Critical Language Scholarship, Gilman, Jack Kent Cooke, and Luce. I have participated in selection interviews for the Congress-Bundestag Youth Exchange (CBYX), observed multiple National Screening Committees for the Fulbright US Student Program, and served on the 2022 Finalist Selection Committee for Truman. Each of these experiences informed my practice as a fellowships advisor.

First, and perhaps most importantly, reading twenty to thirty applications for an award helps identify both positive and negative trends in essay writing. Approaches that may have seemed unique or innovative can seem cliche when they appear over and over in the same pool. This has helped me encourage my students to be more specific in their writing. While many essays will cover the same general ideas—the value of studying abroad, the importance of cross-cultural exchange, the importance of learning from failure—the essays that stand out are those that ground assertions in specific lived experiences. Essays that deploy an unexpected metaphor or provide a compelling connection between a childhood experience and the author's current goals quickly stand out. Subsequently, I have felt more confident in encouraging my students to be creative in their work and to lean into the quirks and idiosyncrasies that make them unique. When digging through dozens of essays, I pay close attention to what resonates so that I can identify those features in my own advisees' writing more quickly. I have also learned that there are many approaches to essays that can be compelling, and so I encourage my students to take risks in their writing. These experiences have helped me deconstruct my preconceived notions of what a good essay should look like. It has also helped me expand my conception of what a good candidate can look like and thereby inspired me to cast a wider net during outreach and recruitment.

Similarly, observing and participating in these processes has reinforced just how subjective selection processes can be. Several of the awards for which I have read incorporate a two-stage process in which each reviewer first reads individually then meets with fellow reviewers to discuss the candidates and make final selections. I can think of countless times when an application that resonated with me has been less well received by another reviewer, and vice versa. Taking the time to discuss these situations reminds me that each reviewer brings their preferences, priorities, and biases to these selection processes. This perspective has been particularly useful in helping me to identify patterns in how I read and what I tend to value in an application and thus to elucidate areas where I need to be more conscious of my own biases when reviewing applications. Sharing these experiences with my advisees—without divulging confidential information—can help them understand that once the application is submitted, they no longer have control over the outcome. Sometimes an excellent application will not move forward through no fault of the student simply because there were not enough spaces for every qualified application.

As I have mentioned, much of the value of participation has come in the form of my own increased confidence in advising students. Being able to say that I have witnessed the process in action builds credibility with my students. But it also helps build credibility with other campus stakeholders. I have found this particularly true as a nonfaculty member who does not have a terminal degree. Sometimes a faculty member will be more willing to accept my perspective about what makes a strong candidate when I can share that I have served on a national selection committee for an award.

Finally, I have drawn on this experience in developing internal selection processes. I write better essay prompts and design preliminary applications that are better at drawing out important components. For example, in our current Truman preliminary application, rather than simply asking students to share a leadership experience, we ask students to share an experience in which they were able to influence or lead others toward a solution, to share the measurable outcomes of the experience, and to clearly articulate their role in the process. While this prompt is a bit complicated at first glance, it helps applicants better understand how to present their work in a way that will be more compelling to a reader.

Specific Reflections on the Truman Process

Serving on Truman's Finalist Selection Committee in 2022 was particularly valuable. Of course, the perspectives here are mine alone. I am writing as an individual fellowships advisor and not as a representative of the National Association of Fellowships Advisors, New York University, or the Truman Foundation.

I was on a committee of three, and each committee had 100–150 applications to read. Each application was read by two committee members, and then applications on the bubble or with significant scoring discrepancies were given a third read. We were expected to select up to eleven finalists per region, but it was up to us to distribute those among the states in the region. Although we were encouraged to aim for at least two finalists per state, we were not pressured to meet this target if fewer than two viable candidates were available.

At times, reading more than 100–150 applications in two days felt like a Herculean undertaking. I read a lot of perfectly fine applications. I read a lot of bland applications. I read maybe three or four applications that genuinely excited or moved me. Most of the applications had solid qualifications but lacked a coherent vision or strategy for change. Even most of the finalists suffered from that flaw as well. Here are a few things that stood out that can take student applications from weak to solid or from solid to exceptional.

While each reviewer had a style and strategy for reading applications, I always started with the endorsement letter. The best endorsement letters came out in paragraph one with a clear statement of the student's focus: "Jordan is working to improve maternal mortality rates among women of color," or "Isha is building a career developing more effective water conservation policies in the agricultural sector." I wanted to know the focus area immediately so as to have the appropriate context for the rest of the application. My favorite letters were plainspoken "Frankly, Blaise is a divisive presence on campus. Some administrators love them; some hate them. But everyone agrees that they are effective." They were straightforward: "Ping chose to take a semester off to focus on their mental health," without making excuses or attempting to compensate for perceived deficiencies. The best letters summarized the applicant's strengths and contextualized their accomplishments without overselling them.

Next, I read the Washington Summer Institute (WSI) question (which asks if the applicant is selected as a Truman Scholar, would the student apply for the WSI the following summer). This was the application's secret weapon. It was the first opportunity for applicants, in their own words, to tell the reader what they are about. And, for me, it was imperative that the topics, goals, and vision introduced align with Q 9 and Q11–13 (see Truman Appendix for a list of prompts). The best responses named the organization that the applicant wanted to intern with and highlighted a specific initiative or project that they wanted to be involved in.

I then read through Q1–6 to see how the student had built a foundation and body of work around the issue and topics that were introduced in the endorsement letter and WSI answer. This was a totally underutilized section of the application. I found it helpful when students used as much space as they could to describe and contextualize their experiences.

Useful Q2–5 Examples:

Activity: Queer Network for Change: Created the first LGBTQ+ union in public health department. Led and succeeded in an initiative to make the department's bathrooms gender inclusive. Supported initiative with a proposal and petitions signed by classmates.
Offices: Co-organizer & Advocacy Chair
From: Feb 2021
To: Present

Type of Work: Legal Intern: I reviewed case facts and evidence on cases ranging from criminal to medical malpractice law. I also drafted, scanned, and filed legal documents for attorneys and paralegals.
Employer: Davies & Davies LLC Midsouth
From: June 2020 and June 2019 (Employed for two summers)
To: Aug 2020 and Aug 2019 (Employed for two summers)
No. Hrs/Week: 40

I was never looking for a set number of activities or a particular distribution of them. But by the end of Q6, I wanted to have a solid vision in my head of how applicants spend their time.

For Q7, I did not particularly care what type of experience applicants wrote about. But I wanted to see engagement that transcended "successfully doing the job that I was assigned" or even "I successfully managed this team." In my view, management and leadership are different skills, and I was looking for people who were able to identify a problem, discuss their approach, and demonstrate clear outcomes. The best Q7s also felt earnest, like they could have started with "Let me tell you about this wicked cool thing we did last semester."

For Q8, I was looking for answers that gave me insight into their motivation for their topic or approach. Frankly, I was more compelled by Q8s that focused on a specific project or initiative rather than a broad reflection on a job or internship. I tired of "serving during my congressional internship made me realize the value of constituent engagement," as that theme showed up frequently.

By this point in strong applications, I had a solid sense of what applicants cared about and how they built a body of work around an issue (or how the issue emerged out of their body of work). I was also starting to make some internal guesses about what their Q9 was going to focus on. Therefore, when Q9 strayed away from what the application had led me to expect, it undermined the application's cohesion. While the connection did not have to be completely on the nose, in the best applications it was at least related to the answers that preceded it. For example, I would expect that a student who had volunteered in a prison education program, interned in a DA's office, and done research on recidivism would be writing about some element of criminal justice reform. The best applications lead to the specific topic within the broader issue (e.g., sentencing reform, pretrial bail, prison labor), but that was exceedingly rare.

The strongest Q9s were able to dig clearly into a larger issue in a way that set up their precise graduate and career path. Broad discussions of health disparities or the myriad needs for environmental regulation were less compelling. I found myself regularly muttering to myself things like "Yes, we know that LGBTQ+ young people have worse mental health outcomes and higher suicide rates.... Tell us that you understand WHY this is the case."

I typically skipped straight from Q9 to Q11–13. (I found Q10 useful for filling in gaps but not for my major decision-making). I was looking for a few things here:

1. Cohesion: The graduate path in Q11 should be a step toward specific training or knowledge required to solve the issue in Q9.
2. Specificity: The best applications had a specific rationale for the graduate program as it pertained to their future goals.
3. A balance of ambition and pragmatism: Truth be told, specific job titles or organizations that were named in Q12–13 were not of great importance because plans change. Some fellow panelists, however, were much more concerned, especially in law. One of my co-readers pointed out that "I want to become a staff lawyer for the ACLU right after law school" is entirely unrealistic and that a quick internet search would have made that clear to the applicant. Candidates need to be ambitious about where they need to go to effect change but also realistic about how to get there.

My take on the application was firmer by the end of Q13. I looked to Q14 to see if it provided any new information (i.e., family background, different articulation of motivation, filling in gaps on resume or transcript). I then made sure the policy proposal was at least in some way connected to Q9/11–13 and made sure the letters of recommendation were consistent and corroborated the claims in the application. I looked at a transcript only if I had specific questions (e.g., Is this philosophy major who says they are pre-med taking enough prerequisites?).

Reviewing applications at the national selection committee level in this way has made me a better reviewer of students on my own campus, and I hope these insights benefit other advisors as well.

Foundation Perspective: Advisors as Reviewers for the Truman Scholarship

Tara Yglesias, Harry S. Truman Scholarship Foundation

The Harry S. Truman Scholarship Foundation—the federal memorial to our thirty-third President—awards merit-based scholarships to college students who plan to pursue careers in government or elsewhere in *public service. Truman Scholars receive up to $30,000 for graduate or professional school, participate in leadership development activities, and have special opportunities for internships and employment with the federal government.*[4]

Advisors have been part of the Truman application review process since before the creation of NAFA itself. The requirement that applicants be nominated coupled with the early recognition that reaching out to fellowships advisors was much more effective than trying to reach students directly ensured that advisors would have a fair amount of input in our process. Indeed, the past thirty years of advice from the Truman Foundation has its origins in materials created by a veritable roll call of early NAFA legends. Their participation in our selection process and the feedback they provided have shaped our selection process for the better. It is difficult to imagine a selection process that does not include advisors at nearly every stage.

Selection Process

The Truman application process includes two levels of scrutiny: a review of the paper applications by the Finalist Selection Committee (FSC) to select finalists and then an in-person interview for those students designated as finalists by a Regional Review Committee (RRP). Our FSC is my focus here.[5]

FSC is comprised of eighteen to twenty-one readers who meet in person over three days in Annapolis, Maryland. These readers generally fall into the following categories: Truman Scholars, graduate school admissions professionals, representatives of other fellowship programs, and fellowships advisors. We divide the readers into teams of three, who review between 100 to 150 applications over the course of FSC meeting. The applications are divided into regions and then subdivided into states (e.g., a team that has the Philadelphia region includes applications from Delaware, New Jersey, and Pennsylvania). Each application is read by at least two of the three readers. After an entire region is read, the team selects the top candidates from each region to advance as Finalists. Given the time constraints, readers are expected to spend no more than ten to fifteen minutes on each application. Readers are also required to engage with the other members of their team for a robust and far-ranging discussion to select the appropriate Finalists for the region.

We look for readers who understand and value our program, can follow our guidance, advocate for their choices, and have the stamina to read quickly and with accuracy over a very short time period. A surprisingly high number of people are weeded out using these criteria. It can be difficult for potential readers to put aside their own ideas about our program and priorities. Scholars and advisors can become fixated on a historical version of Truman Scholars or an outdated notion of prestige. Some potential readers are too timid to push back against veteran readers. In the realm of more quotidian concerns, shockingly few people want to spend Valentine's Day weekend sequestered in a room in an "upscale harborside hotel" with two strangers arguing about the relative merits of Model UN.

Beyond these basics, we are also looking for readers to represent a broad range of disciplines and viewpoints. Our applicants come from a dizzying array of institution types and represent a boggling variety of disciplines. We cannot possibly cover all possibilities, but we do our best to ensure a broad range of interests and perspectives in our readers. Readers must be intellectually curious and flexible enough to entertain different notions of public service, even if they lack personal experience in the subject.

Benefits

Fellowships advisors come in especially handy in this regard. With the possible exception of our graduate school admissions reviewers, few other readers can better understand the range of students on college campuses than advisors. They can contextualize student experiences and react more quickly to generational shifts. They are the first to see trends in leadership style or service interests long before they show up in graduate school or the workplace. Advisors are also able to help balance out the expectations of our occasionally disenchanted public service practitioners. For many, it is very difficult to remember being a college junior. Fortunately, advisors are given constant reminders.

Perhaps the most important feature of advisors as readers is their ability to understand and advocate for different types of institutions. Varying selection criteria to properly evaluate the broad range of participating institutions is always a challenge. Having advisors representing those types of institutions can be critical to ensuring all applications are read equitably.

Advisors as readers also help the foundation gain perspective on the application process itself. These advisors have a full view of the entire process from recruiting to interview preparation. Much of the best feedback comes from these members of our selection committee. They can identify barriers to participation by applicants, recognize campus trends before we see them, and suggest improvements to administrative processes. For instance, it was advisors on our reading committee who first pointed out that unofficial transcripts would be much easier to read and less expensive for students. They were also able to suggest solutions for security issues posed by unofficial transcripts. Every time advisors upload an advising transcript and skip a trip to the registrar, they should thank their fellow advisors, who have served as application reviewers.

But aside from all these tangible concerns, the main driver for including advisors as readers stems from the foundation's long-standing commitment to transparency. Allowing advisors to see the process up close helps them not only to understand what we are looking for but also provides insight into the occasional disappointment. The most difficult thing to understand about our (or any) selection process is that sometimes the favored candidate does not prevail. The reasons for that may be varied, difficult to accept, or downright upsetting, but by providing a window into the process, we hope that these decisions are at least somewhat understandable.

That is not to say involving advisors as readers is without challenges. The first that comes to mind is also the easiest to address—conflicts of interest. In our process, readers cover specific regions, so it is simple enough to ensure no advisor is even in the same room as their applicants.[6]

The other challenge is that we have many more qualified advisors wanting to serve as readers than we have spots. Our panel is not large, and turnover is shockingly rare. While it may be difficult to understand why someone would subject themselves to the eye strain and heartbreak of a weekend with applications, the reality is that most of our readers want to come back. We also feel that using veteran readers improves our process—both in terms of consistency and accuracy.[7] Unlike larger programs, we do not have the option of adding observers, although the idea of a largely silent Greek chorus in the corner of the hotel room has its appeal.

To mitigate these issues, we have set aside one or two slots on FSC as "NAFA slots." These slots are understood to turn over every year to allow more NAFA members to serve. We are always accepting requests to be considered for these spots; however, the list is already very long. During the 2013 Atlanta conference, we also conducted a mock reading session to allow more NAFA members to have the experience of reading for Truman, even if it was just a half-day preconference activity. These mock sessions are likely the only way for us to catch up with demand, but they present their own challenges.[8]

The foundation has also encouraged those advisors who participate in our reading panel to share their thoughts with the broader NAFA group as another way to include more advisors in the process. Previous readers have written blog posts, reflective pieces, or essays to share broadly. We do not attempt to control what the advisor writes. Most advisors have shared a copy as a courtesy, but they are not obligated to do so. Some advisors may decline to share at all because they worry that too many people will come to them for "answers," even though participating in our reading panel left them with even more questions.

The lessons advisors learn from the process have been instructive and occasionally surprising. Most advisors leave the experience with the lesson that we would expect—selection is difficult, often subjective, and occasionally lonely work. But because advisors know how the application works, they can focus on the elements that the rest of us take for granted. Mid-career Truman Scholars critique an applicant for not having a coherent theory of change; advisors can point out that the problem began when the applicant could not answer the question about the Washington Summer Institute with any sort of authority or clarity. Graduate school representatives lament a weak and generic discussion of an applicant's graduate school plans; advisors are able to identify that the problem started when the applicant could not effectively discuss their most important courses.

That is not to say that including advisors as readers is not a little bit frightening. Their familiarity with the process both makes them stronger readers and makes them more likely to spot problems. If they find a problem, they have a variety of channels at their disposal to telegraph and discuss the issue at length. While public critique of our program is often valuable, it is rarely enjoyable or well-timed. But the benefits of including advisors as readers far outweigh the mildly terrifying aspects. Advisors bring valuable perspectives, provide insight into different types of institutions, and can be the catalyst for improvement and refinement of processes.

Conclusion and Call to Action

For foundations, we have found that the benefits of including advisors in review panels can outweigh the challenges. In addition to advisors' diverse academic backgrounds and perspectives, foundations benefit from longer-term improvements to the quality of applicant pools, greater awareness in review panels of factors that shape applicants' approaches, and a strong understanding of deadlines. Including advisors can also raise the profile of an award. Foundations that can include advisors in their selection process should.

For advisors, we have found that the learning outcomes, professional growth, service to the profession, and other benefits typically outweigh the challenges of reading for foundations. After referring to institutional policies and discussing the possibility of reading with their supervisors, advisors who can participate should. In addition to the benefits of doing so, advisors have also found that participating in these processes has strengthened their relationships with the foundations themselves and enabled them to feel more comfortable reaching out to a foundation representative. On many campuses, fellowships advising is a niche role, and it can be easy to feel isolated in this work. In some competitions, the more advisors who volunteer, the smaller the workload for each reviewer. Participating in these processes is a great way to provide service to the broader community, build connections beyond an individual campus, and strengthen confidence in working with students.

Advisors who are interested should watch for solicitations from the following awards, which frequently include fellowship advisors on review panels:

- Boren Awards
- Critical Language Scholarship Program
- Congress-Bundestag Youth Exchange
- Luce Scholars Program
- Gilman Scholarship
- And sometimes (in limited numbers and depending on qualifications): Udall, Truman, Fulbright

Advisors interested in a particular award (even those not listed here) may wish to contact the foundation's NAFA representative to inquire about participating.

Boren Appendix

For the first round of selection, the overall applicant pool is divided into panels (depending on volume and interest) with a regional focus or by special initiative. For the Fellowship selection panels, all three of the reviewers on the panel should hold a doctorate-level degree. Two of the three reviewers should have expertise and/or experience in the panel's region. The third reviewer is not required to have specific regional experience, although there must be one reviewer for each region who has STEM expertise to assist with students with STEM backgrounds.

Table 9.1
Example of Fellowship Panel Requirements (All Doctorates)

East & Southeast Asia Panel 1	East & Southeast Asia Panel 2	East & Southeast Asia Panel 3
1 w/ regional experience	1 w/ regional experience	1 w/ regional experience
1 w/ regional experience	1 w/ regional experience	1 w/ regional experience
1 w/ STEM experience	1 regional experience not needed	1 regional experience not needed

The first round of selection panels for the Boren Scholarships is like that of the Fellowships. Applications are again divided up into either regional panels or special initiatives. Each panel also consists of three reviewers, although for Boren Scholarships, two out of the three reviewers should hold a doctorate-level degree. Of these two reviewers, one must have experience/expertise in the region. Boren does not require that the third reviewer hold a doctorate-level degree; instead, this third reviewer must have experience advising on either study abroad or fellowship/scholarship programs.

Table 9.2
Example of Scholarship Panel Requirements

Every panel requires
1 doctorate + regional experience
1 doctorate + regional experience not needed
1 study abroad or fellowships advising background, doctorate not required

Truman Appendix

The first six questions on the Truman application ask for information about education, activities, employment, and honors or awards. The remaining prompts are as follows:

- Q7: Describe one specific example of your leadership.
- Q8: Describe a recent particularly satisfying public service activity.
- Q9: Describe the problem or needs of society you want to address when you enter public service.

- Q10: What are the three most significant courses you have taken in preparation for your career?
- Q11: Describe the graduate education program you intend to pursue if you receive a Truman Scholarship.
- Q12: What do you hope to do and what position do you hope to have upon completing your graduate studies?
- Q13: What do you hope to do and what position do you hope to have five to seven years later?
- Q14: What additional personal information do you wish to share with the Truman Scholarship Foundation?

Notes

1. Kurt Davies and Lindsay Lawton, together with Michael Saffle (Boren/IIE) and Caitlin Ting (CLS/American Councils), participated in a panel that gave rise to this chapter at the 2023 NAFA conference.
2. And let's be frank: I still forget and am surprised when the call comes around again.
3. This section is not a direct quotation. It is typical verbiage Boren uses in outreach and is paraphrased and condensed from the DLNSEO's own website: https://www.dlnseo.mil/Programs/National-Security-Education-Program/.
4. See "Bulletin of Information," Harry S. Truman Scholarship Foundation, https://www.truman.gov/apply/applying/bulletin-information.
5. In general, we do not involve advisors in our Regional Review Panels due to the inability to control for conflicts. Since the panels are geographically determined, advisors would likely encounter their own applicants. The only method to deal with that conflict would be recusal, so it makes little sense to include advisors at this stage.
6. "Simple" is a bit misleading. We prevent anyone with an institutional affiliation from reading any application in the region, not just the state. Therefore, our reader who works at Stanford Law School does not touch any region that contains an application from Stanford, even if the reader has never met the student. Of course, we would also prevent anyone who knows or has contact with an applicant. With a reading panel of busy public servants—a full third of whom are affiliated with a college or university—managing these conflicts means that all that time spent practicing LSAT logic puzzles has finally come in handy.
7. During FSC and as part of our annual process review, we review the materials from every reader to ensure accuracy and identify areas of concern.

If a reader demonstrated bias or an inability to follow our directions, they are removed. Given that many of our readers are long-time veterans, the need to remove people is rare. Generally, spots open only when readers retire for good or have conflicts for that weekend.
8. There is a reason why this session was only done once. It was, as they say, a heavy lift—literally. At the time, we were still reading with paper applications, so we had to produce copies for the more than forty attendees. Electronic applications would make replicating this session easier, but it would still require several hours of conference time in an already packed schedule.

10

The Logic and Lessons of the Prestige and Practicality Forums

RACHEL BALL-PHILLIPS, JESSIE MCCRARY,
ERIC MYERS, TERUMI RAFFERTY-OSAKI,
JAYASHREE SHIVAMOGGI, AND CHRISTIAN TANJA

This chapter details the origins of the Prestige and Practicality Forum, a large-scale and highly attended session that was held just after the opening remarks of the National Association of Fellowship Advisors (NAFA) biennial conference in New Orleans in July 2023. We outline and reflect on the experience of working as a committee (and subcommittee, at times) to conceptualize and prepare first, a virtual forum and later, this in-person forum, in order to meet goals central to the work of NAFA's DEI Committee (now Committee on Belonging). We share what worked and did not work, as well as the premise for holding such a large and central event with broad parameters. We provide insight on survey data collected from members, which were reported in real time during or just after their participation in the forum. Importantly, we share our experiences and findings to inform advisors on the work and to reflect on what we can do toward supporting inclusive education moving forward. This chapter provides important transparency and lessons learned in an ever-complex landscape of diversity concerns within higher education, as this work is caught in the tension of the competing needs of justice and diversity.

A transformative piece that captures this tension is "The 'Colorblindness' Trap: How a Civil Rights Ideal Got Hijacked," a 2024 essay by Nikole Hannah-Jones in the *New York Times*.[1] Here, the author highlights the tension between the competing priorities of justice and diversity as they play out in higher education. In a powerful opening, Hannah-Jones describes how institutions such as Howard University are navigating pushes to topple its justice-based admission practices to its College of Medicine, which were forced off balance by the Supreme Court's 2023 ruling on *Students for Fair Admissions, Inc. v. President and Fellows of Harvard College* and now are hobbling through a barrage of barriers calling for the revocation of its mandate supporting the advancement of Black students of enslaved ancestry. These trends show little signs of stopping anytime soon. What shifts we experienced over the years in the context of prestigious, named fellowships have given us a lot to consider about our roles in this privilege-tinged work. Paired with ongoing DEI-informed practices, complexities like the ones Hannah-Jones outlines force us individually to look to the future and ask what we can do to shape it. We must embrace the truth that we cannot do this alone. Instead, we must deepen our understanding of the interlocking systems at play.

As of this writing, we are seeing how the 2023 ruling is being used to challenge racial justice programs in and beyond higher education to claim wrongdoing by initiatives that are designed to accommodate those with a farther starting line. The ruling has been used to block efforts that address racial inequity by using "colorblindedness" as an argument for "fairness" and against race-conscious policies. Furthermore, the Supreme Court's decision to promote this colorblindedness maintains racial disparities by blocking affirmative action aimed to reduce racial disparities. The original purpose of affirmative action was to improve conditions for the descendants of slavery. However, in the late 1970s, another Supreme Court decision, *Regents of the University of California v. Bakke,* made the use of racial quotas in university admissions unconstitutional. This signaled a shift to prioritize diversity in college admissions, which diluted the original intent of the policy to uplift those with an enslaved ancestry. The unintended consequence made admission policies vulnerable to attacks and further entangled these two separate and important initiatives of justice and diversity. Racial justice is a crucial foundation for our democracy. The true architects of democracy were unfree at America's founding, who fought for changes that were carried forward through generations by civil rights leaders of minority backgrounds.[2] We continue to see the effects of this inclusion work play out today. The dismantling of DEI initiatives nationwide is occurring despite an increasingly multiracial democracy.

What does this mean for those who work in the fellowship space within colleges and universities? This topic is big and broad, but what do recent legal and administrative shifts mean for the fellowships we support applications to and for our work as advisors and foundations in our institutional and professional spaces?

Access to the prestigious institutions themselves and knowledge of fellowships offices on campus are grounded in the issue of equity. Further, inclusion issues arose when institutions of higher education were rocked with news of "Operation Varsity Blues," the 2019 college admissions scandal involving famous actors, business moguls, and other professionals paying for placements at top universities. This was not the first time this occurred, but it does highlight how finances play a significant role in college admissions.[3]

Issues of access are already at play in college admissions, and fellowships advisors are keenly aware of the ways in which students arrive at campus holding some implicit assumptions about who "prestigious fellowships" are "for." Self-selection and self-elimination are already existent challenges for fellowships advisors and inform the work we do in recruiting students from all backgrounds who may be interested in and competitive for national scholarships and fellowships. The interplay between assumptions of "prestige" (and inherent assumptions of "privilege") and the very practical reasons our students and alumni have for pursuing the funding, networking, and other professional and academic benefits of nationally competitive awards was the inspiration and central tension the NAFA DEI committee hoped to explore in virtual and physical conversation spaces. Thus, we named the forums "Prestige and Practicality."

Further complicating matters are recent state mandates regarding DEI legislation and restrictions in higher education. These state mandates appear to be in response to the reversal of affirmative action protections in *Fair Admissions v. Harvard* as well as being influenced by more generalized "culture wars" playing out via book bans, anti-LGBTQ policies and laws, removal of Advanced Placement African American history courses from high schools, and misguided interpretations of Critical Race Theory (CRT). For example, as part of the State University System in Florida, administrators with terminal degrees, such as directors of fellowships offices, can often have an appointment at their institution as a faculty member. With the passage of HB233, students now can secretly record professors (predominantly for use in the classroom), but it is unclear whether this could be utilized for fellowships information and advising sessions.[4] Also unclear is how the faculty appointment affects the work of fellowships advisors beyond recruitment efforts. This lack of clarity was demonstrated when the state of Florida collected "all written or electronic communications, including but not limited to emails, texts, and social media messages" from anyone associated with DEI from January 2021 to February 2023.[5] While fellowships offices were not directly affected, those who served on or were associated with the DEI offices were audited as part of the process. Finally, while anti-DEI legislation is passed in order to reaffirm "colorblind" admissions, two groups in particular are also vulnerable to the sweeping changes: veterans and people with disabilities, which grew in number under the pandemic.[6] This is one example of how sweeping state legislation impacts the work of fellowship offices as part of a systemic overhaul of higher education.

Multiple layers of prestige and practicality are involved in fellowship applications. This was highlighted when a University of Pennsylvania student embellished her Rhodes Scholarship application with more graphic details of trauma because she described her sense that students applying for scholarships "sometimes felt confused and pressured to be someone they were not amidst their application process."[7] After *Fair Admissions*, students of color now wonder whether they should include any mention of race in admissions essays. This uncertainty highlights the important issues of identity politics, socioeconomic status, and race in future fellowship applications.[8]

The many and complex realities applicants to nationally competitive opportunities face make these critical matters for fellowships advisors to consider, discuss, and commit to influencing where we can. This brief overview of DEI challenges within US higher education over the first few years of the 2020s provides important context for the work of the NAFA Committee on Belonging during the Prestige and Practicality forum. The rest of this chapter outlines the decisions leading to this session, as well as what we learned from NAFA members who participated in it.

Formation of the DEI Committee and Establishment of Goals

One of the hallmarks of NAFA is that student development through the process of fellowship applications embodies the ideals of the American education system to advance personally and professionally. To this extent, the richness and changing face of the profession also represents the aspirational ideal of "a more perfect union." In the late 2010s, institutions throughout the country began to make DEI central to their missions. In 2019, NAFA began efforts to codify more explicitly the organization's goals regarding DEI actions and support of its members. In the same year, systemic racist practices within higher education institutions motivated NAFA members to complete an assessment of the organization's DEI work, especially its limits and opportunities. This was particularly important since NAFA was founded with the goal of broadening access to fellowships opportunities and to widen the field of professional advisement beyond Ivy League contexts. LaNitra Berger and Alsace-Lorraine Gallop, along with the incoming president of NAFA, Cindy Schaarschmidt, were at the forefront of efforts to create a DEI Committee in the wake of the Minneapolis biennial conference in 2019. The importance of integrating DEI into the organization reflected NAFA's advancements in supporting its members and creating more opportunities for those advising students and applicants to communicate with foundations. For two years, Jacob English and Alsace-Lorraine Gallop led efforts to establish the goals of the nascent committee. This was accomplished through community outreach, including a series of town hall meetings in the spring 2020, held against the backdrop of COVID, and during the summer of Black Lives Matters protests following the murder of George Floyd. This period was particularly stressful in higher education, given the contraction of positions and enrollment, the addition on many campuses of furloughs, and general funding uncertainty. Nevertheless, the NAFA Board continued to conduct its formal work throughout this period. During that summer, NAFA hired Cody Charles as a DEI facilitator for monthly board meetings. By the fall and into the winter of 2021, DEI work within NAFA slowly moved from reactive to proactive, integrating and facilitating conversation and creating space for discussion across NAFA committees.

By the 2021 virtual NAFA biennial conference, the DEI committee created the three goals that would ground the committee's work and influence within the organization. The organizing group recruited committee members and established the committee's mission, vision, and three goals. These guiding ideas were distributed to members and are reproduced below:

> **Mission Statement**: The National Association of Fellowship Advisors Diversity, Equity, and Inclusion (NAFA DEI) Committee will nurture and sustain a culturally responsive environment for NAFA members, students, alumni, and fellowships applicants whom we serve. To foster these inclusive spaces, we will develop and implement programs and guidance that promote DEI in the field of fellowships advising.
>
> **Vision Statement**: The NAFA DEI Committee seeks to equip fellowships advisors with inclusive practices designed to affirm and celebrate each student's unique qualities, experiences, and capacity to succeed in their pursuit of award and fellowship opportunities.
>
> **Goal 1**: Promote and prioritize diversity, equity, and inclusion within NAFA.
> - Initiative 1: Publish a diversity plan.
> - Initiative 2: Establish online resources about DEI to inform applicant advisement and staff and faculty recruitment.

- Initiative 3: Create inclusive spaces for open, difficult, and transparent conversations through annual programming.
- Initiative 4: Establish protocols for embedding DEI into conferences, workshops, and study tour participation.

Goal 2: Enhance communication flow between and among the executive board, committees, and NAFA members to develop a more inclusive environment within the organization.
- Initiative 1: Support NAFA's professional management association, executive board, committees, and the NAFA community to ensure an accessible, consistent, and standard communication workflow.
- Initiative 2: Establish and maintain ongoing bi-directional conversations with foundation representatives about diversity, equity, and inclusion.

Goal 3: Promote and retain a diverse membership.
- Initiative 1: Develop a scholarship program to create access to NAFA membership and programming.
- Initiative 2: Establish a recruitment strategy that ensures a diverse membership and leadership.
- Initiative 3: Establish an Excellence and Innovation in DEI Award for NAFA members.
- Initiative 4: Construct an assessment plan to evaluate NAFA programming to inform diverse, equitable, and inclusive membership, programs, and resources.

Once the committee set these goals, additional members were recruited to join the committee to collaborate toward achieving them. The Prestige and Practicality Forum, initially created for a virtual space and then expanded to a large-scale, in-person forum, was the outcome of committee members working in a subcommittee toward Goal 1. Specifically, the forum was created as one outlet to "Create inclusive spaces for open, difficult, and transparent conversations through annual programming," as Goal 1, Initiative 3 states.

Goals of the Prestige and Practicality Forums

Prestige and Practicality Forum, November 2022

The first NAFA Prestige and Practicality Forum was held in November of 2022. The purpose of this workshop was to introduce the DEI Committee to all NAFA members and to create space for dialogue and discussion. The session was structured according to topical, question-based breakout rooms, hoping smaller groups would encourage an atmosphere for fruitful discussion, questions, and listening. Each themed breakout room had a facilitator who was a member of the DEI committee; the intention was for them not to lead discussion, but rather to listen and guide the discussion gently, especially asking questions and allowing for silence and for others in the room to speak.

The themes for the five breakout sessions were (1) allyship, (2) bias awareness, (3) working with graduate students, (4) the rhetoric of prestige, and (5) the language of prestige and practicality. The last two, while very similar in title, were intended to cover different aspects and audiences within our work. These themes were driven by the questions and considerations DEI committee members were observing or experiencing themselves, and brief descriptions were created to help members participating in the Prestige and Practicality forum to decide where they wanted to spend time. Attendees were able to choose which breakout room they wanted to join.

During the opening of the forum, the leaders of the session provided a set of discussion norms. Because we received feedback that these were productive guiding norms, we include them here in the hope they may be used by others creating similar spaces for challenging, open discussions:

- This is an open forum for all in which we aim to challenge ourselves.
- Step up/step back. Share airtime and take turns.
- Use "I" statements. Do not be afraid to say it ugly.
- Give respect. Assume goodwill. Bring light, not heat.

- Engage in ways that make the most sense for you: listening, taking notes, speaking up, taking turns in conversation, etc.
- Expect and accept non-closure. Continue the discussion at lunch and onward.

From the start, it was clear from registration and attendance that NAFA members were interested in and desired this kind of space for discussion. Approximately, 170 people registered for the event on Zoom, and 120 individuals attended the virtual session. This also meant the small-format breakout rooms would be hard to achieve, as the five themed breakout rooms had to accommodate twenty to thirty people.

After the session, the committee sent a feedback survey to understand what worked and what could be improved for future sessions. Unsurprisingly, we received feedback that the sessions were too large to foster conversation and space for everyone who was present. Future sessions could have more, smaller breakout rooms, and we could even allow multiple rooms to cover the same central topics and themes (i.e., have three breakout rooms discussing allyship). Other feedback suggested we could instead have more granular themes and rooms (i.e., name rooms based on region or state, type of institution, or specific need or question). Feedback suggested we should keep the breakout sessions long, even make them longer, to give ample space and time for open, honest conversations. In addition, we heard that providing a follow-up message to participants, via email or digital document format, with some takeaways, resources, and other essential information would have been helpful. We also received positive feedback on key aspects of how we arranged the sessions, especially using breakout rooms, encouraging open dialogue, initial norm-setting, and an icebreaker (offered via the chat function in Zoom). Participants felt that the themes could have been published more than just a few days ahead of the event so that folks had more time to decide and prepare.

Already, given the discussions that took place, the high turnout, and the constructive feedback, we knew it would be useful to hold more sessions, ideally at least once per semester. However, given time constraints and with other committee obligations and an impending biennial in-person NAFA conference, the subcommittee turned efforts toward hosting an in-person Prestige and Practicality session.

Prestige and Practicality Forum—New Orleans, July 2023

After the Goal 1 subcommittee held the first Prestige and Practicality forum in November 2022, we used feedback from participants to begin building what the next forum might look like. Much of the feedback was to hold more, smaller discussion groups (Zoom breakout rooms, for example) on the same thematic subjects as we had in the first session so that more people could participate, and in deeper ways.

Based on those ideas, we began the process of translating our initial goals into the kind of large-scale forum space we would be filling on the conference agenda. Quickly, we decided that it would be impossible to continue to hold the forums without first knowing what our members hoped to gain from them, why they were there, and how the DEI committee might best support their programmatic and individual DEI practices. Therefore, instead of continuing the same conversation tables we had started in the first virtual forum in November 2022, we went back to the drawing board with simpler, starting-point questions for NAFA members. Those were the questions on the slide deck on the projector screens in July 2023:

- What should a NAFA DEI community forum look like?
- What tools, facilitation, and resources would make our DEI community forum most useful?
- Where might the forum take place, how often?
- Should we focus on specific themes or more general guiding questions/topics?
- What elements of your DEI work could be centered in future forum spaces?

During the Prestige and Practicality conference forum, we asked participants to use a form to input ideas, challenges, and discussion points from their individual perspectives or to summarize them from table's perspective. The prompt on the form said simply: "What were some of the key themes, takeaways, questions, observations, or ideas to come from your table discussion?" The planning committee hoped the open format of both the discussion tables and the input form would encourage a variety of conversations and ideas for how the DEI committee could best serve NAFA members.

An important takeaway, based on feedback both at the conference and in the input form, was that an open format was challenging for such a diverse group. For conversations on DEI to be effective, they must be organized with consideration of (1) where individuals are on their DEI journeys, (2) the institutional and state contexts they are operating in in their roles as fellowships advisors or foundation representatives, and (3) the goals the planning committee hopes for the table conversations. The committee heard clearly that while the conference format worked for some, it was too open-ended for others, who left the forum a bit uncertain about what to take away from it.

On the other hand, the forum planning group had much to consider from the fifty-nine submitted responses. Many took the time to summarize ideas from their tables, and others found the forum a meaningful space to share their concerns, questions, and disappointments. The committee took all these into consideration and created a list of key recommendations for how the DEI committee can best use its time to meet the needs of NAFA community members. Those recommendations were based on a qualitative review of the survey data and are reported in this section. We have also coded the survey data and provided our findings more formally, which we report in the following section.

In our initial assessment, we first noted the recommendations that address consideration 1 above, providing resources to support individuals on their various and diverse points along ongoing DEI journeys. Key recommendations that support this goal include (1) establish a DEI resource hub; (2) facilitate advisor training by and for NAFA members (as well as from outside DEI facilitators) on various topics related to advising, student success, and other best practices; and (3) compile a list of DEI-promoting scholarships and opportunities, including input from foundations on their DEI efforts. Recurring input suggests demand for expert-led DEI training for NAFA members. This training would provide workshops for different levels of knowledge and engagement (entry-level, mid-level, and advanced discussions). A summary of inputs also suggested the need to create a database for NAFA members of DEI-focused awards, establishing best practices for inclusive scholar selection, and implementing unconscious bias training.

Second, we noted the recommendations that addressed consideration 2, the institutional and state contexts in which members are operating in their professional capacities, running fellowships offices, advising, administering awards via foundations, and other aligned roles. To best support the variety of contexts, key recommendations included (1) provide structured space and opportunities for members to collaborate on DEI issues, such as regional discussion groups and thematic/topic-based forums; and (2) consider sustainable ways members might engage, given the many ways we are already spread thin or overcommitted.

We also received recommendations for longer-term initiatives. Members noted the importance of gathering baseline demographic data within NAFA. Others noted we could broaden the reach of DEI content beyond current social media channels such as LinkedIn to foster regular DEI discussions through reading groups or similar formats. One idea was to enhance the NAFA website as a tool for students, especially given the uncertainty of DEI-focused support in specific states and institutional contexts. Another idea was to expand resources supporting LGBTQ+ award recipients abroad. We also heard the continued calls for accountability among foundations and agencies sponsoring awards on their efforts to recruit and support diverse applicants and recipients.

The way the planning group designed this forum and its intended goals created further questions for our consideration. One evergreen question is whether the goal of the DEI committee is to serve and support the NAFA board and structure by provide guidance on DEI practices for the organization or whether our goal is to provide resources and support on DEI practices for its members. Certainly, the action items listed in the inputs from members summarized above suggest there is much to do, and great demand for it, to support our members. However, the limits of the labor of one committee are a real barrier to successfully meeting so many of the important suggestions and recommendations we received.

Finally, based on the initial review of survey feedback, we determined that a key area the DEI committee must consider is NAFA accessibility. We heard concerns about NAFA membership affordability as an access barrier. To address this, NAFA and the DEI committee could provide input and support for the creation of sustainable, well-conceived funding to support NAFA membership and participation. Importantly, the DEI committee is called to consider the balance between two broad goals: developing DEI leaders and engaging the broader membership in DEI conversations, training, and inclusive practices alongside the potential NAFA has as an organization to leverage its institutional power for advocacy at state and national levels.

Forum Outcomes, Questions, and Concerns

In the 2023 optional survey we asked forum participants to submit, the conversations and questions that arose at their respective tables provides valuable information for the DEI committee to use as we move forward serving NAFA members. In real time during the forum on the first day of the conference, we asked participants to share a word to express how they were feeling at their tables (see Figure 10.1). In analyzing these and based on conversations, questions, and feedback,

Figure 10.1. Word cloud generated during the July 2023 Prestige and Practicality Forum.

we identified clear themes pertaining to what NAFA can do in order to create a more equitable process for students as an organization, with DEI committee members leading the charge in the coming years amidst a constantly changing higher education landscape.

Using the responses from the community input forum, we coded each unique response (N = 58) to ascertain the perceived need of the respondent after the presentation and roundtable discussion. To do this, two reviewers independently assessed every response and classified it for addressing the following needs: institutional, organizational, and foundation-based. During the classification by need, the reviewers determined whether the need was one that could be addressed at an institutional level (e.g., at an institution of higher education), within the organization of NAFA, or at a foundation-level (i.e., a granting agency such as the Fulbright US Student Program). These areas were chosen to address potential pathways forward for NAFA (organizational) and its members (institutions and foundations).

To situate the responses, every answer was coded to address those needs. Whereas some responses indicated only one need (e.g., institutional), many responses noted multiple needs. This is reflected in Table 10.1. It highlights the fact that an overwhelming majority of responses (93.10 percent of the fifty-eight responses) noted that the needs were organizational in nature, while the institutional and foundation needs were equal, with thirteen mentions each (22.41 percent each).

It is particularly telling that 93 percent of all responses indicated that the needs have to do with the ability of the organization (NAFA)

Table 10.1
Breakdown of Overall Needs

Type of needs	Occurrences in responses	Percentage of specific issue when need coded
Institutional needs	13	22.41
Foundation needs	13	22.41
Organizational needs	54	93.10

to assist in delivering support and guidance on DEI issues. This is underscored by the fact that only 22 percent of all responses indicated needs associated with institutions or foundations. These results could suggest that the respondents, predominantly fellowships advisors, are yearning for support in these matters and the perception is that NAFA could or should be providing that support. An overwhelming majority of the responses collected during the forum highlighted a call from the organization to engage with membership on DEI concerns. The question is, What is the capacity and desire of NAFA and its leadership to provide this level of support?

To understand the needs identified by the respondents, it was necessary to break down the specific issues that could be addressed, whether by an institution or a foundation or by the organization. Tables 10.2–10.4 represent the breakdown of specific issues that reappeared in responses.

Table 10.2
Institutional Needs by Specific Issue

Specific issue	Occurrences in responses	Percentage of specific issue when need coded
Legal restrictions	1	7.69
Recruitment	3	23.08
Internal processes	7	53.85
Student support	3	23.08

Table 10.3
Foundation Needs by Specific Issue

Specific issue	Occurrences in responses	Percentage of specific issue when need coded
Financial support/awareness	3	23.08
Collaboration	2	15.38
Transparency	6	46.15
Accountability	4	30.77

Table 10.4
Organizational Needs by Specific Issue

Specific issue	Occurrences in responses	Percentage of specific issue when need coded
Legal restrictions	9	16.67
Collaboration	4	7.41
Resources	18	33.33
Forums/workshops	17	31.48
Small groups	8	14.81
Virtual meetings	5	9.26
Advocacy	11	20.37
Membership	5	9.26
External facilitation	6	11.11
NAFA transparency	5	9.26

Institutional needs were areas where the respondent noted that the need was something that could and/or should be addressed on their individual campus. Examples include promoting typical diversity fellowships on campus; navigating Title VI and IX discrimination policies; and how individual offices could "measure" DEI initiatives through appropriate assessment tools.

For this need, the reviewers coded the responses into legal restrictions, recruitment, internal process, and student support.

As highlighted in Table 10.1, only thirteen responses mentioned institutional needs. In those thirteen responses fourteen specific issues were addressed. This could suggest that respondents felt they only had so much control over the implementation of DEI practices on their own campuses; however, 53.85 percent noted a need to consider the implications of DEI within internal processes (e.g., rigidity of deadlines and its impact on underserved student populations). This supports the notion that fellowships advisors are keenly aware that there is only so much they can do to influence practices outside of their offices' authority. Still, they do have the power to control and refine the internal processes that affect the selection of applicants.

Foundation needs were areas where the respondent noted that the need was something that could and/or should be addressed by foundations. Examples include selection transparency on behalf of funding agencies; insight into how DEI is being addressed within foundations; and increased representation of underserved populations within applicant pools and selections.

For this need the reviewers coded the responses into financial support/awareness, collaboration, transparency, and accountability.

It is again important to note that only thirteen responses indicated foundation needs, which could mean that fellowship advisors feel the same level of authority to shape the policies and practices of foundations as they do of external DEI measures on their campus. This is supported by the fact that of the thirteen times that foundation needs were mentioned, 46.15% of responses noted the specific issue of transparency and particularly the notion that foundations needed to provide more insight into their selection processes. This could be directly related to the internal processes noted in Table 10.2 (institutional need) and underscores that advisors notice a need to address DEI within the selection processes of foundations as well as at their institutions.

Organizational needs were areas where the respondents noted that NAFA needed to take a larger role in addressing DEI issues, with potential nationwide impact. Examples include regularly scheduled DEI forum meetings; broader conversations around DEI issues; and more tools to help advisors address the changing field of higher education and the intersections with DEI issues.

From these needs, the reviewers coded the responses into legal restrictions, collaboration, resources, forums/workshops, small groups, virtual meetings, advocacy, membership, external facilitation, and NAFA transparency.

Again, it cannot be overemphasized that almost all responses indicated a desire to see NAFA take a role in addressing DEI. Of the issues that came up to address member needs, the most commonly mentioned were resources (eighteen mentions) and forums/workshops (seventeen).

While it is not unfair to suggest that according to the responses, NAFA needs to address and undertake various DEI issues and initiatives, it should be noted that doing so might serve to make institutional and foundation processes more equitable. Therefore, responses could indicate that members are turning to NAFA in order to help develop, implement, and control for DEI needs that they feel powerless to address on their own campuses and with foundations.

The Future: Considerations, Strategies, Questions

As the word cloud in Figure 10.1 illustrates, the concept of DEI sparks a wide array of responses. But the two words that seem to best encapsulate this experience are *frustration* and *hopeful*. *Frustration* perhaps points to the DEI mission as confusing or even unreasonable, as many institutions lack intention, understanding, and, most importantly, resources, especially as administrative responsibilities continue to grow. *Frustration* may also be heightened by the culture of leadership on campuses and at the local and state levels. While the results of the 2023 survey may already seem distant, indicative of a different era of DEI in higher education, our analysis of the data—direct feedback and suggestions from NAFA members—points to an important set of considerations in terms of what resources NAFA provides members in order to meet the DEI aspects of its mission and vision as the organization moves forward. In response to the survey, a community listening session titled "Since New Orleans" was held in June 2024, intended to create a space for discussion of the many new and complex considerations related to our work across campuses, which had emerged in just a year's time.

While it is clear from the responses collected during the 2023 forum that membership is turning to the organization to provide structure and support when addressing DEI issues, the question is, What is the capacity and desire of NAFA and its leadership to provide this structure and support? Given the labor and financial constraints of a volunteer professional organization, it will be challenging for NAFA to meet the needs and desires of members reflected in the survey we present here. However, there does seem to be an opportunity for general members to support one another and continue to address the NAFA core values of collaboration, learning, equity, inclusion, respect, and transparency. Outside of individual member actions, what role can the NAFA board and the committees of the organization play to facilitate this endeavor? The responses of members provided during the Prestige and Practicality Forum provide evidence that efforts toward these endeavors will be worthwhile investments for leadership within and beyond NAFA's DEI committee and executive board. And as noted above, since the inception of the NAFA DEI committee, the question about who the work of the committee is *for* (organization leadership, members, students served by our work, or some or all of these groups) is central, and it remains a central consideration, given what we have reported in this chapter. We hope that our findings here will provoke continued thoughtful discussion with our colleagues and that some of them will guide the DEI committee's investments and planning for future work.

Notes

1. Nikole Hannah-Jones, "The 'Colorblindness' Trap: How a Civil Rights Ideal Got Hijacked," *New York Times*, May 13, 2024.
2. Nikole Hannah-Jones, "Black People and the Promise of Democracy," part 1, episode 3, in *Black History, Black Freedom, & Black Love*, dir. Nicole Rittenmeyer and Maeyen Basssey (MasterClass, 2022).
3. Graham Cates, "Lori Loughlin and Felicity Huffman Among Dozens Charged in College Bribery Scheme," *CBSNews*, March 12, 2019; Matt Hamilton and Harriet Ryan, "USC's Central Role in College Admissions Scandal Brings Anger and Dismay," *Los Angeles Times*, March 13, 2019. For more information see Adeel Hassan, "A History of College Admissions Schemes, from Encoded Pencils to Paid Stand-Ins," *New York Times*, March 15, 2019.
4. Claire Goforth, "Florida Professors Consider Fleeing the State After DeSantis' 'Un-American' Mass Search of Texts, Emails," *DailyDot*, February 9, 2023, https://www.dailydot.com/debug/florida-college-university-desantis-diversity-inclusion-equality/; United Faculty of Florida, "Update on Speaker Renner's Request for Information Related to DEI Faculty," January 30, 2023, https://uff-uf.org/update-on-speaker-renners-request-for-information-related-to-dei-faculty/.

5. See also Francie Diep and Emma Pettit, "DeSantis Asked Florida Universities to Detail Their Diversity Spending. Here's How They Answered," *The Chronicle of Higher Education*, January 19, 2023, https://www.chronicle.com/article/desantis-asked-florida-universities-to-detail-their-diversity-spending-heres-how-they-answered.
6. Megan Landry, Sydney Bornstein, Nitasha Nagaraj, et al., "Postacute Sequelae of SARS-CoV-2 in University Setting," *Emergency Infectious Diseases* 29, no. 3 (March 2023): 519–27, https://www.ncbi.nlm.nih.gov/pmc/articles/PMC9973677/.
7. Rachel Aviv, "How an Ivy League School Turned Against a Student," *The New Yorker*, March 28, 2022, https://www.newyorker.com/magazine/2022/04/04/mackenzie-fierceton-rhodes-scholarship-university-of-pennsylvania.
8. Gabe Cohen, "Black Students Weigh Mentioning Race in College Admissions Essays After SCOTUS Affirmative Action Ruling," CNN, December 26, 2023. More recently, see Bernard Mokam, "After Affirmative Action Ban, They Rewrote College Essays with a Key Theme: Race," *New York Times*, January 20, 2024, https://www.nytimes.com/2024/01/20/us/affirmative-action-ban-college-essays.html. For more detailed information regarding the inextricable link between socioeconomics and college admissions essays, see Arvind Ashok, "The Persistent Grip of Social Class on College Admissions," *New York Times*, May 20, 2021 https://www.nytimes.com/2021/05/26/upshot/college-admissions-essay-sat.html; Elijah Megginson, "When I Applied to College, I Didn't Want to 'Sell My Pain,'" *New York Times*, May 9, 2021; and Scott Jaschik, "Do College Application Essays Favor the Wealthy?," *Inside Higher Ed*, May 31, 2021, https://www.insidehighered.com/admissions/article/2021/06/01/do-college-application-essays-favor-wealthier-students.

11

Approaching Endorsement Letters

How to Do Justice to Your Student, Represent Your Institution Well, and Keep Your Wits About You

LISA GATES, KATYA KING, CHRISTINE OVERSTREET, AND CINDY STOCKS

Introduction

A certain amount of mystery surrounds letters of institutional endorsement. Combined, the four authors of this essay have more than sixty-five years of fellowships advising experience and have written countless letters of institutional endorsement, yet in comparing notes, we discovered that we all questioned the effectiveness of our letters. Over the years, we have heard foundation representatives say that even the best letter of institutional endorsement would not make a winner out of a weak candidate. On the other hand, the Truman Foundation's website states, "Enthusiastic, carefully-written letters from Faculty Representatives help good candidates advance to the interview—even if they have one or two weak points. Ordinary letters are a disservice, even to strong candidates."[1] Were our letters tipping the balance in favor of our students and making the readers want to interview them or—despite our best efforts—were the readers finding our letters "ordinary"?

To tackle this question, we took the unusual step of sharing with each other letters we had written for successful and unsuccessful applications. Together, we read, analyzed, critiqued, and debated at length the strengths and weaknesses of the shared letters. We emerged from the process not with black-and-white answers but with more confidence in our approach. This chapter summarizes much of what we discussed, and we hope it will help advisors, especially those new to this process, have more confidence as well.

We acknowledge that fellowships advising looks different across campuses. The four of us lead fellowship offices at small, well-resourced institutions. On other campuses, the person writing the letter of institutional endorsement could be a faculty member with a full teaching load. Some individuals write just one or two letters annually, while others write dozens. Wherever advisors fall on this spectrum, and whether they are new to the field or even have years of experience, the goal of this chapter is to help advisors prioritize where to focus time and energy when writing letters of institutional endorsement.

What Are Endorsement Letters?

Letters of institutional endorsement—also referred to as letters of institutional nomination—are a unique form of writing, which carry the responsibility of presenting both the applicant and the institution. While each application component (e.g., an essay, transcript, and recommendation) provides insight into the applicant's suitability for the particular fellowship, the letter of institutional endorsement can help the reader understand how all the pieces fit together and present the applicant's candidacy as more than the sum of its parts.

Like letters of recommendation, endorsement letters are read by multiple constituencies, including campus mock interview panels, application readers at the national level, and the foundation's interview committee members. But while both types of letters highlight the candidate's strengths, the endorsement is written from an institutional perspective, not from that of an individual. This is an important distinction. An endorsement letter addresses how a candidate stands out within the context of the institution's student body, not in one professor's course or even among the cohort of students a professor has taught throughout their career.

Although each national fellowship foundation's guidance about what to include in the letter of institutional endorsement varies, a well-crafted letter of institutional endorsement holistically presents the candidate to the reader, while weaving in information about the institution. To accomplish this, the writer should balance summarizing information shared by the applicant and recommenders with new information. Summarizing can emphasize certain points or accomplishments mentioned elsewhere in the application. Any new information should provide context about the applicant, personal background, accomplishments, and the institution, or clarify something mentioned by the candidate or a recommender.

Deciding what to summarize and what new information to include comprises the art of writing effective letters of institutional endorsement. Rather than following a template, most effective letters require the advisor to think strategically about the fellowship's selection criteria, individual candidates, and the strengths and weaknesses of their candidacy vis-à-vis the particular fellowship. We often involve the applicant in these strategic decisions, discussing early on what topics are best addressed by the applicant and what is better conveyed in the endorsement letter. Although we are aware that some fellowships advisors may share part or all of an endorsement letter with the applicant, our practice is to treat these as confidential documents.[2]

Campus culture and the guidance provided by the foundation will dictate who signs the letter. Some national fellowships stipulate that the endorsement letter be signed by the president or another member of the senior staff, while others are less prescriptive. Foundations provide this information through a variety of means, including public websites, application system portals, or email or other direct communication to advisors. Regardless of who signs the letter, it is the fellowships advisor or a member of the campus nomination committee who most commonly drafts the letter.

What Should an Endorsement Letter Include?

Space is limited, often by a word or character count set by the foundation. But even without stated space constraints, there are limits to the reviewers' patience when they encounter an extremely long letter attached to all the other materials in an application. One and a half to two pages is a reasonable length. A good strategy is to start with the core components. Once those are in place, endorsers can add more to further inform and persuade the readers of the applicant's competitiveness for the fellowship. These core letter components should do the following:

- **Declare endorsement.** Somewhere in the text—usually at the beginning or the end (or both)—advisors should make a clear statement of support on behalf of the institution.
- **Address how the applicant meets the foundation's selection criteria.** All foundations lay out clearly the qualities that matter to them. Even if endorsers have been advising for years and feel they know the criteria by heart, reviewing the material again before starting to write can help appropriately orient their thinking. If an applicant is endorsed for more than one fellowship, endorsers may certainly duplicate some material in the letter, but they should still adapt it to fit the particular award for which students are being endorsed.
- **Provide an executive summary of the materials.** No one contributor to the application packet—except the scholarship representative—has seen everything in it. Typically, applicants do not see their recommendation letters. Recommendation writers may have seen one or more of the essays, but perhaps not the transcript(s); they almost certainly will not have seen the other writers' letters. Advisors are in a unique position to notice common threads in the materials and bring those to the reviewers' attention. While we do not advise quoting large portions of recommendation letters, endorsers might include a few words or phrases that emphasize an applicant's extraordinary academic aptitude or character.
- **Clarify the chronology.** Some applications force candidates to list their activities by category (e.g., leadership, research, and service) and do not allow room for a resumé to be uploaded; it can be challenging for reviewers to figure out how the applicant moved from one internship, job, or volunteer assignment to another. Gap years, academic leaves, study

abroad, and transfers among institutions can make it even more confusing. Letters of endorsement should help reviewers understand the applicant's trajectory.

- **Explain any anomalies in the applicant's academic record.** Applicants often want to use precious space in their personal statement to explain why their grades dipped, but an explanation from an endorser will have more authority and likely be seen as more objective. Sickness, family difficulties, the death of a loved one—anything that can be independently verified and that is beyond the normal challenges a student might face—might be offered as reasons. Students sometimes also bite off more than they can manage, realize it, and learn from it. While it is not necessary to explain everything that is not an A grade, hoping the readers will not notice a big drop in grades could be a mistake.

Contextualizing the Core Components

In addition to what the foundations ask endorsers to address in the institutional letter, advisors may choose to include information that gives context to the application. Letters may provide the following:

- **A snapshot of the college or university.** While readers will recognize the names of large state universities and the Ivies, they may not be able to place lesser-known schools. And colleges that are famous on one coast may be little known elsewhere. A *brief* description of the location and character of the institution may be helpful.
- **The context for the applicant's accomplishments within the institution.** Even if readers are familiar with the institution, they are unlikely to know details about specific campus activities or organizations, the prestige level of campus awards or scholarships, how difficult it is to get a summer research position, what it means for a candidate to be asked to be the student representative on a key campus committee, or how unusual it is for a student to go off campus to volunteer. What

is obvious to someone from the university or college may be opaque to them.
- **The university's grading and honors system.** Colleges and universities vary widely in terms of grading rubrics, standards for Latin honors or for Honors College participation, and requirements for a senior/honors thesis. It is hard to say what is typical because there are so many variations. A brief explanation of the institution's policies as they pertain to the applicant's accomplishments may be warranted.
- **The campus committee and endorsement process.** Campus endorsement processes vary widely. If the process is quite rigorous, it may be worth mentioning in *one sentence* that the decision was made by a group of institutional faculty and staff and not simply by the person who signs the letter.

Beyond the Core Components

If the endorsement letter *only* declares endorsement, points out how the student meets the foundation's criteria, and summarizes or clarifies the application materials, it will suffice. But the letter will be more compelling if it outlines something about applicants *not* included or emphasized elsewhere. The new information should bring to the fore special characteristics of applicants—something, perhaps, that brings out their humanity in ways that will make the readers want to meet them. (See the "Stocking Your Pantry" section below for ideas on how to find such material.) The endorser may want to include:

- **Something noteworthy from the campus interview.** The committee may have been wowed by the applicant's answer to a particularly tough question or impressed by coolness or diplomacy under pressure. As a result, endorsers may decide to include a quotation from a committee member.
- **A testimonial from someone who knows the candidate well but was not among the recommenders.** Very accomplished applicants often have more people willing and able to testify to their accomplishments than the application will

allow. People such as coaches and extracurricular organization directors often work closely with candidates and have seen their grit or compassion demonstrated in a specific incident with teammates or co-workers. A quick phone call or in-person chat with these individuals may yield useful quotations and illustrations that can be effectively woven into the letter. As a practice, the authors do not include quotations from peers or family members for the same reasons most foundations do not solicit recommendation letters from such individuals.

- **Needed context for an existing recommendation letter.** Some letters in the packet may lack detail to substantiate included praise or refer to situations that may need more context in order for the reviewers to understand. Check in with the writer and ask for more information and then include it with a direct reference to what that recommender said or let it stand on its own.
- **Information from a candidate's previous applications or recommendations.** Advisors who have essays or recommendation letters from a former application may be able to mine them for useful information. If drawing from such letters, however, advisors should ask permission from the writer.
- **Information from conversations with the applicant.** Whether it is notes about first impressions, responses to specific questions, or something about a student's background gleaned during a meeting prior to writing the endorsement letter, the endorser may want to include a revelatory anecdote or observation that comes straight from the nominee.

Getting Started

Before putting pen to paper (or fingertips to keyboard), here are some basic items to check off. Depending on the institutional processes, much or all of this can be done well in advance of deadlines. By working through these items and mapping out a work plan on the calendar, advisors will have time to collect information, write the endorsement letters and have them reviewed, signed, and submitted by the foundation's deadline.

Below are key items to remember:

- **Review submission deadlines for application materials and endorsement letters.** Place them on the calendar at the beginning of the application cycle. These are not necessarily the same as the candidate's deadline; advisors often need an extra day or two for letters once all the student's materials have been submitted. Pay attention to the timestamps and time zones. It is advisable to submit all materials when there still may be help available on the foundation side, just in case of last-minute emergencies.
- **Check the word or character count.** Write it down. It might be helpful to actually place the information on the calendar due date as well. It is far better to know the aimed for goal in the drafting stage than to find a sudden need to cut 200 words the day a letter is due.
- **Reserve calendar time to write letters.** It is good practice to estimate the amount of time needed for this work and mark that time on the calendar. The amount will vary depending on the length of the letter, the anticipated work volume, and who is responsible for writing the letter: Sometimes the advisor is solely responsible for writing letters; for some awards, members of the nominating committee write drafts or letters in their entirety. Depending on the timing of the nomination processes, advisors may be able to get a head start on writing or at least drafting letters before the fall semester begins.
- **Understand how to work with the president, dean, or provost.** For endorsement letters signed by the university president, provost, or dean, it is important to develop a good working relationship with that individual and office. Advisors need to understand the level of engagement the office expects in this process. In some cases, advisors only need to send the endorsement letter to the senior official and their assistant for review and signature. In other cases, that senior official may

want to meet with the nominees briefly or even add a line or paragraph to the letter before reviewing, editing, and signing it. Alternatively, endorsers may want an assistant or communications colleague to review and edit before they sign. It is vital to know what to expect and incorporate that in the timeline. Whenever there is a presidential transition, advisors should make an appointment to introduce themselves and their role and talk about the current process and any change the president or the staff would like to make. It is also imperative that advisors reach out early—about a month in advance is usually sufficient—to find out whether the senior official will be available to review and sign the letters in the proposed window of time. If they cannot, find out what will work for them and integrate that into the calendar.

Stocking Your Pantry

We recognize that advisors have varying amounts of time to devote to the crafting of an endorsement letter. We can often spend four hours writing a single letter, an amount of time that some may judge to be excessive or simply not possible. In this section, we outline the sources of information to collect for potential use in an endorsement letter.

Gather Institutional Information

Gathering the information below can help an endorser stay on top of relevant information about the institution and student body. Much of this, advisors can do well in advance of crunch time.

- **Keep a folder of institutional policies and data.** Part of the job in this letter is to place the candidate within the institutional context. That includes knowing specific details about the institution and nuances that may be relevant to highlight. Items that should be kept at the ready include thesis policies, grading policies, course credits, distribution requirements,

Latin honors, internal awards—both university-wide and departmental—and student demographics. The registrar's website, an academic policy handbook, eligibility requirements for Phi Beta Kappa and other honor societies, and information about an honors program or the institution's Honors College can prove helpful.
- **Read the student newspaper regularly.** It is a great way to keep abreast of emergent student issues and concerns. Doing so can help contextualize the applicant's leadership and other accomplishments.
- **Have a brief summary of the nomination process handy.** If needed, it can easily be added to the letter. Brevity here is key.

Gather Information About the Candidate

Now to the candidate. Endorsers have drafts of student essays and some or all of the letters of recommendation. What additional information would be important to provide an authentic and compelling portrait? Getting more information about the candidate's background, undergraduate experiences, aspirations, accomplishments, and challenges is particularly helpful. Advisors may also have specific questions about the candidate's proposal that need clarification. Below are different ways to acquire needed information.

- **Check the disciplinary standing of all candidates.** This work should be done at the internal application stage, often through a form or waiver. It is an obvious step but can be overlooked. Most candidates have no infractions or minor ones that do not merit inclusion in an application or letter. Occasionally there is something more significant (which we discuss in the next section).
- **Ask the candidate for a chronologically organized resumé.** Many online applications organize resumé items in thematic clusters. It is helpful to understand the chronology of the applicant's activities and accomplishments when crafting a narrative about the student.

- **Have the candidate write a brief autobiography or complete a questionnaire with additional tailored questions and/or interview the candidate.** These methods provide a quick, effective way to get to know the candidate in greater depth and discover important accomplishments to highlight in a letter. An applicant may have an unusual hobby that speaks to character. Perhaps there is an important aspect of the student's athletic, musical, or student government activity that does not appear in the essay or letters. In some cases, a paragraph about the applicant's personal background can illuminate their motivation for what they do. Again, advisors should ask the candidate's permission when using personal information they provide. This way, they will be prepared if it comes up in an interview.
- **Strike a balance between the letter and the application.** There may be relevant information about the candidate that they did not have the space to include or that may be better for the advisor to address. Some advisors take on the task of covering aspects of the applicant's personal history in the endorsement letter, allowing the applicant to focus their essays on other facets of their candidacy. This can be a good strategy for candidates trying to save space or to avoid crafting essays in which their personal stories overshadow their accomplishments. Advisors may also want to explain the significance or context of particular accomplishments. If relevant, explanations of personal challenges, gaps in the academic record, or other personal information may be more appropriately addressed in the endorsement letter. Again, in all cases, advisors should have the candidate's permission to share personal information and tell them what will be included in case it comes up in an interview.
- **Verify the candidate's claims.** It does occasionally happen that candidates embellish an accomplishment. Sometimes this is done innocently; other times candidates may feel a need to impress. Knowing what is an appropriate representation of the student can facilitate clarifications and necessary

conversations about the importance of accurate representation of accomplishments.

- **Do a digital search of the candidate.** Sometimes students forget to share interesting and relevant information. Sometimes they do not share important but negative information. A search at the start will help prevent unwelcome surprises. Discovering information early can lead to important conversations with the candidate.

Formatting and Style

Formatting is easy; style, less so. In formatting the letter, follow the specifications outlined in the fellowship application or guidance document. Stick to word and character counts or page limits, check if there is a salutation preference, and note if this is a pdf upload on letterhead with signature or content added to a text box. When sharing a letter for a president, provost, or dean, make sure they know what the format is as well.

Style, however, is more challenging. The first question is, Who signs the letter? Fellowships advisors, who are signing the letters in their own names, can take more liberties with language and content. It is still a professional letter, to be sure, but it is written in the advisor's voice and reflects a personal engagement with the candidate. If the advisor is writing on behalf of a president, provost, or dean, then tone and style become more complicated. The task is not only to do the candidate justice and be persuasive to the selection committee, but also to do so in someone else's voice and from their subject position, so it can be useful for the advisor to be familiar with writing style in question before beginning a draft.

In crafting the letter, advisors may want to consider the following suggestions:

- **Review content carefully.** Take time to review the content that has been collected and think about what is important to include. Look for illustrative examples or quotations about the student. Think about how the evidence supports the selection criteria and personal qualities or accomplishments that should be highlighted. An endorser may wish to give more space to one criterion over another, especially if that one is only weakly attested to in the recommendation letters. Pointing to how the candidate possesses all the criteria will demonstrate that the student is a good fit for the fellowship. Advisors always want to consider what key institutional and personal contexts to include.

- **Organize the structure of the letter.** The most straightforward approach aligns with the fellowship selection criteria. Think about the criteria mapped onto a six-paragraph essay: (1) introduction, (2) academics, (3) leadership, (4) extracurriculars, personal or other additional information, university/community context, (5) post-graduate purpose, and 6) conclusion. But depending on the fellowship and who is signing the letter, the advisor may want to experiment with this structure. Move paragraphs around and see how that changes the impact of the letter. If a candidate is unusually strong in one area, the essay might begin with that section. Once the organizational structure is set, it can become a model for other letters as long as it is appropriate to student and to award. Writing letters that feel and read formulaic can be problematic, but when pressed for time, it can be helpful to have a few models to use as a starting point.

- **Use specific examples and quotations to provide evidence to support generalizations.** It is much easier for a reader to grasp why someone is "a leader of outsized impact" if there are specific details outlining the leadership engagement and its impact. For example, an advisor might provide the number of students affected by the applicant's initiative, describe how a campus policy was changed as a result of their work, or explain how they garnered involvement from a large number of peers.

- **Keep paragraphs short and writing concise.** Delete the adverbs; use adjectives sparingly. In short, practice the advice that writing coaches give candidates.

- **Attend to font, size, line spacing.** Start with the instructions given for the endorsement letter as there may be specific guidance offered there. If a text box is provided and not an upload option, advisors will often have specific instructions about how to indent paragraphs (or not) and separate paragraphs. Font and font size will automatically be selected for the endorser. For pdf letter uploads, there may be less information. A rule of thumb is to make the letter easy to read. Typically, this means choosing a twelve-point font and single-spaced paragraphs with a space between paragraphs.
- **Get feedback on a near-final draft.** Ideally, this would be from someone on the committee who interviewed the candidate, but a colleague with excellent writing and editing skills is also a good choice. Catching any error is always helpful, but capturing the student well is also important. A letter reviewer can really help in the process by answering questions such as, Is the candidate represented appropriately given the selection criteria for this particular fellowship? Is the content organized in an effective way? Is the writing compelling?

Ultimately, the objective is to make the work of the awards committee readers as easy as possible. The endorser already knows the candidate's strengths, talents, and goals. The crucial question is whether readers will be able to understand those same strengths quickly and powerfully.

A Word About Generative AI

ChatGPT, Claude, Gemini, and other generative AI platforms have the potential to streamline the work of writing endorsement letters and perhaps even inspire ideas for composition and content. However, using AI also raises ethical questions and concerns about the writing process, content accuracy, overall quality of written work, and originality. Another consideration is that it is a rapidly changing technology that educational institutions are now grappling to understand how best to use. What we write here, for example, may be out of date by the time of publication. Yet it is a tool we encourage fellowships advisors to experiment with to discover its affordances and drawbacks.

For endorsement letters, we have found generative AI platforms to be helpful in suggesting an organizational structure or edits to an existing letter to meet the word or character count. The quality of the writing generated currently is far too general to replace the bespoke quality of an endorsement letter, or depending on the platform, it may add information that may or may not be true for the candidate.

With AI platforms, be mindful of privacy issues. In writing prompts, do not include personal identifying information, such as names or email addresses. Information shared through a prompt could potentially be shared in responses to other users. This is the reason we have not experimented with entering draft letters into AI platforms for suggested edits, relying instead on trusted human colleagues. These platforms vary in the degree of the writer's control over use of their information, so it is worth reviewing specific AI platform policies before selecting a platform.[3] Advisors should also be aware of specific AI guidance from foundations and home institutions. This, too, is a shifting landscape, particularly as enterprise AI systems become a staple of our workplaces. The best course is to become educated. Like any technology, generative AI may save time in some aspects of our work, but currently does not replace the detailed and individualized work that goes into crafting an endorsement letter.

Confidentiality, Truth, Bias, and Other Sticky Wickets

Confidentiality

There is nothing in a candidate's application that cannot be discussed in the endorsement letter. Everything in the application materials is fair game, from grades to any disclosures candidates make in their essays. As the endorsement letter writer, the advisor does not need to be concerned about violating the Faculty Educational Rights and Privacy Act (FERPA) when referring to information stated in the application materials since students are explicitly making that material available for review.

Sensitive Information

Generally, it is not advisable to disclose sensitive personal information about the candidate. Sometimes, however, to fully convey to the reader who the applicant is, advisors need to make judgment calls about including references to family history, traumatic events, identity, disability, and physical or mental health. Of course, advisors should always consult with the candidate about including this type of material.

Bias

As higher education professionals, we are conditioned to check our biases, especially negative ones. But what about positive bias? Many candidates for competitive awards are easy to like and admire, and we may try extra hard to promote these students in whose success we feel a personal investment. It is important to examine one's own partiality and ask, Is everything I am saying about the student fully true? Can I back up my claims? Am I giving this candidate excessive praise for my own personal or political reasons? Could I stand by my statements if called by a member of the national selection committee? Overselling and over-promising is not in the candidate's best interest at any point in the process. If the student receives a national interview, a mismatch between expectations produced by the letter and the candidate's actual performance could be disastrous for the student and may also affect the endorser's credibility. Save highest accolades for that once (or twice) in a lifetime candidate.

Conduct

Institutional endorsement implies that the endorser understands the foundation's selection criteria, that the candidate meets them, and that no relevant information about the student is being withheld.

In most cases, a student's transgressions and consequent disciplinary actions are relatively minor events in their college experience. If the candidate does have a significant conduct violation or a criminal record, advisors may be expected to disclose that information to the foundation. Contact the foundation regarding its expectations. Advisors should also consult with the institution's deans and legal counsel—and the candidate—for the best way to move forward.

Endorsements ≠ Evaluations

No one is perfect, and even the best candidates will have flaws. Should endorsement writers address their candidates' limitations? Here it is best to look at the foundation's directives. Is there a request to assess the candidate by comparing them to others? In such a case, follow the directions, even if it hurts. Is there explicit encouragement to balance the good with the bad in the letter? If so, endorsers should focus on the student's potential for growth. Generally, writers should tread carefully, keeping in mind the purpose of the endorsement, which is institutional support for the nominee.

On "Trying Too hard"

Don't Try Harder

Regarding endorsement letters, Truman Foundation Deputy Executive Director Tara Yglesias writes, "Everyone's trying too hard."[4] This is a function of the high stakes of the Truman competition and other prestigious fellowships—for the candidate, for the candidate's institution, and for the individual advisor. So, should advisors spend an extra hour trying to understand, then explain, the applicant's theoretical physics project? We believe the answer is no. There is no need to become an expert on the candidate's work or even to understand it well. It is the job of the candidate, and secondarily of their recommenders, to explain to the reader the significance of the candidate's research. Stepping back and letting the nominee's application do its own persuading frees the endorsement writer to present the candidacy in a positive—but not blinding—light, using straightforward language that conveys relevant information.

Let Go of Ego

Most endorsement writers have had moments of struggle, whether with writer's block, a dearth of persuasive arguments, pressure stemming from writing on behalf of a superior, and so on—all while facing tight deadlines. It is important to let go of an attachment to the student's success, a need to impress the readers, and any excessively high standards. The endorsement letter is just one of many parts of a fellowship application, and it represents only a small part of the advisor's work with the candidate.

Accept the Good (Enough)

We find that the exercise of writing the endorsement can be clarifying. When an advisor struggles to come up with things to say about a candidate, it may indicate that there is not, in fact, all that much to say. In this situation, advisors should feel comfortable writing a good but not stellar letter. On the other hand, if the struggle is which of the candidate's many accomplishments to highlight, then the advisor may quickly realize the candidate is truly competitive.

Conclusion

Writing a letter of endorsement for a stellar candidate should be a positive experience. It stands as a coda for the process of working with a great applicant, and it is an opportunity to showcase that work to the senior administrators signing the letters. It is also a chance to represent the institution well and allow it to take pride in their nominees' contributions to society. But in the pressurized atmosphere of the application season, advisors rarely take a moment to reflect on their role in the success of individuals and institutions. Do take that moment. Excellent candidates will do well (whether or not they are called to interview) in part thanks to the time endorsers took to do their jobs properly.

Notes

1. Harry S. Truman Scholarship Foundation, "Notes for Advisors," n.d., accessed February 28, 2025, https://www.truman.gov/apply/advisors/notes-advisors.
2. Foundations generally expect endorsement letters and letters of recommendation not to have been shared with candidates. We confirmed this assumption through email communication with representatives of several major foundations, including the Rhodes Trust, the Truman Foundation, and the Beinecke Scholarship Program in January 2025.
3. Michael Alexander Riegler, "AI Assistant Privacy: What Claude, ChatGPT, and Gemini Users Should Know," Medium, June 26, 2024, https://medium.com/@michael_79773/ai-assistant-privacy-what-claude-chatgpt-and-gemini-users-should-now-7d3f5cae9e5d.
4. Tara Yglesias, "Making a Good Truman Nomination Letter Slightly Better," conference presentation handout, National Association of Fellowships Advisors Biennial Conference, "Focusing on the Scholar in the Scholarship Process," Atlanta, GA, July 2013.

12

NAFA at Twenty-Five

The Origin Story

JANE MORRIS

The National Association of Fellowships Advisors has turned twenty-five in 2025—amazing! In her 2013 essay, "Expanding Access through Organized Support—The History and Purpose of the National Association of Fellowships Advisors,"[1] Beth Powers chronicled the growth of the organization from the early days of ad hoc scholarship advising for a handful of scholarships, to small conferences held by foundations for facilitating communications with campus representatives, to the first national conferences where advisors gathered to share best practices for democratizing the process of fellowships advising. My aim in this chapter is to explore the motivations for the founding of the organization through conversations with some of the founding and early members about the experience of fellowship advising pre-NAFA and the realizations of the benefits that students, institutions, and foundations derived from participation in nationally competitive scholarships.

In thinking about how to tell the story of NAFA's beginnings, I considered approaching the topic from the lens of wisdom-mining. From decision-making in the board room to knowledge extraction in data centers, the concept of what Aristotle called *phronesis*—practical wisdom—is making a comeback. The University of Chicago's Center for Practical Wisdom defines this wisdom as "practical decision making that leads to human flourishing."[2] The decisions made by the NAFA founders were without doubt the result of such practical wisdom.

As a former scientist, I have always been fascinated by the crystalization process—the establishment of a highly structured substance from a single seed. Nucleation occurs only when the conditions are ideal (typically when a system is under stress) for the formation of a new thermodynamic phase of matter. Like the formation of a highly structed three-dimensional crystal lattice, NAFA grew from the seed of a good idea forged by the intention to make these transformational opportunities more broadly accessible.

To explore the stressors that drove the phase shift creating NAFA, I developed a set of questions[3] that I sent to eight founding or early members of NAFA.[4] I later brought the group together for a conversation to dive deeper into the stories about the founding and the problems they were trying to solve by starting the organization. We examined how fellowships advising has changed since the founding of NAFA, and we considered what scholarship advising might look like as colleges and universities evolve. The conversation was facilitated by Andrew Ceperley, a higher education executive coach and consultant with extensive experience in university administration, career management, experiential education, student life, and alumni development complemented by expertise in corporate and nonprofit recruitment, strategic communications, and diversity and inclusion.[5]

Discussing NAFA origins is not possible without first including the voices of two iconic figures who were never part of NAFA yet played a critical role in its founding: Nancy Twiss and Louis Blair. In the years before NAFA, Nancy Twiss advised applicants for nationally competitive scholarships at Kansas State University for sixteen years, amassing an impressive record of sixty recipients for the Rhodes, Marshall, Truman, and Goldwater scholarships. On her retirement from KSU in 1996, Twiss served as a consultant to other universities seeking to establish similar advising practices at their schools. One such consultation was at Baylor University in 1999 at the invitation of associate dean Elizabeth Vardaman. In her essay, "Reflections on the Value of Being in the Room Where It Happens," Vardaman recalled her lasting impression of Twiss from that consultation: "She radiated a commitment to students and also embodied a gratitude for and devotion to the genius of scholarship programs and the foundations that funded the scholarships: 'Because of them, students all over the country are identifying issues central to their concerns, weighing what they want their lives to count for, and determining concrete steps toward achieving those ends.'"[6]

In a September 14, 2001, interview with *The Chronicle of Higher Education*, Twiss commented on the value of scholarship advising:

> Most of us will not find answers to the causes of cancer, or solve the problems of homelessness, or defuse international conflicts, but we feel that through our advising, we may be able to make a small but pivotal contribution to our students' ultimate work. . . . It seems to me that [our students] represent an unequivocal reply to Margaret Mead, when she famously said: "Never doubt that a small group of thoughtful, committed [people] can change the world. Indeed, it's the only thing that ever has."[7]

Clearly, Nancy Twiss's wisdom in appreciating the value of the scholarship advising process serves as a foundation for the purpose of NAFA to "promote educational, ethical, and equitable fellowships practices" by "envisioning a higher education landscape that recognizes, prioritizes, and honors the transformative value of fellowships processes."[8]

The Harry S. Truman Scholarship Foundation also played a vital role in creating the framework for NAFA. Established through an act of Congress in 1975, with the mission to educate future leaders and public servants, the Truman Foundation awarded the first scholarships in 1977–1978.[9] With this focus on education and public service, the Truman Foundation contributed to the establishment of NAFA through the efforts of Louis Blair, who served as the executive secretary from 1989 to 2006. Blair, with a master's degree in engineering from MIT and a career in government service before taking his leadership role for the Truman Foundation, hosted workshops for Truman campus representatives in 1997 and 1998 in Roanoke, Virginia, and Valley Forge, Pennsylvania, respectively, to communicate with campuses more effectively about the scholarship.

In 1999, Blair hired Mary Tolar as the Truman deputy executive secretary. Tolar, a Truman and Rhodes Scholar from KSU, had been mentored by Nancy Twiss. That was the year that the Truman Foundation and Marshall Aid Commission joined forces to hold a conference for campus representatives at the University of Arkansas, hosted by Suzanne McCray and where Nancy Twiss was the keynote speaker. This event was the seed crystal that led a group of fellowships advisors, organized by Mary Tolar, to a meeting in Chicago in the summer of 2000. The National Association of Fellowships Advisors was thus established, and the first official conference was held the following summer in Tulsa, Oklahoma.

When asked about early stories of NAFA, Mary Tolar reflected on Louis Blair's motivation for bringing the campus representatives together after hearing from the newly selected scholars at the Truman Scholars Leadership Week about their experiences with their advisors:

> The Truman Scholarship application was designed as a learning and discovery tool, not solely a means of informing selection. The scholarship itself also had stated commitments and goals for geographic and other diversity, so the foundation was invested in reaching students across all institutions—invested in access. So, he [Blair] began by inviting Truman Faculty Reps to meet—to recognize their critical role in the Foundation's work, learn from their work with students, and share best practices—and start building a network, a community.[10]

The idea of NAFA was recognition in these gatherings of the growing interest and investment in scholarship competitions among institutions, the value the process had for student growth and development, and the ethical requirements and obligations associated with working with students and for institutions in competitive settings. And if convenings were the source of addressing these shared concerns and opportunities, perhaps a larger, diverse group could assure greater access and participation—among institutions and sponsors/foundations.

With this understanding about the history of NAFA's roots, what led campus scholarship advisors in the late 1990s to join Tolar in Chicago? When asked about their experiences prior to NAFA, the early NAFA founders whom I interviewed described their work as isolated—either as faculty with scholarship advising duties or operating in an office of one—and uniquely pressured by their administrations—"Any winners this year?" The opportunity to meet with others similarly positioned at their institutions offered advisors a community and a professional identity. In sharing experiences and best practices, it also provided an ethos for the practice of scholarship advising. What evolved was a framework for defining the benefits of participation in nationally competitive scholarships beyond "winning," i.e., the "value of the process" that we all share.[11] Ann Brown, NAFA's first secretary, explained what led her to joining the founding NAFA Board:

> It [NAFA] is founded on solid values and ethical principles. On wanting the best for the students and having honest and clear conversations about these important issues. Scholarship advising is both an art and a science, and NAFA helped demystify the process. The job is often a one-person operation on a campus, and no one [outside the office] understands the work, so NAFA provides a network for people to find support.[12]

Democratizing the scholarship advising process—a core NAFA value—allowed for a greater range of institutions and students to engage in scholarship application processes.[13] As institutions became more invested in the fellowships enterprise, there was also an emphasis on promoting and supporting co-curricular experiences such as undergraduate research and study abroad, which enriched academic learning and helped students build credentials that not only made them more competitive for scholarships, but also created greater opportunities for postgraduate education and careers. Some schools launched courses such as the "Windows to the World," a seminar focused on current events, writing, and interview skills created by Bob Graalman at Oklahoma State University. Many institutions developed multipurpose offices combining fellowships advising with undergraduate research, international studies, or career services. Such synergies have contributed to the competitiveness of student participants, helping them with both experiential learning and reflection on that learning as they develop their scholarship applications under the guidance of their advisors.

The establishment of NAFA also provided foundations with broader outreach to colleges and universities beyond those institutions that had typically participated in their competitions. This co-evolution of campus and scholarship foundations, forged by NAFA, resulted in greater representation among scholarship recipients and their institutions while creating more opportunities for students as foundations refined their goals and their processes. The recognition of student successes by the foundations and the schools producing those students enhanced institutional reputations and facilitated outreach efforts by the scholarship foundations. The Fulbright Top Producers list each year is a perfect example of this dynamic, as news stories of freshly minted Fulbrighters appear in campus publications, on social media, and on websites where the Fulbright badge of recognition is proudly displayed.

In the early days of NAFA, there were no postgraduate degree programs focused on scholarship advising. How did this community of advisors find their way to fellowships advising? For most, it was an indirect path; for many, it was equal parts serendipity and industry. NAFA's fifth president, Paula Warrick, who has a PhD in art history focused on portraiture in the late eighteenth and early nineteenth centuries, had been teaching art history and lecturing in a museum setting when she learned about a scholarships advising position at American University. About the connections between her training, her experience, and scholarship advising, she reflected:

> A few different aspects of my training and early professional background drew me to scholarships advising. I am drawn to the issue of how people choose to represent themselves to the world when they have to be selective in order to convey a message [about] their identity. I also appreciated the way in which studying portraits, which

often entails reading private diaries and letters, allowed me to connect with another person across the barrier of time.[14]

The NAFA founders had a wide range of academic backgrounds and experiences. Bob Graalman, NAFA's first president, has a PhD in English and was assistant to the dean of arts and sciences at Oklahoma State University before becoming the founding director of OSU's Office of Scholar Development and Undergraduate Research. Many of the founding members were honors program directors, who, like John Richardson, recognized the need for scholarship advising and established a role within their programs to best serve applicants. Some of us pivoted to higher education from careers outside academia. Ann Brown worked as a nurse and taught nursing at a technical college before moving to Ohio University, first as a development officer and later as an assistant dean in the Honors College. I had a career as a research scientist in the pharmaceutical industry before finding my home within higher education and fellowships advising.

Beth Powers, with an undergraduate degree in French, experience as an English teaching assistant in China, and a master's degree in education, found her way to scholarship advising at Kansas State University by taking a detour away from a job offer as an undergraduate pre-major advisor to a position in scholarship advising with Nancy Twiss. She observed:

> Somewhere between the job offer and my start date, I was asked to consider the scholarships position. Knowing little about national scholarships, I reached out to a high school friend, Mary Tolar, recalling that she had won some of these awards. Little did I know that I was going to get the opportunity to be mentored by Nancy Twiss, a veteran advisor who had helped many K-State students win major national awards in the 70s, 80s, and 90s. Fortune found me prepared to take advantage of learning from this wonderful person whose guidance helped set my professional trajectory.[15]

Those who entered the nascent field of scholarship advising in the early days of NAFA were frequently entering newly established roles at their schools and had little direct experience with nationally competitive fellowships. What qualified them for advising scholarship applicants were highly transferrable skills from their prior academic and life experiences. One of the many successes of NAFA is that scholarship advising has become recognized as a profession in higher education with opportunities for career advancement. One needs only to observe the evolution of the NAFA "Survey of the Profession" from a six-page document in 2012 to twenty-plus pages in 2023, to understand how the work has grown—both in scope and importance—over the years.

The profession of scholarship advising has had a profound impact on the early NAFA members I interviewed. For many of them, it set the path to leadership roles within their institutions. Mary Tolar, who is now the dean of the Staley School for Leadership at Kansas State, explained how her path started as a student applicant:

> The four questions that shaped my own fellowship advising journey—from candidate to advisor—continue to shape how I approach my work as a dean supporting students across the university. It's how I understand my work in higher education. Who am I? What do I care about? What kind of contribution do I want to make in the world? How am I going to get there? Being asked, and responding to those questions as a college sophomore, changed my trajectory. Continuing to respond to those questions at various times in my life affirmed or altered my trajectory. Asking and listening to others respond and share their aspirations has motivated me, inspired me, and given me hope.[16]

Suzanne McCray, the vice-provost for Enrollment Management at the University of Arkansas, reflected on how scholarship advising widened her perspective and opened her to new career possibilities:

> Being an advisor, who encourages students to be ambitious and put themselves out there, had a significant impact on my own life when a professional opportunity opened up for me. Early in my career, I might have been more reluctant to embrace it. I remember

thinking—what would I encourage a student to do? I jumped outside my comfort zone, and it was a great decision to do so.[17]

What started as an organization for supporting the process of fellowships advising for undergraduate students has grown in important ways as higher education—and society—have evolved over the years. NAFA has changed in that its outreach includes advising graduate students as well as undergraduates. There is also far greater emphasis on centering diversity, equity, and inclusion in our work. During her tenure as president, Paula Warrick prioritized both the development of a five-year strategic plan and the first iteration of the NAFA code of ethics. She offered her observations about the important ways NAFA has grown over the years:

> The early history of NAFA has entailed putting an infrastructure in place to give the organization legs. A tremendous amount of work was done in those early years, including obtaining 501(c)3 status, establishing founding documents, putting the organization on a sound financial footing, establishing a code of ethics, and creating the conference proceedings, which gives us an identity as a body. I am impressed by the grassroots efforts of our members that led to wonderful outcomes—such as our summer workshops and international study tours. I have been impressed by the way in which scholarship programs and foundations have contributed to the growth of NAFA. The most notable recent developments I have seen in NAFA have to do with grappling with equity and inclusion and reassessing some of the standard narratives that appear in autobiographical essays.[18]

Before we concluded our conversation, founders were asked to consider the following question: "Given that higher education is changing and facing a variety of challenges, what do you see as the future of fellowships advising on college campuses?" Reflecting the efforts of colleges and universities to build greater diversity on their campuses, NAFA maintains a strong commitment to diversity, equity, and inclusion, one of our founding principles, despite challenges such as the Supreme Court decision of 2023 have posed and the current political climate. NAFA conferences, workshops, and publications focus on best practices for developing broader outreach in order to address issues of inclusion and equity.

Another area of change and growth is technology. Bob Graalman, who retired from fellowships advising in 2013, recalled visiting his former office and observing how much information was available online that had not been in the past. He pointed to the impact of technology and social media on advising work. Since the pandemic forced advisors to move work with students and faculty to Zoom, we have adapted to engaging in a virtual environment, making it far easier to convene faculty committees and offer advising to alumni and students who are away from campus. Maintaining advising notes and managing applications have become more manageable with platforms such as Handshake, Slate, and SurveyMonkey Apply.

Now artificial intelligence and large language models such as ChatGPT have entered the world of scholarship advising. Even as many of our student applicants are proposing research using AI systems to improve society, we are facing ethical challenges concerning the use of ChatGPT for scholarship applications. The Rhodes Scholarship "Information for Candidates" recently added instructions for using this technology in preparing application materials.

Change is inevitable, and one of the factors that has contributed to the success of NAFA over the years is its ability to evolve as new issues on campuses and in the world arise. This adaptability was woven into the principles on which NAFA was founded, as Elizabeth Vardaman, associate dean and director emeritus of Engaged Learning for the College of Arts and Sciences at Baylor University, noted when reflecting on the success of NAFA:

> NAFA addressed a need that was pervasive in college cultures. It also provided excellent resources and enriched conversations for the professionals who run these programs as well as for the foundations that seek to help us identify great potential leaders across many fields. Working toward many common goals, both foundations and universities within NAFA are identifying and nurturing students who may become leaders in their fields. In many ways, NAFA has filled a gap in

higher education and enhanced the college experience for countless students, whether or not they ultimately grasp the desired scholarship's golden ring.[19]

As we approach NAFA's silver anniversary, I would like to take a moment to reflect on the virtue of wisdom. On the website of the University of Chicago's Center for Practical Wisdom, Howard Nussbaum, the director, explains their mission: "We seek to understand the foundations of wisdom such as perspective taking, reflection, epistemic humility, insight, emotional intelligence, and perseverance in intellectual struggle."[20] There is no better evidence for the success of NAFA and the impact of "practical decision making that leads to human flourishing" than the thank you note Jane Curlin received when she was a scholarship advisor before becoming the director of Education Programs for the Udall Foundation. The message was brief, but it was profound: "You almost make me believe I am worth it."[21] With gratitude to the NAFA founders for their wisdom, I am excited to see what the next twenty-five years brings. The seed crystal that was started in Chicago at the turn of the century is still growing—and it is beautiful.

Notes

1. Beth Powers, "Expanding Access Through Organized Support: The History and Purpose of the National Association of Fellowships Advisors," in *All In: Expanding Access Through Nationally Competitive Awards*, ed. Suzanne McCray (Fayetteville: University of Arkansas Press, 2013), 119–26.
2. University of Chicago Center for Practical Wisdom, "The Scientific Understanding of Wisdom," n.d., accessed February 28, 2025, https://wisdomcenter.uchicago.edu/.
3. Interview questions:
    - Tell me about yourself in the time before NAFA
        ◦ Schooling
        ◦ Career path
    - How did you find your way to fellowship advising?
    - As founding or early members of NAFA, can you share some stories about the early days of NAFA?

- What were the issues that first prompted organizing fellowship advising as a profession?
- Who organized the first meetings to discuss and brainstorm about forming NAFA?
- Who was involved in those first meetings?
- When was the first study tour? How did it go?
- How has NAFA/fellowships advising changed over the years?
- How has fellowships advising changed you?
- How do you measure success in fellowships advising?
- Why do you think NAFA has been so successful?
- Other thoughts/observations/recommendations?

4. The group of early NAFA leaders who were kind enough to share their experiences for this essay are: Mary Tolar, dean of the Staley School for Leadership at Kansas State University (former Deputy Executive Secretary of the Truman Foundation); Suzanne McCray, vice provost for Enrollment Management and dean of Admissions and Nationally Competitive Awards at the University of Arkansas (past NAFA president and founding member); Robert Graalman, former director of Scholar Development & Undergraduate Research at Oklahoma State University, (founding NAFA president); Elizabeth Vardaman, former associate dean and director of Engaged Learning for the College of Arts and Sciences at Baylor University, (founding board member); Beth Powers, director of Scholar Development and Undergraduate Research at Kansas State University (past NAFA President); John Richardson, former professor of chemistry and director of the Honors Program at the University of Louisville, (founding—and long-serving—NAFA treasurer); Ann Brown, former director of the Office of Nationally Competitive Awards at Ohio University, (founding NAFA secretary); Paula Warrick, director of the Office of Merit Awards at American University (past NAFA president); Jane Curlin, former director of Education Programs for the Morris K and Stewart L Udall Foundation, (founding board member).

5. See Andrew T. Ceperley and Associates, webpage, n.d., accessed February 28, 2025, https://andrewtceperley.com/about/.

6. Elizabeth Vardaman, "Reflections on the Value of Being in the Room Where It Happens," in *Roads Less Traveled and Other Perspectives on Nationally Competitive Scholarships*, ed. Suzanne McCray and Joanne Brzinski (Fayetteville: University of Arkansas Press, 2017), 161–69.

7. "Scholarship Advising, A View from the Trenches," *Chronicle of Higher Education*, September 14, 2001, https://www.chronicle.com/article/scholarship-advising-a-view-from-the-trenches/.

8. NAFA, "About NAFA: Purpose, Vision, and Strategic Approach," n.d., accessed February 28, 2025, https://www.nafadvisors.org/about-us/purpose-strategic-approach-and-vision/.
9. Harry S. Truman Scholarship Foundation, "Our History: A Living Memorial," n.d., accessed February 28, 2025, https://www.truman.gov/about-us/our-history.
10. Mary Tolar, personal communication, August 2023.
11. Suzanne McCray (ed.), *Beyond Winning: National Scholarship Competitions and the Student Experience* (Fayetteville: University of Arkansas Press, 2005).
12. Ann Brown, personal communication, August 2023.
13. NAFA, "ABOUT NAFA: Values and Code of Ethics," n.d., accessed February 28, 2025, https://www.nafadvisors.org/about-us/values-and-code-of-ethics/.
14. Paula Warrick, personal communication, August 2023.
15. Beth Powers, personal communication, August 2023.
16. Mary Tolar, personal communication, August 2023.
17. Suzanne McCray, personal communication, August 2023.
18. Paula Warrick, personal communication, August 2023.
19. Elizabeth Vardaman, personal communication, August 2023.
20. Howard C. Nusbaum, "Welcome from the Center Director and Founder," University of Chicago Center for Practical Wisdom, n.d. accessed February 28, 2025, https://wisdomcenter.uchicago.edu/welcome-center-director-founder.
21. Jane Curlin, personal communication, August 2023.

NATIONAL ASSOCIATION OF FELLOWSHIPS ADVISORS MEMBERS

Executive Officers

President: Megan Friddle, Emory University (2023–2025)

Vice President: Robyn Curtis, Clemson University (2023–2025; president 2025–2027)

Communications Director: Cassidy Alvarado, Loyola Marymount University (2023–2024); Jennifer Staton, University of Alabama at Huntsville (2024–2025)

Secretary: Anne Wallen, Rutgers University (2023–2025)

Treasurer: Dana Kuchem, University of Richmond (2021–2025)

Foundation Representative

Christian Tanja, Knight-Hennessy Scholars (2022–2025)

Members at Large

Susan Albrecht, Wabash College (2023–2025)

Heidi Bauer-Clapp, University of Massachusetts–Amherst (2023–2027)

Kylla Benes, University of Montana (2024–2025)

Brittany Davis, University of South Florida (2023–2027)

Kurt Davis, New York University, (2021–2024)

Alsace-Lorraine Gallop, North Carolina Agricultural and Technical State University (2021–2025)

Alicia Hayes, University of California Berkeley (2024–2025)

Ashley Kuntz, Florida International University (2021–2025)

Eric Myers, Princeton University (2023–2027)

Terumi Rafferty-Osaki, Northeastern University (2021–2025)

Meredith Raucher Sisson, Virginia Commonwealth University (2023–2027)

Shania Siron, Reed College (2023–2024)

Foundations

American-Scandinavian Foundation
American Society for Engineering Education
Amgen Foundation (Harvard University)
The Asia Foundation
Astronaut Scholarship Foundation
Carnegie Endowment for International Peace/James C. Gathier Junior Fellows Program
Carnegie Mellon University Rales Fellows Program
Center for the Study of the Presidency and Congress
Clinton Foundation: Clinton Global Initiative University
Critical Language Scholarship (CLS) Program
DAAD German Academic Exchange Service (Deutscher Akademischer Auslandsdienst)
Diplomatic Fellowships, Howard University
Ellison Scholars Program
English-Speaking Union of the United States
Fulbright Commission Hungary
Gates Cambridge Trust
General David H. Petraeus Center for Emerging Leaders
Goldwater Scholarship Foundation
Harry S. Truman Scholarship Foundation
Hertz Foundation
The Honor Society of Phi Kappa Phi
Institute of Current World Affairs
Institute of International Education—Boren Awards
Institute of International Education—Fulbright US Student Program
Institute of International Education—Gilman International Program
Institute of International Education—Quad Fellowships
Jack Kent Cooke Foundation
James Madison Memorial Fellowship Foundation
Knight-Hennessy Scholars, Stanford University

Luce Scholars Program, Henry Luce Foundation
Marshall Aid Commemoration Commission
McCall MacBain Scholarships at McGill
Meridian International Center
The Morris K. Udall and Stewart L. Udall Foundation
NAACP Legal Defense Fund Marshall-Motley Scholars Program
The National Bureau of Asian Research
Pat Tillman Foundation
Paul and Daisy Soros Fellowships For New Americans
Payne Fellowship Program
The Posse Foundation
Princeton in Asia
Public Policy and International Affairs Program
The Rhodes Trust
Samvid Ventures
Schwarzman Scholars
Stephen S. Schwarzman Educational Foundation
Thomas R. Pickering Fellowship
US-Ireland Alliance & Mitchell Scholarship Program
US-UK Fulbright Commission
Victims of Pan Am Flight 103 Legacy Award
The Washington Center for Internships and Academic
Watson Foundation
The Winston Churchill Foundation of the United States

UK Members

Durham University
Imperial College London
Queen's University Belfast
University College London
University of Cambridge
University of Nottingham
University of Sheffield
University of St. Andrews
University of Warwick

University Members
Adelphi University
Albert Einstein College of Medicine
Alma College
American University
Amherst College
Anderson University
Appalachian State University
Arizona State University
Arkansas State University
Auburn University
Augsburg University
Babson College
Ball State University
Bard College
Barnard College
Baruch College, City University of New York
Bates College
Baylor University
Belmont University
Bennington College
Binghamton University
Birmingham City Schools
Boise State University
Boston University
Bowdoin College
Bowling Green State University
Brandeis University
Bridgewater State University
Brigham Young University
Brown University
Bryn Mawr College
Bucknell University
Butler University
California Institute of Technology

California Polytechnic State University, San Luis
California State University, East Bay
California State University, Monterey Bay
Carleton College
Carnegie Mellon University
Case Western University
The Catholic University of America
Central College
Central Michigan University
Centre College
Christendom College
The Citadel
City College of New York
Claremont McKenna College
Clarkson University
Clemson University
Coastal Carolina University
Coe College
Coker University
Colby College
Colgate University
College of Charleston
The College of New Jersey
College of Saint Benedict
College of Staten Island
College of the Holy Cross
Colorado College
Colorado School of Mines
Colorado State University
Columbia University
Concordia College
Connecticut College
Cornell University
Dartmouth College
Davidson College
Denison University

DeSales University
Dickinson College
Doane University
Dominican University
Drake University
Drexel University
Drury University
Duke Kunshan University
Duke University
Duquesne University
Eastern Kentucky University
Eastern Michigan University
East Tennessee State University
Eckerd College
Elizabethtown College
Elmhurst University
Elon University
Embry-Riddle Aeronautical University
Emerson College
Emmanuel College
Emory University
Fairfield University
Florida Atlantic University
Florida Gulf Coast University
Florida International University
Florida State University
Fordham University
Fort Hays State University
Franklin & Marshall College
Fulbright University Vietnam
Furman University
George Mason University
Georgetown University
George Washington University
Georgia College and State University
Georgia Institute of Technology

Georgia State University
Grand Canyon University
Grand Valley State University
Grinnell College
Gustavus Adolphus College
Hamilton College
Hampden-Sydney College
Harding University
Harvard College
Harvard University
Haverford College
Hobart and William Smith Colleges
Hope College
Hunter College
Indiana University, Bloomington
Indiana University, Indianapolis
Iowa State University
Jacksonville University
James Madison University
John Jay College
Johns Hopkins University
Juniata College
Kalamazoo College
Kansas State University
Kennesaw State University
Kenyon College
Knox College
Lafayette College
Lawrence University
Lebanon Valley College
Lehigh University
Lehman College, City University of New York
Le Moyne College
Lewis & Clark College
Liberty University
Louisiana State University

Loyola Marymount University
Loyola University Chicago
Loyola University Maryland
Lubbock Christian University
Luther College
Macalester College
Marist College
Marquette University
Marshall University
Massachusetts Institute of Technology
McKendree University
Mercer University
Miami University
Michigan State University
Middlebury College
Middle Tennessee State University
Millsaps College
Minnesota State University Mankato
Mississippi State University
Mississippi Valley State University
Missouri University of Science and Technology
Montgomery College
Morgan State University
Mount Holyoke College
Mount Mary University
Mount Saint Mary's University, Maryland
Muhlenberg College
Murray State University
New College of Florida
New Jersey Institute of Technology
New Mexico State University
New York University
New York University Abu Dhabi
New York University Shanghai
North Carolina Agricultural and Technical State University
North Carolina State University

Northeastern University
Northern Arizona University
Northern Illinois University
North Park University
Northwestern University
Oberlin College
Occidental College
Ohio Northern University
The Ohio State University
Ohio University
Oklahoma State University
Old Dominion University
Oregon Institute of Technology
Oregon State University
Pace University
Pacific Lutheran University
Pennsylvania State University
Pennsylvania State University Erie
Pierce College
Pitzer College
Pomona College
Portland State University
Prairie View A&M University
Pratt Institute
Princeton University
Providence College
Purdue University
Queens College, City University of New York
Ramapo College of New Jersey
Reed College
Rensselaer Polytechnic Institute
Rhode Island College
Rhode Island School of Design
Rhodes College
Rice University
Ringling College of Art and Design

Roanoke College
Robert Morris University
Rochester Institute of Technology
Rollins College
Rowan University
Rutgers University–Camden
Rutgers University–Newark
Rutgers University–New Brunswick
Saint Joseph's University
Saint Louis University
Salem College
Salem State University
Salisbury University
Samford University
San Diego State University
San Francisco State University
Santa Clara University
Sarah Lawrence College
Scripps College
Seattle University
Siena College
Simmons University
Skidmore College
Slippery Rock University
Smith College
Southern Illinois University, Carbondale
Southern Methodist University
Southwestern University
Spelman College
Stanford University
St. Catherine University
St. Edward's University
Stetson University
Stevens Institute of Technology
St. John's College, Annapolis
St. John's University

St. Lawrence University
St. Mary's College of Maryland
St. Olaf College
State University of New York Geneseo
State University of New York New Paltz
State University of New York Old Westbury
State University of New York Oswego
Stonehill College
Stony Brook University, State University of New York
Suffolk University
Susquehanna University
Swarthmore College
Syracuse University
Tarleton State University
Temple University
Tennessee Tech University
Texas A&M University
Texas Christian University
Texas State University
Texas Tech University
Towson University
Transylvania University
Trinity College
Truman State University
Tufts University
Tulane University
Union College
United States Air Force Academy
University at Albany, State University of New York
University at Buffalo, State University of New York
University of Alabama
University of Alabama at Birmingham
University of Alabama in Huntsville
University of Arizona
University of Arkansas
University of California, Berkeley

University of California, Davis
University of California, Irvine
University of California, Los Angeles
University of California, Riverside
University of California, Santa Barbara
University of California, Santa Cruz
University of Central Arkansas
University of Central Florida
University of Chicago
University of Cincinnati
University of Colorado Boulder
University of Connecticut
University of Dayton
University of Delaware
University of Denver
University of Georgia
University of Hawaiʻi at Hilo
University of Hawaiʻi at Mānoa
University of Houston
University of Idaho
University of Illinois at Chicago
University of Illinois at Urbana Champaign
University of Iowa
University of Kansas
University of Kentucky
University of Louisville
University of Lynchburg
University of Maine–Orono
University of Maryland, Baltimore County
University of Maryland, College Park
University of Massachusetts Amherst
University of Massachusetts Boston
University of Massachusetts Lowell
University of Miami
University of Michigan, Ann Arbor
University of Minnesota, Rochester

University of Minnesota, Twin Cities
University of Mississippi
University of Missouri
University of Missouri–Kansas City
University of Montana
University of Nebraska–Lincoln
University of Nebraska at Omaha
University of Nevada Las Vegas
University of New Hampshire
University of New Mexico
University of North Alabama
University of North Carolina at Chapel Hill
University of North Carolina at Charlotte
University of North Carolina at Greensboro
University of North Carolina at Wilmington
University of North Carolina School of the Arts
University of North Dakota
University of North Florida
University of North Georgia
University of Northern Iowa
University of North Texas
University of Notre Dame
University of Oklahoma
University of Oregon
University of Pennsylvania
University of Pittsburgh
University of Portland
University of Puget Sound
University of Rhode Island
University of Richmond
University of Rochester
University of San Diego
University of South Carolina
University of South Dakota
University of Southern California
University of Southern Mississippi

University of South Florida
University of Tennessee at Chattanooga
University of Tennessee, Knoxville
University of Texas at Austin
University of Texas at Dallas
University of Texas at El Paso
University of Texas at San Antonio
University of Texas Rio Grande Valley
University of the Pacific
University of Toledo
University of Tulsa
University of Utah
University of Vermont
University of Virginia
University of Virginia's College at Wise
University of Washington
University of Washington Bothell
University of Washington Tacoma
University of West Georgia
University of Wisconsin–Madison
University of Wyoming
Ursinus College
United States Coast Guard Academy
United States Military Academy West Point
Utah State University
Vanderbilt University
Vassar College
Villanova University
Virginia Commonwealth University
Virginia Military Institute
Virginia Tech University
Wabash College
Wake Forest University
Wartburg College
Washburn University
Washington and Lee University

Washington College
Washington State University
Washington University in St. Louis
Wayne State University
Wellesley College
Wesleyan University
Western Carolina University
Western Kentucky University
Western Washington University
Westminster College
West Texas A&M University
West Virginia University
Wheaton College
Whitman College
Whittier College
Wilkes University
William & Mary
Williams College
Winona State University
Winthrop University
Wofford College
Worcester Polytechnic Institute
Xavier University of Louisiana
Yale University

CONTRIBUTORS

Rachel Ball-Phillips is director of Graduate Fellowships and Awards in the Moody School of Graduate and Advanced Studies at Southern Methodist University (SMU). Prior to that, Ball-Phillips directed National Student Fellowships and the President's Scholars at SMU. She teaches in both the Department of History and the Department of Human-Centered Interdisciplinary Studies at SMU. Ball-Phillips has been a member of NAFA since 2017 and currently co-leads the monthly "Ask a Grad Advisor" professional development series.

Kristin Bennighoff, senior associate director of the Honors College at the University of Delaware (UD), leads fellowship efforts for the institution. She has served the Honors College for more than twenty years in the areas of academic advising, development and alumni relations, recruitment and admissions, and event planning. Bennighoff holds bachelor's and master's degrees in art history from UD.

Megan Bruening received a bachelor's degree in English from Roanoke College, a master's degree in English from Wake Forest University, and a doctoral degree in English from Lehigh University. Her doctoral program framed literary study and teaching practices within social justice theory. She began her fellowships advising career at Lehigh as a writing specialist for Gilman Scholarship applicants before becoming an advisor. Bruening moved to George Mason University as assistant director of graduate fellowships in 2021 and became the director of the Office of Fellowships in 2023.

Sarah Chow is the application and selection program specialist for the Boren Awards, administered by the Institute of International Education (IIE). She has worked for IIE for the past nine years and specifically with the Boren Awards for the past seven. Prior to working at IIE, she worked with a study-abroad program provider, where she managed study abroad programs in Europe, East Asia, and India. She received a bachelor's from Furman University, South Carolina, in French language and literature in 2000 and a master's in international affairs and global justice from Brooklyn College, City University of New York, in 2023.

Laura Collins is the founding director of the Office of Scholar Development and Fellowship Advising (OSDFA) at Rutgers University–Camden. In this role, Collins oversees the advising and outreach processes for all the nationally competitive awards. Prior to establishing OSDFA in 2017, Collins served for twelve years as assistant dean and associate director for the Honors College at Rutgers–Camden. Collins is also a proud Rutgers–Camden alumna, holding a bachelor's degree in English and psychology and a master's degree in psychology. Collins remains actively engaged in academic research and has deepened her ties to NAFA to connect with colleagues with similar interests, including exploring issues of access and equity and student success.

Kurt Davies is the director of Global Awards at New York University. He came to NYU from James Madison University, where he served as the director of Prestigious Scholarships. He has also worked in the Center for Undergraduate Research and Fellowships at Villanova University and the Alliance for Higher Education and Democracy at the University of Pennsylvania. After a career as a travel agent, Davies returned to college as a nontraditional student, receiving a bachelor's degree in linguistics and anthropology from the University of North Carolina and a master's in higher education from the University of Pennsylvania. They are currently pursuing a doctorate in higher education administration at NYU. He has served on the board of directors for NAFA. Davies received a Fulbright grant in 2010 to research post-Soviet language policy in Kyrgyzstan.

Kelsey Fenner is the associate director and team lead for Nationally Competitive Scholarships, Fellowships, and Awards in Villanova University's Center for Research and Fellowships. Prior to her role at

Villanova, Fenner worked in career development at Cornell University. She holds a bachelor's in English rhetoric from Binghamton University, a master's in higher education from the University of Oxford, and a master's in human resource development from Villanova University. She is a Society for Human Resources Management (SHRM) Certified Professional and received the Fulbright Scholar Program's International Education Administrator's grant to Taiwan in 2024. Fenner has presented nationally and internationally on her work and is particularly interested in researching how university systems can adapt to ensure that they produce graduates who contribute to the economic, social, and civic needs of a changing world.

Craig Filar is associate dean of Honors, Scholars, and Fellows in the Division of Undergraduate Studies at Florida State University. He has entered his twentieth year of fellowships advising at the university. Filar has previously served on the NAFA board as president, vice president, and a board member. He was the co-editor of *Saving the World in Five Hundred Words: Perspectives on Nationally Competitive Scholarships* (University of Arkansas Press, 2024). Filar received both his master's degree and doctorate in music theory from Florida State University.

Paul Fogleman has directed the Office of National Scholarships and Awards at Indiana University, Bloomington, since 2014. As an undergraduate, he majored in international studies and German at the University of Missouri and completed master's degrees in international relations at the City College of New York (2002) and in second language studies at Indiana University, Bloomington (2010). Prior to working at Indiana University, he worked for the Conference on Jewish Materials Claims against Germany administering Holocaust compensation programs.

Nicole Galante is the assistant director of the National and International Fellowships Office at Elon University in North Carolina, where she has served as the university's sole full-time fellowships advisor since 2022. Prior to beginning her career in fellowships, Galante earned a bachelor's in English (2019) and a master's in higher education (2021), both from Elon University. Outside of her direct work, Galante enjoys advising Elon's First-Generation Student Society (Galante is proudly first-gen), serving as an officer for Elon's Phi Beta Kappa chapter, and researching young adult literature.

Bonnie Garcia-Gloeckner has been the assistant director for the Office of National Fellowships at Florida State University (FSU) for the past three years. Prior to fellowships advising, she served for six years as the lead academic advisor for FSU's Department of Biological Science and, in 2021, was the recipient of FSU's Outstanding Undergraduate Advising Award. Garcia-Gloeckner earned a bachelor's in geology, and one in Classical civilization, and a master's in biological science from Florida State University.

Lisa Gates is the associate dean for Fellowships and Research at Middlebury College. She has served as a fellowships advisor since 2006 and been a NAFA member since 2008. Gates holds a bachelor's from Dartmouth College and a doctorate from Harvard University. She has worked in higher education for over thirty years in teaching, administrative, and research positions.

Julia Goldberg is the scholarship and fellowships advisor at Lafayette College. Prior to her work as a scholarships advisor, she served as an editor for Simon & Schuster and taught linguistics, English as a second language (ESL), and communication studies at Cambridge, the University of Nebraska–Lincoln, the University of Wyoming, and the University of Illinois Urbana–Champaign. Her research includes studies in cross-cultural communication, identity negotiation, and conversational analysis. She received her doctorate in linguistics from Cambridge University and holds master's degrees in ESL and Russian and Balkan history from the University of Illinois Urbana–Champaign.

Mitch Hobza advises on graduate-level fellowships at Arizona State University. He received his doctorate in rhetoric and composition, with a focus on writing centers and second language writing, from

Purdue University in 2022. While at Purdue, Hobza worked concurrently as a graduate assistant at the Purdue Writing Lab and the National and International Scholarships Office, which is how he was introduced to fellowships advising. Hobza's dissertation studied how empathy is defined in writing center scholarship and offered a theoretical framework for cultivating empathy as a critical praxis in writing center staff education. Additionally, Hobza holds a master's in literature with a certificate in women's and gender studies from the University of Nebraska–Lincoln.

Kristin Janka has served as the director and assistant dean of the Distinguished Student Awards Office at Michigan State University (MSU) since 2013. Janka is also director of international engagement for MSU's Honors College. She currently serves on several NAFA committees, including Governance; Technology Publications, and Communications; and Research Community of Practice; and she co-led the 2024 New Advisor Workshop. Before a career in fellowships, she spent over a decade working in Latin American studies at MSU. She received Foreign Language and Area Studies (FLAS) grants from the US Department of Education to support her doctoral studies and a Fulbright-Hays Group Projects Abroad grant to lead K-12 educators to Costa Rica for professional development. She earned a doctorate in curriculum, teaching, and educational policy from MSU, where her research focused on international professional development and the Fulbright-Hays Group Projects Abroad program.

Claire Kervin is assistant professor of English and director of fellowships advising at Lawrence University (LU). She holds a doctorate in English literature from Boston University, where she wrote a dissertation on depictions of ecological interconnectedness in contemporary American fiction. As a faculty member at LU, she teaches literature, writing, and environmental studies classes. She began directing fellowships advising at LU in 2019, building on previous work as an academic advisor and a writing center tutor and administrator at the University of Wisconsin–Madison and Boston University. At LU, Kervin serves as the point person for all nationally competitive fellowships and scholarships. She joined NAFA's Best Practice, Assessment, and Consultation Sub-Committee in 2022, co-hosted the Midwest Regional NAFA Day in 2022, and organized a panel titled "It's the Process, Not the Prize" for the 2023 NAFA conference. Across her different roles, Kervin's deepest interest is in the power of stories and how they help us understand ourselves, other people, and the environment.

Katya King is the director of the Office of Fellowships at Williams College. She has been a fellowships advisor and member of NAFA since 2001. She has lived in the Czech Republic, Sweden, Canada, and Germany. King earned a bachelor's from McGill University and a doctorate in Slavic languages and literatures from Harvard.

Lindsay Lawton is the founding director of Scholar Development & Fellowship Advising at the University of Denver. In this role, she works with applicants for fellowships and scholarships and teaches in Leadership Studies as well as the Honors Program. She came to Denver from Yale University, where she served as senior associate director of Fellowships & Funding. She taught English and researched third language acquisition in Berlin as a Fulbright grantee and completed a master's degree and a doctorate in Germanic studies at the University of Minnesota, where she also began her career in fellowships.

Jessie McCrary is associate director of the National Scholarships and Fellowships Program in the Pathways Center at Emory University. She has been working as a fellowships advisor in Atlanta, Georgia, since 2019. Her work on the occluded genre of letters of recommendation in fellowship contexts was published in the journal *Written Communication* in 2024 (co-authors Lauren Tuckley, Catherine Salgado, and Elise Rudt-Moorty are also NAFA members). She has also conducted research on the impact of quality enhancement plans on university Writing Across the Curriculum programs, which was published in *College English* in 2022.

Jane Morris is the executive director of the Center for Undergraduate Research and Fellowships (CURF) at the University of Pennsylvania. Morris provides leadership, vision, and direction for CURF. Morris also oversees two of Penn's academic scholars' programs, the Benjamin Franklin Scholars and University Scholars. Before coming to Penn, Morris served as the executive director of Duke University's Office of Undergraduate Scholars and Fellows and as the director of Villanova's Center for Research and Fellowships. Prior to her career in higher education, Morris had a twenty-year career as a research scientist. Morris holds a bachelor's in biology from Villanova University and a master's in biology from Bryn Mawr College. She is a former president of NAFA. In this role, she participated directly in helping the Marshall Scholarship Program evaluate and revise its selection criteria to include those same qualities of intellectual leadership that define excellence in a broader and more meaningful context.

Eric Myers is assistant director of fellowships advising in the Office of International Programs at Princeton University. Myers first started fellowships advising at his graduate school alma mater, West Virginia University, in January 2020. His research interests focus on how institutions of higher education play a role in creating citizens, both on a national and global scale. He currently serves on NAFA's board of directors.

Mathilda Nassar is the assistant director of national fellowships at the University of Notre Dame, where she develops, manages, and evaluates the campus advising processes. Nassar holds a master's in global affairs with a concentration in international peace studies from the University of Notre Dame and a bachelor's in international relations from Roanoke College in Salem, Virginia. Nassar received a Kroc Institute Fellowship during her master's work, and she received both the Gilman Scholarship and the Freeman-ASIA award as an undergraduate. In between her undergraduate and graduate studies, she worked at a grassroots peace project in Palestine and served to improve English curricula in the US Peace Corps in Dubno, Ukraine.

Christine Overstreet is the director of the Office of Fellowships at Amherst College. She began working in higher education in 2012 as part of Mount Holyoke College's Speaking, Arguing, and Writing Program, then moved to fellowships advising there. She has been at Amherst College since 2016. Overstreet holds a bachelor's in ancient studies from Mount Holyoke College and a master's in religion from Yale University.

Terumi Rafferty-Osaki is associate director of the Undergraduate Research and Fellowships Office at Northeastern University. He began at American University working in the Office of Merit Awards in 2017 before he moved to Florida to undertake an assistant director role at Rollins College and founded the Office of Competitive Fellowships at Florida Gulf Coast University. His research interests examine masculinity and citizenship. He currently serves on the NAFA's board of directors.

Elena Reiss holds a master's degree in English literature and teaching English to speakers of other languages (TESOL). Prior to her current role as an assistant director of fellowships advising at Lehigh University, she worked with multilingual populations in the United States and abroad, fostering intercultural competence through teacher training, professional workshops, and conferences. Her work has focused on researching and implementing best practices for multimodal second language instruction. Passionate about creating an equitable community, Reiss is dedicated to supporting the professional development of multilingual learners and helping them navigate academic environments.

Elise Rudt-Moorthy received a bachelor's in global studies with a minor in psychology from University of Maryland Baltimore County and then a certificate in teaching English to speakers of other languages (CELTA). She worked for two years as an AmeriCorps member in Baltimore to help adults apply for naturalization. For the past eight years, she has worked for the University of Notre Dame as a fellowships advisor, assisting over 300 fellowship winners, and helping Notre Dame break onto the Gilman Scholarship top-producing list. Rudt-Moorthy received a master's in technical communication with a concentration on grant writing and self-sponsorship. She has presented four different conference sessions for the NAFA biannual conference about technological tools for advising, performing research in the field, and trauma's role in fellowship applications.

Jayashree Shivamoggi founded her consultancy, Dr. Jay's College & Career Advising, after twenty-five years of working as a fellowships advisor. During that time, Shivamoggi established two successful offices, first at the University of Central Florida, a large public university, and later at Rollins College, a small private liberal arts college. Shivamoggi is well known in the Central Florida community for her success with and passion for working with underrepresented and first-generation students.

Cindy Stocks has been the director of Student Fellowships and Research at Bowdoin College and a member of NAFA since 2007. Prior to that, she held several other positions in higher education, led an arts nonprofit, and worked for a member of Congress. A proud Mainer, she earned her undergraduate degree from the University of Maine and holds a master's in public administration from the Harvard Kennedy School.

Christian Tanja is the senior assistant director of admission at Knight-Hennessy Scholars, Stanford University's graduate fellowship program. He drives global recruitment, selection, and partnerships, advancing diversity and inclusion initiatives. As a member of Stanford's Graduate Diversity Staff Council and NAFA's board of directors, he is dedicated to expanding access to fellowships. Previously, Tanja recruited for Schwarzman Scholars and the Institute of International Education. Equipped with degrees from University of California, Los Angelos (UCLA), and Teachers College, Columbia University, he is passionate about emboldening first-generation and underrepresented students.

Melissa Vert is the director of the Office of National Scholarships and Fellowships at the University of Michigan in Ann Arbor. Vert has been working directly with scholarship applicants for the University of Michigan for the past seven years. She has a deep interest and enthusiasm for education, international relations, and public policy. Her work experience has included supporting UNICEF, the Bureau of Educational and Cultural Affairs at the United States Department of State, and the Inter-American Development Bank. Vert earned a bachelor's in economics and Japanese from the University of California, Davis, and a master's in international relations and international economics at the Johns Hopkins University's School of Advanced International Studies.

Jesse Wieland joined Florida State University's Office of National Fellowships (ONF) in 2015 as a graduate assistant and has served as the associate director since 2020. His career at ONF has prioritized the recruitment and support of underrepresented students; he was named the Center for Academic Retention & Enhancement's Preeminent Partner in 2019 for his work supporting first-generation college student success. Wieland is originally from Destin, Florida, and is a first-generation graduate of FSU, where he earned a bachelor's in social science education and a master's in higher education.

Tara Yglesias is the deputy executive secretary of the Truman Foundation and has been involved in the selection of Truman Scholars for over twenty years. A Truman Scholar from Pennsylvania, she also served as a Senior Scholar at Truman Scholars Leadership Week and the Foundation's Public Service Law Conference prior to joining the foundation's staff. An attorney by training, she began her career in the Office of the Public Defender in Fulton County, Georgia. She is an active member of NAFA and served as the foundation representative on the board for several years. She holds a bachelor's in policy studies and African American studies from Syracuse University and a law degree from Emory University, where she was a Robert W. Woodruff Fellow.

EDITORS

Doug Cutchins is the director of global awards at New York University Abu Dhabi, a position he inaugurated in 2014. Previously, he served as director of social commitment and assistant dean for postgraduate transitions at Grinnell College from 1999 to 2014. Cutchins has been an active member of the NAFA community throughout his career as a fellowships advisor, including serving on the board of directors and as vice president and president. He is also a returned Peace Corps volunteer (Suriname, 1995–1997), living kidney donor, Ironman triathlete, and co-author of four editions of *Volunteer Vacations* (Chicago Review Press). Cutchins holds a bachelor's in history from Grinnell College and a master's in history from the University of Connecticut, which he attended as a James Madison Fellow.

Suzanne McCray serves as vice provost for enrollment and dean of admissions and nationally competitive awards at the University of Arkansas. She is also an associate professor in the Higher Education Program in the College of Education and Health Professions. She currently serves as a member of the College Board's board of trustees. She has edited or co-edited ten volumes of essays on the topic of nationally competitive scholarships. The most recent include *Saving the World in 500 Words: Perspectives on Nationally Competitive Scholarships* (2024), with co-editors Craig Filar and Kyle Mox, and *Wild About Harry: Everything You Have Ever Wanted to Know about the Truman Scholarship* (2021), with co-editor Tara Yglesias. In 2019, she received NAFA's inaugural exemplary service award. She earned a bachelor's and a master's in English from the University of Arkansas and a doctorate in English from the University of Tennessee.

Cindy Schaarschmidt serves as executive director of International Education at Pierce College District in Washington State. Before coming to Pierce College, Schaarschmidt served as the director of Student Fellowships and Study Abroad at the University of

Washington Tacoma and assistant director of the fellowships office at Drexel University. She is a past board member, vice president, and president of NAFA and currently serves as president of the World Affairs Council of Tacoma. Originally from Germany, she arrived in the United States as a Fulbright Foreign Language Teaching Assistant, and her academic and professional journey has also taken her to Guatemala, the United Kingdom, Russia, and Spain. Schaarschmidt holds a master's in media communications and American studies from the University of Leipzig, Germany.

INDEX

access, 185. *See also* diversity, equity, and inclusion
access to scholarship and fellowships: antiracist practices improving, 8–9, 123–38; bichoronous teaching and advising improving, 165; by community college and transfer, 7, 67–87; diversity, equity, and inclusion practices, 8, 89–103; by historically marginalized students, 8, 105–22; 178–79; interview costs and, 35; overview of, 7–9
advisors on review panels: benefits for advisors on, 148–50, 152, 154–58, 166–68; benefits for foundation of, 153–55, 164–67; conflicts of interest issues, 170nn5–6; encouragement of, 167–68; foundation perspective on, 151–55, 162–67; overview of, 147; as professional development, 149, 156; selection of, 148; strategies for, 148–51, 158–62
affective filters, 119–20
affirmative action, purpose of, 174
affirmative mentorship, 75–76
AI (artificial intelligence), 62–63, 206–7, 222
allyship, 110n17
ambiguity, comfort with, 57–59, 64
American Association of Colleges and Universities (AAC&U), career readiness survey, 43
application contents, uncertainty about, 59

application process: appreciative advising and, 24–26; courses and workshops about, 45–48; as development approach, 49–50; going through as success, 50–51; learning from, 37–38, 79; use of AI in, 62–63. *See also* advisors on review panels; endorsement letters; knowledge transfer; student development from process
appreciative advising: defined, 17–18; other methods compared, 18–19; overview of, 15–16, 19–20, 33–34; phases of, 20–28; satisfaction survey about, 28–36
Aristotle, 130, 141n2, 213
assessment, 48–50, 93
assisted metacognition, 92
Association for Experiential Education, 41
audience, consideration of in writing, 63
authenticity: limited by language conventions, 119; in writing voice, 113, 115, 117, 121–26
autonomy, support for, 80–81
awareness of fellowship opportunities, increasing, 45–48

badges, digital, 51
Bain, Alexander, 130
Baird, Neil, 87
Bazerman, Charles, 124
Beach, King, 87
Beaufort, Anne, 95
Berger, LaNitra, 106, 177

Bhopal, Kalwart, 101
bias, 208
Blair, Louis, 215–16
Boren Awards, 55, 151, 152–53, 168–69
brain development, 56
Brown, Ann, 217, 219, 224n4
Bruening, Megan, 111n17

career readiness, 42–44
CCCC Statement on White Language Supremacy, 115
celebration of application process, 50–51
Center for Practical Wisdom (UC), 213, 223
Center for Research and Fellowship (CRF at Villanova), 44
Charles, Cody, 178
Chow, Sarah, 151–55
classes, about application process, 46–48
CLS (Critical Language Scholarship), 55
code-meshing, 118
code segregation, 118
code-switching, 118
cohesion in applications, 162
collaboration, as core NAFA value, 37, 38
college admissions scandal, 175
college essays, 143n10
"The 'Colorblindness' Trap: How a Civil Rights Ideal Got Hijacked" (Hannah-Jones), 173–74
competency building. *See* skill acquisition
Conference on College Composition and Communication (CCCC), 113–15
confidence, equity and, 77
confidentiality, of endorsement letters, 195, 207–8, 211n2

conflicts of interest, 170nn5–6
courses, about application process, 46–48
credibility, review panel participation increasing, 158
Critical Language Scholarship (CLS), 55
cultural ambassadorship, 110n17
cultural capital, 110n15
culture, office, 26–27
Curlin, Jane, 223, 224n4
curse of knowledge, 25

Davies, Kurt, 155–62
deans, working with, 200–201
deliver phase of appreciative advising, 26–27, 33
Delyla M., 70, 72, 74–76, 82–83
design phase of appreciative advising, 24–26, 32, 36
developmental advising, 18–19, 150. *See also* knowledge transfer; skill acquisition
digital badges, 51
digital searches of candidates, 204
Dilger, Bradley, 87
disarm phase of appreciative advising, 20–22, 29
disciplinary information, handling of, 202, 208–9
discover phase of appreciative advising, 22–23, 24, 30
discussion norms, 180–81
diversity, equity, and inclusion: advisors on review panels helping with, 165; imagination process and, 77; justice and diversity as competing needs, 173–74; NAFA commitment to, 221–22; study abroad and, 100. *See also* inclusive writing pedagogies; Prestige and Practicality Forums

Index | 257

don't settle phase of appreciative advising, 27–28, 34
dream phase of appreciative advising, 23–24, 31. *See also* imagination process

editing, individual lenses in, 57
Elon University, 81, 87, 89. *See also* imagination process
ELT (Experiential Learning Theory), 41
embellishment of accomplishments, 203–4
emotional appeals. *See* trauma experiences
employability, role of advising in, 42–44
endorsement letters: AI use and, 206–7; application review process and, 159; confidentiality of, 195, 207–8, 211n2; contents of, 195–99; context for applicants provided by, 124–25, 197–98, 199, 201–2; defined, 194–95; ethics and, 207–9; formatting and style of, 204–6; information sources for, 201–4; new information in, 195, 198–99, 203; overview of, 193–94, 210–11; preparation for writing, 199–201; trying too hard and, 209–10
English, Jacob, 177
enslaved ancestry, people with, 174. *See also* diversity, equity, and inclusion
Envision, Apply, Embark, 68–69. *See also* imagination process
equity and inclusion. *See* diversity, equity, and inclusion
Erickson, Erik, 39
ethics: AI and, 222; endorsement letters and, 195, 207–9, 211n2; to foundations and to self, 81;

imagination process versus fantasy, 79–80
examples, use of in endorsement letters, 205
exit evaluations, 93
"Expanding Access through Organized Support—The History and Purpose of the National Association of Fellowships Advisors" (Powers), 213
Experiential Learning Theory (ELT), 41
external compensation policies, 156
external readers. *See* advisors on review panels

fantasy versus imagination, 69–70, 79–80
feedback, 25, 206, 207
Finalist Selection Committee (FSC), 163
first-generation students, 38, 72, 74–75
first impressions, appreciative advising and, 20–22
fit for fellowships, 84n12
Florida State University, 16–17. *See also* appreciative advising
foundations: advisors' ethical obligations to, 81, 209; NAFA founding and, 218; perspective on advisors on review panels, 151–55, 162–67; perspective on trauma experiences in applications, 139–41
four Rs, 134
Fulbright Post-Submission Survey, 42–43, 49
Fulbright Program, 42–43, 49, 55–57
future plans on applications: accuracy of, 59–62, 74; multiple applications with different plans, 79; overview of, 55–57, 64–65; uncertainty and, 57–59; use of AI in, 62–63

Gallop, Alsace-Lorraine, 177
Gallup, 43
generative AI, 62–63, 206–7, 222
genre instances, 116
Global and Post-Graduate Opportunities and Fellowships course, 47
goals: advising approach adapted to, 89–90; backward goal-setting process for, 105–6; clarifying with imagination process, 76; developmental goal-setting, 88–89; of Prestige and Practicality Forums, 180–85
Graalman, Bob, 219, 222, 224n4
grading and honors systems, 198
group discussion of study-abroad scenarios exercise, 106–7
growth. *See* student development from process
Guerra, Juan C., 118

Hannah-Jones, Nikole, 173–74
Harris, Muriel, 91
Harry S. Truman Scholarship Foundation, 215–16. *See also* Truman Scholarship
Hart-Davidson, Bill, 116–17
Hartenberger, Laura, 63
honors and grading systems, 198
Horner, Bruce, 124

identity: DEI legislation and disclosure about, 176; of multilingual students, 120–21; saliency of, 106; study abroad and, 99, 101. *See also* diversity, equity, and inclusion; first-generation students
identity crisis, 120
Identity Development Theory, 39–40
imagination process: benefits of, 72–76; context requiring flexibility in, 81–83; for Delyla M.,

70, 72, 74–76, 82–83; equity and, 77; ethics and, 79–81; fantasy versus, 69–70, 79–80; learning who applicant is as person, 68, 78–79; for Megan C., 70–71, 78–79, 82; for Natalie T, 82; for Natalie T., 70–71, 73–74; overview of, 67; start of, 68
inclusion, as core NAFA value, 37, 38. *See also* diversity, equity, and inclusion
inclusive writing pedagogies: authentic voice and, 113, 115, 117, 121–26; bridging of, 118–19; genre instances and, 116–17; identity and, 120–21; purposes of, 121–23; rhetorical awareness development and, 123–24; Students' Right to Their Own Language resolution, 113–15; as tool for advisors, 121, 125–26; types of, 118
indecision, uncertainty versus, 58–59
institutional nominations. *See* endorsement letters
institutions, genre instances reflecting power of, 116–17
Intellect and the Good Life course, 47
intrusive advising, defined, 18

Janka, Kristin, 135
Jones Royster, Jacqueline, 124

Kaplan, Robert B., 123
Keagan, Robert, 40
knowledge, curse of, 25
knowledge transfer: direct facilitation of, 93–94; explicitness about, 92–93; negative transfer and, 86–88; overview of, 85–86; promotion of deeper learning for, 91–92; research on benefitting from considering fellowship

Index | 259

advising, 94–95; shared vocabulary and, 89–90
Kolb, David, 41

language, learning another, 64
language choice, 119
large language models. *See* AI (artificial intelligence)
Lawton, Lindsay, 147–51
learning: as core NAFA value, 37–38; Experiential Learning Theory, 41; metacognition and, 88–89, 92–93, 95. *See also* knowledge transfer
learning management systems, 48
learning outcomes, assessment of, 48–50
letters of endorsement. *See* endorsement letters
letters of nomination, 124–25
letters of recommendation, 124–25, 194, 199
long-term outcomes, tracking, 50
low-income people, barriers for success of, 74–75
Lu, Min-Zhan, 124

Magolda, Marcia Baxter, 40
marginalized identities, 74–75. *See also* first-generation students
McCray, Suzanne, 220–21, 224n4
Megan C., 70–71, 78–79, 82
mental practice, 73
metacognition, 88–89, 92–93, 95
misrepresentations, 203–4
modeling, 91–92
Monolingual/Monocultural approach, 118
Moreno, Rhia, 100
Multilingual/Multicultural approach, 118
mutual intelligibility, 118

NACE Career Readiness Competencies, 42–43

Natalie T., 70–71, 73–74, 82
National and International Fellowships Office (NIFO at Elon), 67, 81. *See also* imagination process
National Association for Colleges and Employers (NACE), career readiness competencies, 42–43
National Association of Fellowship Advisors (NAFA): 2023 conference, 3, 173; changes in over time, 221–23; core values of, 37–38, 215, 217; DEI Committee formation, 177–79; founding of, 213–17, 224n4; interview questions about history of, 223n3; scholarship advising as profession due to, 220. *See also* Prestige and Practicality Forums
National Center for Education Statistics study, 61
nationalism, 100, 109n2
National Security Education Programs (NSEP), 151
negative transfer, 86–88
neoliberalism, 100–101
nomination letters, 124–25
norms for discussion, 180–81
NSEP (National Security Education Programs), 151
Nussbaum, Howard, 223

office culture, 26–27
Office of National Fellowships (ONF at FSU), 16–17
Office of Scholar Development and Fellowship Advising (OSDFA at Rutgers), 45
operational uncertainty, 59
"Operation Varsity Blues" admission scandal, 175
otherness, sense of, 120

panels of reviewers. *See* advisors on review panels
past, easier to focus on than future, 57
pathos. *See* Rhetorical Triangle Revised exercise; trauma experiences
"A Path Revealed: Reflections of a Former Scholarship Advisor" (Tolar), 40–41
Pebble in the Pond exercise, 104–6
peer review for deeper learning, 91
personal statements: addressing anomalies in academic record in, 197; as coursework, 47; genre instances and, 116; inexperience with, 120, 134; workshops to write, 46
phronesis (practical wisdom), 213
plausible fiction, 58
positionality, 99–101
possibilities. *See* imagination process
postgraduate degree programs for advisors, lack of, 218
power, 116–17, 130
Powers, Beth, 213, 219, 224n4
practical wisdom (phronesis), 213
prefrontal cortex development, 56
prescriptive advising, defined, 18
presidents, working with, 200–201
Prestige and Practicality Forums: background for, 173–77; creation of, 179; DEI Committee formation and, 177–79; frustration and, 185, 190; goals of, 180–85; needs and concerns expressed at, 185–89; overview of, 190–91
Preston, John, 101
privacy issues, 207
privilege, prestige and, 175
process, valuing of. *See* student development from process

process pedagogy, 102
professional development, review panel participation as, 149, 156
provosts, working with, 200–201

quotations, use of in endorsement letters, 205

race-conscious policies, challenges to, 174–77
radical belief, 77
radical imagination, 77
reality, keeping in, 69–70
recommendation letters, 124–25, 194, 199
referrals to resources, 25–26
"Reflections on the Value of Being in the Room Where It Happens" (Vardaman), 214–15
Regents of the University of California v. Bakke (1978), 174
reporting, on student development, 49–50
resilience, appreciative advising and, 27–28
resources for applicants, 25–26, 90
re-traumatization, 134–35, 136
review of endorsement letters, 206, 207
Rhetoric (Aristotle), 141n2
rhetorical problem-solving, 95
Rhetorical Triangle Revised exercise, 102–4
Richardson, John, 219, 224n4
role-play, 91
Rosinski, Paula, 95
Rutgers University–Camden, 45. *See also* student development from process

safety, 135, 137
saliency, 101, 106
scaffolding, 94

selection panelists. *See* advisors on review panels
selection process, subjectivity in, 157–58
Self-Authorship Theory, 40–41
self-sponsorship, 132
sensitive information, use in endorsement letters, 208
Serrano, Malaika Marable, 101
shared vocabulary, 89–90
skill acquisition, 41–44, 52. *See also* knowledge transfer; student development from process
social media, impacts of, 222
Standard American Written English (SAWE), inclusive writing pedagogies versus, 114, 117
Statement on White Language Supremacy, 115
"Statement on Writing Transfer" from Elon University, 87, 89
student development from process: assessment of, 48–50; celebration of, 50–51; courses and workshops for, 45–48; learning about self, 79; overview of, 37–38, 52; skill and competency frameworks and, 41–44; theories of, 38–41. *See also* knowledge transfer
student newspapers, reading, 202
Students for Fair Admissions, Inc. v. President and Fellows of Harvard College (2023), 174
Students' Right to Their Own Language resolution (CCCC), 113–15
study abroad: exercises to think about purposes for, 102–7; promoting reflection about during, 108; research on preparation for lacking, 102; stakes in, 99–101; terminology use, 101
submission, appreciative advising and, 26–27

Substance Abuse and Mental Health Services Administration (SAMHSA), 134–35
success, definition of by students, 50–51
"Survey of the Profession" (NAFA), 220
surveys: AAC&U career readiness, 43; about Global and Post-Graduate Opportunities and Fellowships course, 47; appreciative advising satisfaction, 28–36; Fulbright Post-Submission Survey, 42–43, 49; future plans, accuracy of, 59–62; Gallup career readiness, 43; NAFA "Survey of the Profession," 220; Prestige and Practicality Forum feedback survey, 181, 183; writing about trauma experiences, 135–36

technology, impacts of, 222
terminology, shared, 89–90
testimonials, 198–99
textual structure of genres, 117
theory, grounding fellowships in, 39–41
Thibault, Paul J., 119
Tolar, Mary Hale, 40–41, 216, 220, 224n4
transcripts, use of unofficial, 165
transfer. *See* knowledge transfer
translanguaging, 118, 119, 121–23
Translingual/Transcultural approach, 118
transparency, advisors on review panels and, 165
trauma dumping, 131
trauma experiences: context for, 130–32; fellowship office and, 132–34; foundation perspective on, 139–41; overview of, 129, 141; recommendations for advisors about, 134–36; writing process and, 136–39
trauma-informed practices, 134–36

Trimbur, John, 124
Truman Scholarship, 55, 162–64, 169–70, 193
Twiss, Nancy, 214–15, 216, 219

uncertainty, comfort with, 57–59, 64
University of Chicago's Center for Practical Wisdom, 213, 223
University of Delaware (UD), 45. *See also* student development from process
unofficial transcripts, use of, 165
US Student Fulbright Program, 42–43, 49, 55–57

Values and Code of Ethics (NAFA), 37
Vardaman, Elizabeth, 214–15, 222–23, 224n4
Vert, Melissa, 135
Villanova University, 42–43, 44. *See also* student development from process
visibility of scholarship advising, increasing, 46
vocabulary, shared, 89–90

Warrick, Paula, 218–19, 221, 224n4
"What AI Teaches Us About Good Writing" (Hartenberger), 63
why, consideration of, 24, 78
Wick, David, 102
Willis, Tasha, 102
Womack-Wynne, Carly, 100
writing: audience and, 63; authenticity in voice, 113, 115, 117, 121–26; integration into real-world, 95; process pedagogy and, 102; questioning ability, 119–20; reflection on knowledge and beliefs about, 87–88. *See also* future plans on applications; inclusive writing pedagogies; personal statements

Yglesias, Tara, 162–67, 209
Yosso, Tara J., 110n15
You Hit Submit celebration, 51

Zemach-Bersin, Talya, 100, 109n2, 110n15

www.ingramcontent.com/pod-product-compliance
Lightning Source LLC
Chambersburg PA
CBHW031432160426
43195CB00010BB/707